T0305224

The Economics of Energy and the Production Process

NEW HORIZONS IN INSTITUTIONAL AND EVOLUTIONARY
ECONOMICS

Series Editor: Geoffrey M. Hodgson
Research Professor, University of Hertfordshire Business School, UK

Economics today is at a crossroads. New ideas and approaches are challenging
the largely static and equilibrium-oriented models that used to dominate
mainstream economics. The study of economic institutions – long neglected
in the economics textbooks – has returned to the forefront of theoretical and
empirical investigation.

This challenging and interdisciplinary series publishes leading works at
the forefront of institutional and evolutionary theory and focuses on cutting-
edge analyses of modern socio-economic systems. The aim is to understand
both the institutional structures of modern economies and the processes of
economic evolution and development. Contributions will be from all forms
of evolutionary and institutional economics, as well as from Post-Keynesian,
Austrian and other schools. The overriding aim is to understand the processes
of institutional transformation and economic change.

Titles in the series include:

The Evolutionary Analysis of Economic Policy
Edited by Pavel Pelikan and Gerhard Wegner

The Evolution of Scientific Knowledge
*Edited by Hans Siggaard Jensen, Lykke Margot Richter and Morten
Thanning Vendelø*

Evolutionary Economic Thought
European Contributions and Concepts
Edited by Jürgen G. Backhaus

Economic Institutions and Complexity
Structures, Interactions and Emergent Properties
Karl-Ernst Schenk

The Economics of Knowledge Sharing
A New Institutional Approach
Edited by Ernst Helmstädter

The Economics of Energy and the Production Process
An Evolutionary Approach
Guido Buenstorf

The Economics of Energy and the Production Process

An Evolutionary Approach

Guido Buenstorf

Max Planck Institute for Research into Economic Systems, Jena, Germany

NEW HORIZONS IN INSTITUTIONAL AND EVOLUTIONARY ECONOMICS

Edward Elgar
Cheltenham, UK • Northampton, MA, USA

Published by
Edward Elgar Publishing Limited
Glensanda House
Montpellier Parade
Cheltenham
Glos GL50 1UA
UK

Edward Elgar Publishing, Inc.
136 West Street
Suite 202
Northampton
Massachusetts 01060
USA

A catalogue record for this book
is available from the British Library

Library of Congress Cataloguing in Publication Data

Buenstorf, Guido, 1968-
    The Economics of energy and the production process : an evolutionary
    approach / Guido Buenstorf.
        p. cm. — (New horizons in institutional and evolutionary economics)
    Includes bibliographical references and index.
        1. Energy policy. 2. Economic policy. 3. Power resources. I. Title. II. Series.

HD9502.A2B84 2004
333.79—dc22

2003066005

ISBN I 84376 461 X

Printed and bound in Great Britain by MPG Books Ltd, Bodmin, Cornwal

Contents

Figures

Tables

Symbols

b   specific exergy
B   exergy
G   Gibbs free energy
I   information
k   Boltzmann's constant
K   number of interdependent elements
N   total number of elements
o   operation in production process
p   pressure
ρ probability
P   conditional probability
Π profit
Q   heat
R   universal gas constant
S   entropy
T   temperature
V   volume
w   number of microstates
W   work
x   vector of relevant properties
X   state of knowledge
Y   state of system

Preface

When I first started my research into the economics of energy use that resulted in the present study, I had no idea into how many different fields of economics, and academic disciplines more broadly, this project would lead me. Some of the avenues taken would turn out to be dead ends. Others seemed less than helpful at one point in time, and their applicability to the issues under investigation became clear only after other elements of the argument had evolved further. During the production of this study the individual parts of the argument began to fit together in a way that yielded an approach to the economics of energy and production from an unconventional perspective. I think this perspective is fruitful for deriving new insights into the conditions of production processes and their long-term development. In line with the sequential perspective of production to be developed below, I hope that the present output of my production process will not remain a final output but will serve as an input into further research.

In any event I would never have been able to produce the present study without discussions with, comments from and support by a large number of people. Some of them will not have realized their significance for my research at the time, and would be utterly surprised to know about it. But all of them have been crucial. I specifically want to thank (in order of appearance) John Foster, Frank Beckenbach, Malte Faber and Leonard Dudley. Uwe Cantner's contribution went far beyond his official role as member of my dissertation committee. Robert Ayres' critical comments on my work made for a better book.

This book was written as part of an ongoing research project into long-term economic development pursued at the Evolutionary Economics Group of the Max Planck Institute for Research into Economic Systems in Jena (Germany). The Institute provided both the intellectual freedom and the material infrastructure required for this kind of work. I want to thank all researchers and staff for the outstanding working conditions at the Institute. I am particularly indebted to my colleagues and friends of the Evolutionary Economics Group. Thomas Brenner and Christian Sartorius not only read the entire manuscript, their interdisciplinary background and occasional standby tutorials helped wipe out many (hopefully all) of my deficiencies in the physical and biological sciences. Wilhelm Ruprecht was critical in shaping my understanding of some conceptual issues. Last but not least I want to express my gratitude to Ulrich Witt who supervised my thesis work on which the present book is based and who provided much of the vision underlying this book.

The manuscript was revised during my visit at Carnegie Mellon University in 2003. I am grateful to the Max Planck Society for their funding, and to Carnegie Mellon's Department of Social and Decision Sciences, in particular Steven Klepper, for their outstanding hospitality.

Just as some of the ideas and concepts in this book go beyond the traditional boundaries of economics, some important influences on my personal intellectual development did not come from economics or economists. I learned a lot about science in the interdisciplinary setting of BMWG Jahnstraße in Jena, particularly from Jörg Ackermann, Peter Slickers and Anke Neumann.

The most important people are still missing, however. Inken Poßner's impact on this work, both directly and indirectly, as colleague, critic, coach and companion are not to be expressed in words. Anna and Konstantin reminded me that there is life outside research and cheered me up in dark moments. I am grateful to the three of them for tolerating both my absence and my presence during the long final stretch of this work. I am not sure what was harder to bear. Finally, without the encouragement, role models and unconditional support provided by my parents, Klaus and Elke Bünstorf, this book would never have been possible. My father did not live to see the finished book. He passed away only a few weeks after I had completed the revisions to the manuscript. This book is dedicated to his memory.

Pittsburgh, October 2003   G. B.

To the memory of my father

1. Introduction: energy is back on the agenda

1.1 POWER BLACKOUTS IN THE KNOWLEDGE ECONOMY

Throughout most of the twentieth century economics has shown little interest in energy. There have been, however, periods of increasing research into the economics of energy. The ups and downs in the interest in energy closely followed energy-related changes in the world economy. When oil prices exploded in the 1970s, many economists felt that economics had not properly accounted for the importance of energy, and a wave of energy-related research was undertaken.[1] In particular, economists began to study seriously the hazards to economic growth and well-being that might be caused by potential shortages of energy and other resources. Yet it soon emerged that the fears of imminent shortages triggered by the oil price shocks and by pessimistic resource availability scenarios (Meadows et al., 1972) had been exaggerated. Energy prices began to fall, and the development in prices was reflected by a diminishing academic interest in energy during the 1980s. Energy again became an issue in the early 1990s, this time because of increasing awareness of environmental changes such as global warming, which are at least in part caused by the combustion of fossil fuels. Nuclear energy was becoming increasingly controversial after the accidents of Three Mile Island and Chernobyl. However, in these contexts, energy was no longer discussed as a crucial input into economic processes, but the focus was on potential dangers and harms caused as side effects of energy use. The renewed interest in the economics of energy was largely an interest in environmental economics.

---

1. The number of Social Science Citation Index entries on 'energ*' provides anecdotal evidence for this development. Taking into account the upward trend in the total number of entries, 'energ*' entries increased more than threefold between 1973 and 1982, before returning to the previous level by 1988. In the early 1990s, a second rise in 'energ*' entries began, which may be related to the increased public interest in the problem of global warming.

In addition to falling energy prices, another development worked against a sustained interest in the economics of energy in the 1990s. After the oil price shocks of the 1970s, dramatic changes in information and communication technologies had taken place. Economic activity in the Western industrialized economies, in particular in the United States, had rapidly shifted from traditional manufacturing sectors to new technologies and the service industries. During the 1990s, these technological and structural changes became known under the popular labels 'knowledge economy' or even 'new economy.' It became the conventional wisdom that knowledge is the crucial input into economic activities in developed economies. By contrast, the importance of materials, energy, and physical labor as inputs into production was downplayed.

The vision of a dematerialized 'new' economy based on service industries and intellectual rather than material inputs to production has always been more of a popular myth than an empirical phenomenon borne out by statistical facts. Per capita energy use in the industrial economies is still increasing. And even though it is true that energy intensity, i.e. energy input per unit of economic output, tends to decrease in the industrial economies, this is by no means a new development. The decline in energy intensity began many decades ago in all industrial countries. In Britain, energy intensity has been falling since the 1870s, and in the US since the 1920s. There is no evidence for a recent acceleration in the downward trend of energy intensity, either. Reductions in energy intensity can therefore hardly be related to the revolutions in information and communication technologies that underlie the so-called knowledge economy.

Today, in 2003, the vision of a 'new,' knowledge-based economy already looks rather old. Several developments have caused it to lose much of its fascination. Most important, perhaps, was the bursting of speculative bubbles in the high-technology equity markets, and the wave of corporate failures and downsizing that accompanied it. But already before these events, the vision of the knowledge economy had been damaged in a very symbolic way by the California energy crisis of 2000 and 2001. Very suddenly, blackouts, rationing of electricity and strongly increasing electricity prices proved that even allegedly post-industrial places such as Silicon Valley, the global center of the knowledge economy, are fundamentally energy-dependent – if only for the power supply of computers and the air-conditioning of offices, laboratories, and highly sensitive chip production facilities. Electricity shortages began to threaten the functioning of the economy – a phenomenon that was well known from less developed countries, but that one would no longer have expected to see in the leading industrial economies. To be sure, the California energy crisis was not caused by fundamental shortages of energy. It is easily explained by a combination of market power, regulatory failure and some unexpected exogenous factors such as extreme weather conditions (Joskow, 2001; Krugman, 2003). Nonetheless, the California crisis was significant in bringing energy back on the political and economic agenda. The US administration reacted to the crisis with an emphasis on energy policy that would have been surprising some years earlier. An energy task force led by the US Vice President was installed, and significant policy measures were taken in order to secure and increase future energy supplies. Moreover, it has often been suggested that considerations of energy policy exert a significant influence on the foreign policies adopted by the US and other Western governments.

These current developments are in striking contrast to the vision underlying the notion of a knowledge economy. They teach an important lesson. Energy and materials may not have been the most crucial factors driving the recent technological and structural changes in the industrialized economies. These changes have not, however, made energy and material inputs superfluous. They have only been taken for granted. Put differently: What has been dubbed the knowledge economy is far from replacing the more traditional economy. It rather builds on it, and it is dependent on it. Therefore, it is still worthwhile to attempt better understanding of the physical underpinnings of economic activity. This book is a contribution to this endeavor.

1.2 THREE LEVELS OF ANALYZING PRODUCTION

This book develops a new approach to the study of energy use in the production process, and of the ways it changes over time. In subsequent chapters, I will outline a conceptual framework for the analysis of production processes. In investigating the changing role of energy in production, I will make extensive use of the traditional economic concept of factors of production. Although frequently used in economics, this concept is not clearly defined. Economists typically understand as factors of production those categories of inputs into production processes that are sufficiently important to include them explicitly in theories of production, for example as arguments of analytical production functions. Traditionally, capital and labor (and to a lesser degree, land) are considered factors of production. The adequacy of this choice of factors has frequently been questioned. Energy figures prominently among the candidates for alternative factors of production that have been suggested before.

To answer the question whether energy is a factor of production, one first has to clarify the status of the concept of factors of production. In the following chapters, I will therefore both develop a new interpretation of the notion of factors of production, and discuss in what sense energy qualifies as a factor of production.

Before these arguments can be developed in more detail, it appears highly useful to go back one further step and to disentangle alternative levels of analysis at which production processes can be studied. It will turn out that the answers to the above issues critically depend on the chosen level of analysis. I will distinguish between three levels of analysis, which can be called the physical level, the level of goods, and the level of value. Studies of production have focused to varying degrees on the three levels. Researchers interested in the technical specificities of production processes, and those with an interest in the environmental implications of production, have tended to emphasize the physical level, and to define production at this physical level. This resulted, for example, in characterizing production as the application of energy to materials (Chenery, 1953), or as the transformation of energy and matter (Faber et al., 1998). Taking into account that energy and matter transformations also take place spontaneously in nature, an alternative definition of production at the physical level emphasizes that production either accelerates or temporarily decelerates spontaneous transformations (Ayres, 1994a). At the physical level of analysis, energy and matter are straightforward candidates for factors of production, with a more philosophical controversy between authors on whether materials are 'active' factors or only 'passive' substrates of production (see for example, Hall et al., 2001).

In spite of its usefulness for technical and environmental issues, the physical level alone is insufficient to characterize production. Clearly, not all anthropogenic modifications of the physical world can be considered production processes. It is characteristic for production that it pursues an economic purpose: Its aim is to make useful and potentially valuable goods available. The physical level has to be connected to economic considerations. However, the link from the physical level to the economic level can be conceived of in different ways. The dominant conception changed significantly over the history of economics.

Before the subjectivist revolution in economics, classical economists generally adhered to what Mirowski (1989) has called a 'substance theory of value,' which mostly took the form of the labor theory of value. For classical economists, the value of goods was a direct consequence of the impact of value-generating agents such as human labor. Production constituted the process in which goods acquired their value.

After the subjectivist revolution of neoclassical economics in the late nineteenth century, things became more complicated. For the subjectivist neoclassical economists, production of value was not an acceptable notion. According to neoclassical economics, the value of goods is decoupled from their production. Relative prices and therefore exchange values of goods are determined by the marginal utility consumers derive from them, which in turn depends on the relation between supply and demand. By equating value with marginal utility, neoclassical economists came to grips with the paradox of use value and exchange value that had puzzled classical economists.

The following quotation from Eugen von Böhm-Bawerk ([1884] 1959, p. 90f.; emphasis in original; see also Mirowski, 1989, ch. 6) nicely illustrates the neoclassical view of the relationship between production and value:

> *Value* is not produced at all, and cannot be produced. We never produce anything but forms, shapes of materials, combinations of material, that is to say, things, goods. These goods can of course be *goods possessing value*, but they do not bring value with them ready made, as something inherent that results from production. They only *acquire* value from the wants and satisfactions of the economic world. Value has its source not in the past of goods, but in their future . . . The most that production can do is create goods in the hope that, according to the anticipated relations of demand and supply, they will be of value.

Although producers engage in their activities in the expectation of producing valuable goods, the production process itself does not impart value in goods. The only remaining relation between production and value is that, in the Marshallian synthesis (Marshall, [1890] 1997), production costs determine the lower bound of long-run prices.

In spite of their subjectivist value theory, early neoclassical economists did deal with the objective properties of goods. In this context, it is useful to recall Carl Menger's definition of goods.[2] According to Menger ([1871] 1950, p. 52):

> [i]f a thing is to become a good, or in other words, if it is to acquire goods-character, all four of the following prerequisites must be simultaneously present:
> 1. A human need.
> 2. Such properties as render the thing capable of being brought into a causal connection with the satisfaction of this need.
> 3. Human knowledge of this causal connection.
> 4. Command of the thing sufficient to direct it to the satisfaction of the need.

The causal connection of a thing to the satisfaction of needs (Menger's second condition) is the basis of their usefulness (*Nützlichkeit*). Usefulness is thus a necessary condition of 'goods-character' (ibid.) of a thing (or a service). Menger discusses it as an objective property of goods. He further

2. I am grateful to Wilhelm Ruprecht for calling this definition to my attention. An extensive discussion of Menger's position is found in Ruprecht (2001).

classifies goods into various orders of increasingly indirect capacity to fulfill wants. Inputs into production are higher-order goods, because they indirectly serve for the satisfaction of wants. Of all goods, only a subgroup (Menger calls them 'economic' goods) is characterized by scarcity, which in turn is necessary for a good to possess (exchange) value. From this it follows that the capacity of a good to fulfill human needs (directly or indirectly) is necessary but not sufficient for the good to have value. For Menger there is thus a level of goods-character which antecedes price theory and which is based on the objective property of usefulness.

Although Menger rejected the notion of use value (*Gebrauchswert*), his distinction between usefulness and value is equivalent to the classical dichotomy between use value and exchange value.[3] This distinction is also relevant for production theory, because it helps to clarify the character of economic production models. Somewhat paradoxically, most of neoclassical production theory is located at the level of (exchange) value, in spite of the decoupling of value from production. It is, as it were, a price theory of production, which has been developed in analogy to the field concept of neoclassical consumer theory (Mirowski, 1989, ch. 6). The relevant issue in neoclassical production theory is identifying the optimal mix of input factors, which will, in the case of substitutable factors, be reached when marginal factor productivities are equalized. In these production models the value of input factors is imputed from the value of the product. From the perspective of neoclassical production theory it is straightforward to focus attention on those inputs that account for the largest cost shares. A further justification for the neoclassical factors of production, land, labor and capital, can moreover be found in their relevance for distributional issues, as the owners of these inputs hold competing claims to the product. Historically, the legitimacy of these claims has often been a contested political issue.

At the level of pure theory, economists tend to show little theoretical interest in the concrete nature of the factors of production. In the models based on activity analysis (see section 3.1 below), for instance, no a priori restrictions are made as to whether any particular good is an input or an output. Goods become inputs to the economy under investigation simply if their aggregate net output over all activities is smaller than zero, i.e. if a larger quantity of them enters the variety of production processes than leaves them as a product (Arrow and Hahn, 1971). Similarly, the popular textbook by Varian (1992, ch. 1) argues for specifying inputs in as much detail as possible (with regard to quality, time and location, p. 2), but it does not

---

3. In what follows, the term 'value,' if used without further qualifiers, will always refer to exchange value.

discuss what *kinds* of inputs are actually used in production processes. This lack of interest in the nature of inputs into production is analogous to the research interests of neoclassical consumer theory. Consumer theory has become increasingly disconnected from its psychological origins and restricts itself to formal, rather than material, statements on consumers and their preferences (Witt, 2000). At the same time, the agnostic position of neoclassical economics vis-à-vis the nature of factors of production implies that criticisms of the specific set of 'neoclassical' factors of production (such as in Boulding, 1981) miss the point. The choice of factors is not really a matter of theoretical interest in neoclassical economics.

Given the price-theoretic focus of neoclassical production theory, there is no need in neoclassical economics to develop a realistic representation of production processes. However, not all authors have been content with restricting the analysis of production to the level of values and prices. There have been repeated attempts at developing a more faithful depiction of production starting from the neoclassical theory, some of which will be sketched in subsequent chapters. It may be argued that these attempts shift the focus of interest from the level of value to the level of how useful goods are actually produced.

A similar interest will be followed here. In what follows, I will study the production of useful goods that are capable of satisfying human wants, i.e. goods having use value. I do not discuss whether or not these goods also have exchange value, but it is reasonable to assume with Böhm-Bawerk that generating exchange typically is the purpose of engaging in production, even though this goal may not always be achieved. This approach to production means returning to the issue of use value as a property of goods. As the example of Carl Menger has indicated, this was still a relevant issue for early neoclassical economists, even though subsequent economists have tended to neglect it. Only recently, the issue of use value has been rediscovered in the context of evolutionary consumer theory (Ruprecht, 2001; Witt, 2001). The level of use value is also the level at which I will approach the concept of factors of production. The factor concept developed below investigates the way in which particular kinds of inputs are capable of contributing to the production of useful goods. Factors of production derive their 'factor quality' from providing services in production processes that generate goods with use value, which are capable of fulfilling human wants. Insofar, the concepts developed below would even be applicable to an economy in which no exchange takes place.

The present study stands in the broad tradition of evolutionary approaches to economics. The link to evolutionary economics is present in several dimensions of the argument. First, as was implicit in the previous paragraph, the study adopts a 'classical' definition of economics in terms of its subject matter (roughly, as the academic discipline that deals with how humans conduct the material, non-coercive aspects of their lives) rather than in terms of a specific method (such as rational choice, for example). This basic understanding of economics is a prerequisite for integrating concepts and theories from other disciplines into the economic analysis, which is a general characteristic of evolutionary approaches that I will adhere to below. Second, the present analysis of energy use in production focuses on change and development. It highlights innovation and endogenous novelty generated through learning from experience, and also the importance of qualitative change. These issues have long been central to the field of evolutionary economics. Third, the argument is evolutionary also in that the material statements on the nature and characteristics of goods, production processes and factors of production that I will develop below are grounded in findings from the physical, engineering, biological and behavioral sciences. In line with the hypothesis of an 'ontological continuity of evolution' (Witt, 2003b, p. 3), the argument starts from the basic assumption that evolutionary economic processes are constrained and shaped by the needs and capacities of the human nature as it has evolved over the course of human phylogeny, even though their actual dynamics may be quite different from those of the evolutionary dynamics found in nature. Moreover, in the context of the present study the relevant legacy from natural evolution even extends beyond the biological sphere to include basic physical constraints.

1.3   OUTLINE OF THE ARGUMENT

This book studies the contribution of energy to the production of goods, and the changes over time in the human use of energy for productive purposes. Some conceptual groundwork for the investigation has to be laid first. This will be done in the next two chapters with regard to two different aspects. Chapter 2 introduces a number of energy-related concepts. It starts out by giving a brief summary of the treatment of energy in economics, both in more mainstream approaches and in a separate 'energetic' tradition. Such energetic approaches can be traced over a period of more than 100 years. They attempt to reduce economics to the physical level. Subsequently, I introduce some basic concepts of thermodynamics and discuss their implications for the physical aspect of production. Chapter 3 develops the conceptual framework that provides the basis of the further analysis. It emphasizes the sequential character of production, as most production processes are made up by successive stages of manipulating the objects of production. The intellectual roots of this sequential framework are outlined first. They include economic theories as well as concepts from engineering and management. I then define the concepts of workpieces and operations as the basic building blocks of the framework. Workpieces are the objects of the production process, and operations are its individual stages. Operations fulfill specific functions that are instrumental for increasing the good's usefulness. To execute a particular operation, the services of specific factors of production are required (for more rigorous definitions of these concepts, see section 3.3). It is a central tenet of the present approach, which is also supported by the engineering concepts discussed in Chapter 3, that material statements concerning the nature of operations and the required factor services can be made. The chapter concludes with a discussion of the categories of factors of production implied by the approach taken in this book.

The subsequent two chapters study the role of energy in the production process in more detail. In Chapter 4, I first discuss the factor services provided by energy. The discussion is based on the classification of different energy forms made in physics. In addition, I distinguish between two ways in which energy can provide factor services. 'Direct' factor services of energy inputs are utilized to modify energy-related properties of goods. 'Indirect' factor services of energy are required in operations modifying properties of goods that are not related to energy. Chapter 5 traces the historical development of how factor services of energy have been provided over time. The major historical energy innovations are sketched and classified according to the service categories developed before. I moreover suggest a reinterpretation of the aggregate historical pattern in the use of various sources of energy, emphasizing their increasingly specialized use.

Chapters 6 and 7 change the perspective towards studying the dynamics of technological change in a sequential production process. Chapter 6 first discusses a number of general aspects of process innovations in sequences of operations. It then shows how changes in individual operations can give rise to complementarities at various levels. Finally, the chapter analyzes incompatibility problems that arise from changes to production processes with interdependent operations. The relevant issues are analogous to those discussed in the contexts of modular product designs and complex systems theories. In addition, the discussion highlights the long-term variability of interdependencies. In Chapter 7, the tools developed before are utilized to investigate three historical cases of energy innovations: the transition from wood to coal, the introduction of the steam engine, and the electrification of industrial production. Chapter 8 summarizes the findings and concludes the book.

2. The physical perspective on the economy and its limitations

Energy and material inputs do not figure prominently in many recent innovative developments in industrial economies. Yet as I have argued in the introduction, these developments depend on the well-functioning of more basic sectors of the economy; sectors in which energy and material inputs are indeed crucial. The knowledge economy is only a part of the economy. It presupposes the existence of more traditional sectors and infrastructures. Energy still matters.

This chapter summarizes several lines of research that deal with the physical underpinnings of the economy. It starts by giving a brief survey of the discussion of energy in various strands of economics and related disciplines. I then discuss some basic concepts from thermodynamics and how they have been applied to economic issues. A sketch of open systems thermodynamics and the concept of self-organization follows, which allows for the identification of some relationships between thermodynamics and evolution. Based on the earlier discussion, the major implications of thermodynamics for economic production processes are then outlined. Finally, the chapter points to the limits of analyzing economic processes at the physical level.

2.1 A BRIEF HISTORY OF ENERGY IN ECONOMICS

Energy in Economic Theory

Energy has played a marginal role in twentieth century economics.[4] It has rarely been considered as an explanatory factor in production or growth

4. This statement only holds for the level of 'material' statements that are related to energy as a physical variable. As regards analytical concepts, the field formalism that had been developed in physics to deal with the analysis of energy became the very foundation of the neoclassical model. Thus, in the late nineteenth century, both economic energetics (see below) and

models. In standard production models, physical resources are considered only in form of the classical production factor 'land.' And this factor (to which the eighteenth century physiocrats still attributed the exclusive capacity of generating value) has been increasingly neglected over time. If the nature of inputs is specified at all in present-day production models, it is normally only capital and labor that are taken into consideration as relevant factors of production. A possible explanation for the lack of interest in energy was given in the introductory chapter: Standard economic production models have a price-theoretic focus, and the cost share of energy among the inputs to production is in most cases small. To be sure, some particular fields of contemporary mainstream economics pay considerable attention to energy-related issues. Prominent among them are resource and environmental economics, and also studies of industrial organization that deal with market structure, pricing and regulatory issues in particular energy markets. But even in these fields, it is not energy per se that is considered an important issue, but rather the specific economic characteristics of particular fuels, energy forms, and energy technologies. Two lines of energy-related economic research are most relevant for the present discussion: Theoretical work on exhaustible natural resources, and empirical studies of the interrelations between economic growth and energy use.

The economics of exhaustible (non-renewable) resources are closely intertwined with energy economics both conceptually and historically. Conceptually, and this will emerge more clearly from the subsequent analysis, fossil fuels are the prime examples, if not the only valid cases, of exhaustible resources. Historically, the field of resource economics became prominent at the time of the first oil price shock in 1973. In addition to the debate on 'Limits to Growth' spurred by the 1972 Report to the Club of Rome (Meadows et al., 1972), the oil price hikes experienced in the 1970s led to increasing concerns about the adequacy of energy supplies. These concerns, to which some of the early contributions to the field explicitly refer (e.g., Solow, 1974a), provided an impetus for research into resource economics.

The classic contributions to resource economics were made in the 1970s. They built upon Harold Hotelling's earlier (1931) findings, which until then had largely been neglected by the discipline. Hotelling had shown that under competitive conditions the price of a non-renewable resource (net of marginal extraction cost) increases at the market rate of interest. Only at this rate of price increase is the owner of the resource indifferent between extracting and selling it immediately and keeping it in the ground for later sale (see

neoclassical economics were inspired by physics, but they translated the physical concepts into economics in entirely different ways (Mirowski, 1988, 1989).

Krautkraemer, 1998, for a review of theoretical extensions and empirical tests of the Hotelling model). The basic approach of resource economics was to apply the same kind of logic in a dynamic optimization framework, and to identify feasibility and optimality conditions for paths of resource use under varying assumptions about technology and preferences. Specifically, analysts explored three basic mechanisms and their capacity to compensate for the depletion of non-renewable resources: resource-enhancing technological change, substitution of reproducible capital for the exhaustible resource, and the resort to an alternative technology based on a (practically) non-exhaustible resource base. This alternative technology became known as the 'backstop technology' (Nordhaus, 1973).

Resource economists have found that whether or not a positive level of consumption can be sustained indefinitely in the absence of technological change hinges critically on the elasticity of substitution between the exhaustible resource and reproducible capital. If the elasticity is greater than one, production can proceed without the use of the resource, so that the exhaustible resource does not cause any fundamental problems. By contrast, if the elasticity of substitution is below or equal to one, then the exhaustible resource is essential for the production process (no positive output can be produced with zero input of the resource).[5] For a CES (constant elasticity of substitution) production function with elasticity of substitution strictly below one, consumption eventually has to fall to zero (Dasgupta and Heal, 1974). In the limiting case of an elasticity of substitution equaling one (Cobb–Douglas technology), a positive level of consumption can be sustained indefinitely if the output elasticity of capital exceeds that of the resource (Solow, 1974b). This crucial role of the elasticity of substitution between energy and capital for the long-term feasibility of positive consumption levels has given rise to a debate on the empirical value of the elasticity of substitution, which extends into the present (Frondel and Schmidt, 2002).

Technological change provides a second avenue to alleviate the dependence of production on exhaustible resources. There are numerous ways to include technological change in a dynamic optimization model. Using a Cobb–Douglas framework, Stiglitz (1974) shows that a positive per-capita consumption level can be maintained if the rate of resource-augmenting technological change is at least as high as the growth rate of the population. Finally, if a backstop technology is available, the resource problem is reduced to a problem of choosing the least expensive technology

---

5. Formally a resource R is essential in the production function $Q = F(K,R)$ if $F(K,0) = 0$.

with which to produce. Although using the backstop technology may be costly, its existence ensures that a positive consumption level is feasible.[6]

In spite of the close relation between energy and exhaustible resources, they are not entirely equivalent. On the one hand, not all sources of energy are exhaustible. On the other hand, there is a fundamental physical difference between energy and other natural resources (such as metal ores), which is not reflected in the notion of exhaustible resources. Put simply, all non-energy resources can in principle be recycled completely, provided that sufficient energy is available. By contrast, energy is invariably degraded in its use. (This issue will be discussed in more detail below.) Some contributions to resource economics have not accounted for this difference (e.g., Solow, 1974a; Stiglitz, 1974). However, given the long-term perspective of its models, the difference between energy inputs and non-energy natural resources appears important for resource economics. It also implies a fundamental difference between 'backstop technologies' for the two kinds of resources. If a viable energy 'backstop technology' became available,[7] it would at the same time modify the problem of exhaustible non-energy resources, since it would allow for recycling them over and over again. Accordingly, the 'stock' limitation of non-energy resources would turn into a 'flow' limitation of what quantities of these resources can be used at any point in time (Ayres, 1999). The distinction between energy and non-energy resources moreover matters in another context. A crucial condition for sustained consumption is unbounded productivity of exhaustible resources as resource input goes to zero (Krautkraemer, 1998). This condition is satisfied in standard economic production models such as the Cobb–Douglas technology, but it is hard to reconcile with the laws of physics. For non-energy resources, it may be justified on the basis of recycling. For energy inputs, this justification does not hold.

As was noted above, the economics of exhaustible resources are not the only line of more traditional economic research that is relevant for the purposes of the present study. In addition to developing theoretical models of

6. In addition to identifying feasibility conditions for sustainable positive consumption, resource economists have also produced results on the existence and properties of optimal consumption paths, given alternative assumptions on welfare criteria. Dasgupta and Heal (1974) show in an intertemporal welfare maximization framework that optimal consumption may fall to zero in finite time even if positive consumption would be feasible forever. Solow (1974b) explores the implications of a Rawlsian criterion of intergenerational equity for this issue.

7. Nuclear fusion and solar power are frequently referred to as potential candidates for backstop technologies. While the very feasibility of controlled fusion is still uncertain, the large-scale practicability of an all-solar energy supply system is far from established.

resource use, economists have also studied empirical relationships between economic growth and energy use. International comparisons suggest that the development of an economy's energy intensity, i.e. the ratio of energy inputs to social product at the macroeconomic level, follows a robust pattern. Whereas energy intensity increases in the early development of an economy, it tends to fall in more mature industrial economies. For example, the energy intensity of the US has been falling since the 1920s. In the United Kingdom, the decline in energy intensity began back in the 1870s (Setzer, 1998, p. 210). Because of growing output levels, however, per capita energy use can increase, and does in fact increase, in spite of the reductions in energy intensity. It has moreover been suggested that energy intensity may again begin to rise in very highly developed economies (de Bruyn and Opschoor, 1997).

A related set of contributions includes energy in growth accounting estimations. Several authors have found that by regressing output on labor, capital and energy, the growth performance of industrial countries can be accounted for with only small residuals (Kümmel et al., 1985, 1997; Beaudreau, 1998). By additionally including non-commercial energy inputs and a variable reflecting increases in the efficiency of energy use, Ayres and Warr (2001) can explain US growth from 1900 to the mid-1970s, whereas an unexplained residual of some 12 per cent remains for the period afterwards. These studies do not investigate causality relationships between the variables, however. Since the studies do not address the question whether variables are (co-)integrated, it is moreover unclear how valid their results are. Empirical tests for cointegration and Granger causality[8] between energy and output can be found in the literature, but the findings are inconclusive. While earlier tests for Granger causality between energy and output have mostly been negative (Cheng, 1996), Stern (2000) finds both cointegration and Granger causality from energy to output. His analysis uses a multivariate framework and a quality-adjusted energy measure.

Energetic Approaches to Economic and Cultural Development

The growth accounting studies discussed in the previous section have also found large empirical values for the output elasticity of energy (Kümmel et al., 1997). This result has been interpreted as an indication that energy plays a more important role in economic development than is normally acknowledged in economics. Although they are based on traditional

---

8. A variable x_t is said to Granger-cause a second variable y_t if the prediction of the current value of y_t can be improved by including the past value of x_t (Cheng, 1996, p. 74).

economic methods, the growth regressions thus establish a link to the long tradition of energetic approaches to economics and social science more broadly. In these approaches energy plays a central explanatory role. It is not just introduced as a potential constraint, but rather as a driving force of economic and social development. In terms of the levels distinguished in the introduction, energetic approaches constitute a reduction of economics to the physical level. They have mostly been developed outside and at the margins of academic economics, with many of their protagonists coming from engineering and the sciences (see Martinez-Alier, 1987; Mirowski, 1988; Söllner, 1996 for more extensive discussions). The development of energetic ideas can be traced over the past 100 years and across various academic disciplines.

In the late nineteenth century, the energy concept from physics became one source of inspiration for the academic movement of monism. Monism aspired to develop a unified worldview based on the principles of the natural sciences. It became increasingly popular in Germany at the turn of the twentieth century. Several varieties of monist theories were developed, which took different scientific disciplines as their points of departure (Breidbach, 2000). One variant of monism was 'general energetics,' the analysis of all kinds of phenomena in terms of energy (which would go so far as to include the notion of 'psychic energy' to account for emotions).[9] Its most prominent proponent was Wilhelm Ostwald, a German physical chemist and Nobel laureate. Ostwald developed energetic theories both in physics, where he encountered the opposition of Ludwig Boltzmann and Max Planck (Mirowski, 1989), and in the social and economic realms, where his ideas were rejected by Max Weber ([1909] 1985). According to Ostwald, cultural changes follow in the wake of new energy technologies, and the development of culture aims both at making new energy sources available for use and at exploiting the presently used ones more efficiently. In spite of his emphasis on energy, Ostwald did not go so far as to postulate an energy theory of value (Martinez-Alier, 1987), i.e. to argue that the value of a commodity is proportional to the total amount of energy required for its production, both directly and in the production of other inputs (the commodity's 'embodied energy'). This is in contrast to his contemporaries Sergei Podolinsky, Leon Winiarsky and Ernest Solvay, who all adhered to the energy theory of value.

9. The transfer of concepts did not only flow from natural to social sciences, however. An example for a reverse transfer concerns the origins of ecology. Evolutionary biologist Ernst Haeckel, one of the founders of the *Monistenbund*, coined the term 'ecology' and characterized it as 'the body of knowledge concerning the economy of nature' (1870; quoted in Allee et. al., 1949). In ecology, energy flows are often likened to money flows in the economy.

Since the energy theory of value is a form of a substance theory similar to the earlier labor theory of value, adopting it means going back before the subjectivist revolution in economics. It therefore also means a return to the problems that led neoclassical economists away from that explanation, such as the inability of substance theories to account for changing values of unchanged goods, and their deterministic character, which leaves no room for the subjective evaluation of goods (Mirowski, 1988; Söllner, 1996).

Several decades after Ostwald, another Nobel laureate in chemistry, Frederick Soddy, stressed the importance of energy for economic development. Soddy (1933, p. 27) argued that technological progress is caused by the 'successive mastery over the sources of energy in Nature' and that 'Discovery, Natural Energy and Human Diligence' are the 'real factors that underlie the production of wealth' (ibid., p. 61). Like Ostwald, Soddy did not adhere to an energy theory of value. He distinguished, however, between 'real' wealth based on the use of physical inputs and the merely 'virtual' wealth that is created in financial transactions. Based on this distinction, Soddy suggested that financial crises are caused by the incompatibility between the conservation laws of physics and the growth of debts due to compound interest (Cleveland, 1999).

Even more radical ideas were promoted by the 'technocrats,' a movement led by professional engineers that attracted some popular support in the US in the 1920s and 1930s (Akin, 1977). Technocracy was based on such diverse intellectual influences as Soddy's energetic economics, Frederick Taylor's scientific management, and Thorstein Veblen's radical political economy, which it blended with pre-existing anti-market sentiments that were widespread among engineers (Stabile, 1986; Taylor, 1988; Knoedler and Mayhew, 1999). It aimed at replacing both the market economy and the democratic system with the 'scientific' rule of a caste of engineers who were to run both the economic and the political system. In the search for a scientific, unifying concept for social, political and economic analysis, the technocrats again turned to energy. They adhered to an energy theory of value and saw energy as the driving force of economic development.

During World War II, similar energetic concepts surfaced in anthropology. American anthropologist Leslie White proposed a 'law of cultural evolution' according to which 'culture develops when the amount of energy harnessed by man per capita per year is increased; or as the efficiency of the technological means of putting this energy to work is increased; or, as both factors are simultaneously increased' (1943, p. 338). The parallels to Ostwald's thought are obvious. White developed a stage theory of cultural development, with stages being characterized by differences in energy use. His energetic determinism went as far as claiming that, for lack of new energy technologies, there was 'little cultural advance' between the development of agriculture and the beginning of industrialization in the nineteenth century (ibid., p. 344).

Again one decade later, US sociologist Fred Cottrell (1955) published another theory that related the development of societies to their energetic bases. Cottrell's approach is in striking contrast to White's. He does not postulate 'laws' of development, nor does he claim that developments are determined by energy use patterns. Rather, Cottrell argues for an interdependence of the values held within a society and the energy available to it. He stresses the role of institutions and subjective evaluations for cultural development and allows for persistent inefficiency in energy use patterns.

Canadian economist Bernard Beaudreau is perhaps the most recent author within the tradition of energetic thought. Beaudreau (1998) proposed a 'Newtonian' production theory in which output is a function of energy use, energy efficiency, the level of technology, and the degree of supervision in the production process. He moreover developed a stage theory of economic development that distinguishes three stages according to changes in energy use and their organizational consequences. Beaudreau comes close to an energy theory of value. He argues that energy is the most important input into production, that material well-being is proportional to energy consumption and also that energy use is of central importance for the growth performance of an economy. For example, Beaudreau explains recent trends toward automation and offshore production by the impact of the 1970s oil price shocks. The rationale underlying the argument is that after the explosion of oil prices, the factor share of energy, which had been appropriated by capital and labor before the 1970s, was no longer available to satisfy distributional claims. Instead, capital owners now satisfied their claims to the product at the expense of workers.

Energetic Laws of Evolution and Systems Development

Mathematical biologist Alfred Lotka, a student of Ostwald's, was the founding father of another academic tradition in which energy plays a central role. Contributors to this tradition seek to develop a set of general physical laws of evolution starting from the laws of thermodynamics. The interest of this line of research lies primarily in the development of a general theory of systems dynamics, for which economic systems are only one of several fields of application, rather than in detailed economic theories (see Buenstorf, 2000, for a more thorough discussion).[10] Lotka initiated this line of thought in the

10. The primary objective of the literature sketched in this section is to identify the physical foundations of evolutionary biology. The discussion is summarized in Depew and Weber (1995,

1920s by suggesting that the biosphere is an open system evolving to a state far from thermodynamic equilibrium. To explain the direction that this evolution takes, Lotka proposed a 'law of selection' postulating that *'natural selection* tends to make the energy flux through the system a maximum, so far as compatible with the constraints to which the system is subject' (Lotka, 1922, p. 148; emphasis in original). The law of selection implies that, in terms of energy use, there are two viable strategies for survival. According to Lotka, selection favors both those species which use energy flows more efficiently than their competitors, and those which are capable of exploiting flows of energy that cannot be used by their competitors. Selection pressure thus results in two regularities at the aggregate level of the biosphere. First, in an increasing total energy flow through the biosphere (because of the premium on using novel energy sources), and second, in increasing energy efficiency of individual processes (due to selective advantages of efficient energy use). These ideas appear to be heavily influenced by Ostwald.

Lotka was rather cautious as to the implications of his work. He expressed his 'law of selection' in a conditional form, and explicitly allowed for the occurrence of mutations that are detrimental in terms of energy, as long as they are sufficiently advantageous otherwise. The expected regularities at the aggregate level are therefore not claimed to hold as universal physical laws. Moreover, their realm of validity is restricted to the evolution of the biosphere. Lotka himself was skeptical about whether they could be applied to other realms (Söllner, 1996).

In spite of Lotka's own skepticism, several later authors tried to derive general evolutionary laws from his work. Howard Odum turned the conjecture of increasing energy flow, which he referred to as the 'maximum power' principle (Odum and Pinkerton, 1955), into the foundation of a general systems ecology. In one of the most reductionist contributions to economic energetics, he later applied the maximum power principle to the analysis of human societies (Odum, 1971). In Odum's work, the regularities conjectured by Lotka are turned into universal laws, whereas the behavioral basis of competition and natural selection is abandoned. More recently, Wicken (1980, 1986) used Lotka's contribution as the basis of a proposal for general thermodynamic laws of evolution, ruling both natural and economic systems, and Adams (1981, 1988) advocated a theory of social evolution based on Lotka's principles and the self-organization concept (see below). Weinel and Crossland (1989) tried to derive the direction of technical change from thermodynamic laws.

ch. 17). Starting from the controversies in biology, Foster (1994, 1997) explores the capacity of the approach to provide a conceptual foundation of evolutionary economics.

Biophysical Economics

Yet another energy-based approach to economics developed in reaction to the oil price shocks of the 1970s: 'biophysical economics,' which was to become one of several approaches within the field of ecological economics (Cleveland, 1999). Biophysical economists advocate an energy theory of value, and have made considerable efforts to validate that theory empirically. In his influential contribution to this line of research, Costanza (1980) utilized a multi-sector input–output model to demonstrate the proportionality between economic valuation and the energy requirements of production. Costanza was able to show a close relation between sectoral outputs in monetary terms and energy inputs, but to do so he relied on a controversial method (see Huettner, 1982; Costanza, 1982; Costanza and Herendeen, 1984; Söllner, 1996, for a discussion). A fundamental problem is caused by the data on which the empirical research is based. Because of a lack of data on physical flows, the empirical input–output model is based on money flows between the sectors. Implicitly, the proportionality of money flows and energy flows therefore enters the model as an assumption, which renders the finding of the very proportionality little surprising (Söllner, 1996). A further problem derives from the static character of the input–output method. Even if the embodied energy theory of value holds for any given period, the finding of intertemporal differences in the energy intensity of production remains to be explained (Huettner, 1982).

Problems of Energetic Approaches to the Economy

What can be learned, then, from this review of how various approaches to economics have dealt with energy? First, the discussion clearly shows that even though energy plays only a marginal role in the economic mainstream, there has been no shortage of alternative approaches with more emphasis on energy. That the economics of energy may be more important than is recognized by mainstream economics is an old and recurrent theme. Second, however, none of the energetic approaches was able to attract widespread and sustained academic interest. This failure may be due to the reductionist character of economic energetics, which studies economics exclusively at the physical level of analysis. In subsequent chapters, I will begin to develop a different approach to the economics of energy. This approach does not reduce economics to the physical level, but rather tries to bridge the physical and economic levels of analysis. In particular, I will highlight the role of physical factors for the satisfaction of human wants, i.e. the degree to which the use value of goods depends on these factors. Before delving into that endeavor, however, another line of prior research has to be discussed: the long tradition of approaches that take thermodynamic concepts as their point of departure for studying the physical preconditions of economic activities.

2.2   THERMODYNAMIC CONCEPTS AND ECONOMIC APPLICATIONS

Thermodynamic concepts are a useful point of departure to derive several fundamental relationships about the physical level of economics. Numerous economists have taken this avenue of research, and in doing so they were able to arrive at important results. These thermodynamics-based approaches differ from the economic energetics discussed above in that they do not require a reduction of economics to the level of physics. Some of these approaches use the reference to thermodynamics to identify necessary conditions and regularities at the physical level of economics, without suggesting that these are sufficient to explain economic valuations or patterns of development. In this section, I briefly review some basic thermodynamic concepts and their implications for economics. This review will be helpful to put the arguments of subsequent chapters into perspective.

The First and Second Laws of Thermodynamics

The first and the second laws of thermodynamics are the fundamental physical laws of energy.[11] The first law of thermodynamics states that the energy of an isolated system is constant. To appreciate this statement, one has to know a little terminology of thermodynamics. In thermodynamics, systems are all entities of matter and energy for which boundaries can be specified so that the system can be distinguished from its environment. A system is called 'isolated' if it exchanges neither energy nor matter with its environment. There is at best a single real-world isolated system – the universe as a whole – but even that is controversial among physicists. A 'closed' thermodynamic system is one that has exchanges of energy with its environment, but no exchanges of matter. The planet earth is a straightforward example of a closed system, as it receives energy flows from the sun and radiates heat into space, whereas there are (practically) no mass flows to and from the earth. Finally, a system is 'open' if both energy and matter can flow from and to the environment.

---

[11] The material covered in this section can be found in physics textbooks. Faber et al. (1996, ch. 6) provide an accessible treatment informed by the perspective of ecological economics. The present discussion draws on their exposition.

Given the non-existence of isolated systems in the real world, one might wonder about the relevance of the first law. This relevance goes beyond isolated systems, however, and lies in the principle of energy conservation: It follows from the first law that if the energy of a system changes over time, the change can only be caused by energy flows between the system and its environment. Energy can neither be created nor destroyed. In addition, as all matter contains energy, and since the transformation of matter into energy is possible only at the level of nuclear processes, the conservation law also extends to matter. The first law therefore postulates the conservation of matter in any closed system in which no nuclear processes (such as fission and fusion) take place.

By an appropriate delineation of boundaries to their non-economic environment, economic entities such as production processes, as well as entire economies, can be interpreted as thermodynamic systems. In any such system, all changes in the quantities of energy and matter must be effected through inflows from or outflows to the environment. For production processes, the first law of thermodynamics simply implies that all energy and material resources entering the process must eventually leave the process, either as desired products or undesired wastes (which include waste heat; see Ayres and Kneese, 1969; Ayres, 1998). No energy and no matter is created or lost in the process. The same argument also holds for larger economic systems including the entire global economy (which is conveniently defined as the aggregate of all anthropogenic processes, see also section 2.3 below). All energy and matter that enters the economic sphere from the environment (for example, through the tapping of natural resources) will eventually leave the economic sphere again. Because stocks of matter and energy in the economy may change over time due to capital accumulation, buildup of inventories and the like, energy and mass flows need not be balanced at any single point in time. All differences between inflows and outflows are temporary in nature, however.

The second law of thermodynamics has been expressed in a number of ways. Its classic formulation is due to German physicist Rudolf Claudius who in 1865 stated that the entropy S of an isolated system can never decrease:

$$dS \geq 0 \qquad (2.1)$$

with strict inequality holding for all irreversible processes that proceed with higher than infinitely low velocity, i.e. for all real-world processes. Intuitively, entropy is a measure of the 'unavailability' or 'lack of quality' of energy. The higher the entropy of a system, the smaller is the amount of work that can be done by the energy contained in the system. The entropy of a system increases in irreversible energy conversions and reaches its maximum when the system is in thermodynamic equilibrium.

Heat flows between bodies of different temperature invariably result in a loss of available energy. This loss is measured by the increase of entropy in the combined system. To repeat an oft-cited example (see Faber et al., 1996, ch. 6): If a cold cabin is heated by burning wood in a fireplace, the total energy of the cabin as a thermodynamic system does not change (assuming that no heat is lost to the environment). Some of the cabin's energy changes its form, however. Chemical energy of the firewood is converted into thermal energy of the fire. Temperature gradients in the cabin are reduced by heat transfers from the hot fireplace to the colder air elsewhere. Associated to these heat transfers is an increase in the cabin's entropy. This is because the chemical energy stored in the firewood could have done more work (as a steam-engine fuel, say) than the dispersed thermal energy of the cabin's air can do. The entropy law thus reconciles the first law with the intuition on energy following from day-to-day use of the term: Although the energy of an isolated system is constant according to the first law, it may become less available as a consequence of irreversible processes that the system undergoes.

The classical definition of entropy S is

$$dS = \frac{dQ}{T} \qquad (2.2)$$

where Q stands for heat and T denotes temperature. Equation (2.2) gives the infinitesimal change of the system's entropy associated with an infinitesimal heat flow. The equality in (2.2) only holds for reversible processes of infinitely slow velocities. By integrating both sides of the equation, the change of entropy between two states of the system (along a reversible pathway) can be calculated. For irreversible processes, the equality has to be replaced by an inequality:

$$dS > \frac{dQ}{T} . \qquad (2.2')$$

In the cabin example, the entropy of the system increased due to the heat transfer between the fireplace and the air of the cabin. Heat transfers, which also result from all irreversible conversions of energy, necessarily reduce the capacity of the system's energy to do work. This is due to a fundamental asymmetry between heat and other forms of energy. Whereas all forms of energy can completely be converted into heat, the reverse conversion from heat into work and other forms of energy is necessarily imperfect. Because of this asymmetry, physicists consider heat to be a low-quality form of energy. The theoretical maximum of work W that can be derived from a given amount of heat depends on the difference between the temperature T_1 of the available heat source and the temperature T_0 of the environment. It is given by the formula for the conversion in reversible Carnot engines (Chapman and Roberts, 1983):

$$W = Q\left(1 - \frac{T_0}{T_1}\right). \tag{2.3}$$

Two aspects of the classic formulation of the entropy law are unsatisfactory from the perspective of physics. First, it is limited to processes of heat exchange, whereas increases in entropy may also result from other forms of homogenizations in the composition of a system, for example from homogenizations caused by mixing. Second, Claudius' formulation of the entropy law is a phenomenological one. It is consistent with the empirical observation of increasing entropy in all irreversible processes, but it cannot explain the observation. To deal with these shortcomings and to provide a microfoundation of thermodynamics, the entropy concept of statistical mechanics has been developed, which goes back to the works of Ludwig Boltzmann.

The entropy law of statistical mechanics is based on a hypothetical isolated system of an ideal gas. For this system, a distinction is made between the macrostate of the system, which is given by observable variables such as temperature and pressure, and its microstate, which specifies the (non-observable) positions and velocities of all gas molecules.[12] The entropy of the system in a particular macrostate is expressed as a function of the probabilities ρ_i of all possible microstates corresponding to that macrostate:

$$S = -k\sum_i \rho_i \ln \rho_i \text{ with } k = 1.38 \times 10^{-23} \frac{\text{Joule}}{\text{Kelvin}} \text{ (Boltzmann's constant)} \quad (2.4)$$

For the simplest case of equal probability ρ of all microstates, the system's entropy is given by:

---

12. As a simple illustration of the distinction between macrostates and microstates, think of a board game using two dice. Obviously, in such a game extreme results ('macrostates') such as 12 are less likely than intermediate outcomes such as 7, since the latter can result from a larger number of actual combinations ('microstates') than the former (1-6, 2-5, 3-4, 4-3, 5-2, 6-1 versus 6-6).

$$S = k \ln w \qquad (2.4')$$

where $w = 1/\rho$ is the number of microstates.

In the formulation of statistical mechanics, the second law of thermodynamics postulates that any isolated system develops toward its most probable macrostate. The most probable macrostate is the one that corresponds to the largest number of possible microstates. According to formula (2.4), it also has the highest entropy of all macrostates. This state of maximum entropy is attained when the molecules are diffused equally throughout the system, i.e. when there are no gradients in concentration.

The standard way of illustrating the entropy concept of statistical mechanics is to think of a system containing a number of balls, which are located in one of two containers. Any macrostate of this system is characterized by the number of (unspecified) balls in each container. Any microstate is defined by a complete list of the positions of all individual balls. The system attains its maximum entropy in that macrostate where an equal number of balls is found in both containers. This is the macrostate that can be realized by the largest number of microstates and that is therefore most likely to be attained. Moreover, if the state of maximum entropy (equal distribution of balls) is attained, the containers cannot be distinguished on the basis of the number of balls they contain. It is easy to see how this non-distinguishability of partial systems in the state of maximum entropy suggested the popular generalization of entropy as disorder, even though this generalization is not generally valid.[13]

The entropy concept of statistical thermodynamics provided the foundation of information theoretic concepts that are sometimes utilized in economic applications. Information theory interprets information as a reduction of uncertainty about the state of a system. In this context, entropy S is a measure of ignorance about the state of system Y conditional on the available knowledge X. It is expressed in terms of the probabilities ρ_i of possible states i of the system (Tribus and McIrvine, 1971):

---

[13] There is a fundamental difference between the entropy notions of phenomenological and statistical thermodynamics. According to phenomenological thermodynamics, the entropy law is deterministic – the entropy of a system can under no circumstances decrease. In the formulation of statistical thermodynamics, it is a probabilistic law. According to this law, the entropy of a system may temporarily decrease, although this is very unlikely to happen. This switch from a deterministic law to a probabilistic one has resulted in some controversy in physics, and although the entropy formulation of statistical thermodynamics is commonly utilized in physics, not all physicists accept it as a general foundation of thermodynamics (Prigogine and Stengers, 1984).

$$S(Y|X) = -A\sum_i \rho_i \ln \rho_i \quad \text{with A: constant.} \qquad (2.5)$$

A system's informational entropy is at its maximum when all states are attributed equal probability, i.e. when no information is present on the basis of which the probabilities of different states can be distinguished. On the other hand, entropy becomes zero when one state can be assigned probability one, i.e. when it is known with certainty that this state is attained.

The information I contained in a message is defined as the reduction of entropy that results from knowledge of this message (where X stands for the state of knowledge before and X' for the state of knowledge after the message was received):

$$I = S(Y|X) - S(Y|X'). \qquad (2.6)$$

Economic Applications of Thermodynamic Concepts

Thermodynamic concepts are often used in economic contexts. Most frequently references are made to the notion of entropy. There are, however, numerous different ways in which thermodynamic concepts have been transferred to economics. Since these transfers differ with regard to important aspects, they have to be distinguished.

A first kind of reference to thermodynamics in economics is a heuristic one that can be encountered in methodological contexts. It refers to the second law as a fundamental law showing the irreversibility of real world processes, and holds that it undermines the standard approach of modeling economic processes, because the latter is based on the reversible concepts of classical mechanics. This kind of reference to the second law is not a very powerful argumentative device against economic models. As has been observed by Baumgärtner (2000), it is easily possible within the standard models to exclude reversible processes by assumption, and economists such as Koopmans (1951) have indeed done this. In addition, reference to the second law suggests a general tendency for decline that is difficult to reconcile with the historical record of economic development. Accordingly, it has been argued that as a heuristic for economic irreversibility, the thermodynamics of open systems (discussed in section 2.3 below) are more appropriate than the entropy concept (Proops, 1986; Foster, 1994).

Second, the laws of thermodynamics can be used to demonstrate the necessity of energy inputs into economic processes. At the physical level, no production process is feasible without an input of low-entropic energy. This reference to thermodynamics in order to clarify the physical basis of economic processes is indeed highly useful. It will be dealt with in more detail below.

Third, there has been some controversy about whether concepts from statistical thermodynamics can be applied to economics. The most prominent proponent of introducing thermodynamic concepts into economics, Nicholas Georgescu-Roegen (1971, ch. 6), rejected the relevance of statistical thermodynamics altogether. At the same time, Georgescu-Roegen argued that not only the dissipation of energy, but also the dissipation of matter implies entropic limits to economic development. As this argument cannot be derived from the existing laws of classical thermodynamics, Georgescu-Roegen (1986) proposed a 'fourth law of thermodynamics' postulating that all processes on earth dissipate matter. Georgescu-Roegen's 'fourth law' implies that complete recycling of matter is impossible, so that the amount of resources available for economic processes is permanently decreasing. This position gave rise to a prolonged controversy within ecological economics (see Faber et al., 1996, ch. 7, for a summary). As a result of the controversy, it has been established that the 'fourth law' is not consistent with physics. Given sufficient amounts of available energy, there is no absolute limit to the efficiency of recycling (Ayres, 1999).

In spite of the problems with his 'fourth law,' Georgescu-Roegen's contribution has been very influential. It was the starting point of an entire line of research in ecological economics. In addition, his reasoning provided a major source of inspiration for what might be called the 'doomsday uses' of the entropy concept. These applications of the entropy concept – exemplary is Rifkin (1980) – argue that absolute limits to economic growth derive directly from the second law. The alleged limits to growth are caused by the irreversible reduction of all stocks of low-entropic resources. Rifkin discounts the fact that the earth is not an isolated system for which the entropy law would directly apply, but that it receives low-entropic energy inflows from the sun. The relevance of this kind of argument is highly questionable, however, particularly since when compared to the entropy resulting from natural processes, anthropogenic entropy generation is of minuscule quantities. Kaberger and Mansson (2001) estimate that the natural entropy generation at the earth's surface (through dissipation of solar energy) is some 7500 times larger than anthropogenic entropy generation. With regard to the availability of resources, it is not the entropy law, but the dependence on fossil fuels or the lack of workable recycling technologies that may limit economic development in the foreseeable future.

Yet another transfer of thermodynamic concepts into economics has applied the entropy concept of statistical mechanics to analyses of resource extraction (Faber et al., 1995). In terms of thermodynamics, purification of a mined resource is a process of unmixing. Unmixing is the opposite of a diffusion process and causes a decrease in the resource's entropy. To achieve the (local) reduction in entropy, an input of low-entropic energy is needed for the purification process. The required quantity of low-entropic energy can be calculated (see equations (2.11) and (2.12) below). For two reasons, this calculation is of limited practical applicability, however. First, as is acknowledged by its proponents, it involves some rather 'heroic' assumptions (Faber et al., 1995, p. 124). For example, concentrating copper requires operations of crushing, grinding and flotation to separate the copper ore from rock. These operations require substantial amounts of energy, which do not enter the calculations of changes in entropy from unmixing. Second, the approach analyzes resource extraction exclusively as a physical process of increasing the concentration of a resource. It abstracts from changes in chemical composition, which are important for many resources, including those metals which can be used in industrial processes only after having been reduced from minerals found in nature. As a consequence of these limitations, theoretical results for energy requirements of resource extraction derived from applying the entropy law tend to be much smaller than those observed in real-world processes (Chapman and Roberts, 1983).

Using entropy as a general measure of environmental disruption (see, for example, Faber et al., 1995) seems even more problematic. In this context, the problem with thermodynamic quantities is that they cannot capture the specific problems caused by environmental pollution. For example, there typically exist critical thresholds in an ecosystem's capacity to inactivate pollutants or to reintegrate anthropogenic immissions into biological cycles. These thresholds differ between ecosystems and kinds of pollutants, and the differences cannot normally be derived from thermodynamic considerations (Sartorius, 1999). It is conceivable that total dispersion of a pollutant (i.e. maximum entropy) would do less harm than partial dispersion that exceeds the threshold values of some of the affected ecosystems.[14]

Information theoretic entropy measures were originally developed for applications to communication technology. Applying them to economic issues requires on the one hand that all possible states of the system and their corresponding probabilities are known. This knowledge is not available in situations involving novelty and genuine uncertainty (Knight, 1921). On the other hand, information theory abstracts both from the content of a message (its semantics) and from its practical effects (its pragmatics). As these are the core conditions of economic relevance of a message, information theoretic

---

14. The same limitations also apply to proposals of environmental indicators that are based on other general thermodynamic variables such as exergy (Ayres, 1998). Exergy will be discussed in the following section.

concepts are of limited usefulness in economics (Binswanger, 1992). In this context, it is frequently noted that energy and information are equivalent from the perspective of physics. Accordingly, the information theoretic entropy concept can be used to show the minimum energy requirement for acquisition of a bit of information (9.57×10^{-24} *Joule/Kelvin*; see Tribus and McIrvine, 1971, p. 184).[15] Again, this equivalence is not very relevant for economics, because actual energy requirements of communication strongly vary between different technologies and typically exceed the theoretical minimum by orders of magnitude (ibid.).

Analogies to thermodynamics are another way in which the entropy concept has been applied to economic contexts. Such analogies are often based on interpreting entropy increases as losses of order. They tend to invoke the second law of thermodynamics to prove the necessity of monotonic developments in some economic variables. In other words, thermodynamic variables are replaced by economic ones, and even though the arguments thus derived have no physical meaning, the validity of the physical laws is postulated. As a consequence, analogical applications of thermodynamics are questionable at best (see Söllner, 1996, for a more thorough critique and examples).

Finally, entropy is also used as a descriptive statistical measure of variety (Saviotti, 1996). For example, Frenken (2001a, ch. 5) has adopted entropy measures to describe the development over time of technological designs. The statistical entropy measure is formally equivalent to the entropy concept of statistical thermodynamics. It has no thermodynamic connotations, however. In particular, in applying entropy as a descriptive statistic, no recourse is made to the second law as a cause of particular dynamics. It is therefore crucial to distinguish the descriptive use of the entropy concept for statistical purposes from the analogies mentioned in the previous paragraph.

This section has indicated the variety of ways in which the entropy concept has been transferred to economic reasoning. This variety has been confusing and at times even misleading. As a consequence of loose references to entropy as disorder and of unfounded thermodynamic analogies, the notion of entropy moreover seems discredited to many economists. Nonetheless, as I will argue later in this chapter, thermodynamic concepts are valuable for the analysis of the physical level of production, and the fundamental relevance of thermodynamic laws for the physical level of economic processes is beyond doubt. Fortunately, however, the application of thermodynamic concepts to economics does not depend on the notion of

15. This figure equals ln 2 times Boltzmann's constant k (see Tribus and McIrvine, 1971, p. 181).

entropy. As an alternative to entropy, the variable 'exergy' will be defined and outlined in the following section.

Exergy: an Encompassing Thermodynamic Variable

In this section, some further thermodynamic relations are outlined which are of importance for economics.[16] The exposition is based on the notion of exergy that was first developed by Rant (1956, 1957) and has primarily been adopted in engineering. Exergy provides a general measure of the available energy of a thermodynamic system. It can be defined as 'the amount of work obtainable when some matter is brought to a state of thermodynamic equilibrium with the common components of the natural surroundings by means of reversible processes' (Szargut et al., 1988, p. 7). As opposed to energy, exergy is not subject to a conservation law (roughly speaking, exergy is what in day-to-day discourse is understood by energy). Since the exergy of a system is a function of both the system itself and of the state of its environment, it is defined relative to a reference state only. The specification of the reference state necessarily involves a degree of arbitrariness, because the earth is not in thermodynamic equilibrium, and no absolute criterion for the specification exists.

A formal definition of exergy B has been developed by Szargut et al. (1988). This definition has four components:

$$B = B_{pot} + B_{kin} + B_{phys} + B_{chem} . \qquad (2.7)$$

(Gravitational) potential exergy B_{pot} stems from differences between system and environment in terms of elevation. Kinetic exergy B_{kin} results from the state of motion that the system has relative to its environment. Physical exergy B_{phys} is due to differences in temperature and/or pressure. Chemical exergy B_{chem} is caused by differences in the chemical compositions of system and environment. Equation (2.7) is a simplified definition that was originally developed for engineering purposes. It concentrates on the practically most relevant forms of exergy and excludes nuclear, magnetic, radiant and electric exergy and also interfacial effects. It is worthwhile to look at the individual components of equation (2.7) in a little more detail. In this way, the relationship between exergy and entropy can be demonstrated, and also the way in which order, or more precisely distinguishability, can be expressed in terms of exergy.

16. The present section draws on Szargut et al. (1988), Spiegler (1983), and Ayres (1998).

The exploitation of natural gradients in potential exergy B_{pot} and kinetic exergy B_{kin} provides the basis of important energy technologies. Water power utilizes the kinetic energy of falling water, which in turn stems from its potential energy, and converts it into mechanical work. Similarly, wind power exploits the kinetic exergy of wind, i.e. its motion relative to the ground. In addition to utilizing natural gradients in potential and kinetic exergy, economic processes may also establish new gradients. A system's potential exergy B_{pot} is modified in all processes where the transportation of materials and objects changes their elevation. Gradients in kinetic exergy are generated in a wide variety of economic processes, including both transportation and production processes that physically modify materials and objects.

Physical exergy B_{phys} gives a measure of the amount of work that could be obtained if the system were taken in reversible processes from initial temperature T and pressure p to the environment's temperature T_0 and pressure p_0. B_{phys} derives both from temperature and pressure differences between the system and its environment, and from the existence of temperature and pressure gradients within the system. The physical exergy of an internally homogenous system is given by:

$$B_{phys} = -T_0(S - S_0) + p_0(V - V_0) \qquad (2.8)$$

where S stands for entropy, V for volume, and the subscript 0 denotes variables pertaining to the environment (Spiegler, 1983). Neglecting changes in pressure, losses of B_{phys} are caused by heat transfers from the system to its environment and by equilibration of internal temperature differences. Equation (2.8) indicates that physical exergy and entropy of a system are inversely related. The physical exergy of a system decreases as its entropy increases:

$$\Delta B_{phys} = -T_0 \Delta S \qquad (2.9)$$

The fourth right-hand term of the exergy definition (2.7), chemical exergy B_{chem}, denotes the work that could ideally be done by the equilibration of differences in chemical composition, both between the system and its environment and within the system. Chemical exergy accounts for the bulk of exergy inputs into economic processes. Most importantly, the combustion of fuels exploits their chemical exergy to obtain heat and work. Chemical exergy moreover provides a measure of the possibility of distinguishing the chemical composition of a system from that of its environment. The higher a system's chemical exergy, the more different it is chemically from its environment and/or the more pronounced are internal differences in the chemical composition of different parts of the system.

As chemical exergy B_{chem} is a measure of a system's available chemical energy relative to its environment, evaluating it requires prior specification of the environment's chemical composition. In Szargut et al. (1988), the average chemical compositions of the atmosphere, of the ocean, and of the earth's crust are adopted as environmental 'reference states' for the different chemical elements. Compounds found in these reference states are selected as so-called 'reference species' for the chemical elements. For example, CO_2 is adopted as the reference species for carbon, and Fe_2O_3 for iron, because these compounds are the prevalent forms in which the elements occur naturally in the chosen reference state. Dependent on the abundance (mole fraction) of the reference species in the reference state, the standard chemical exergy of the reference species is calculated such that components less abundant in nature (such as xenon) have higher chemical exergy than more abundant ones (such as nitrogen).

Since the theoretical minimum of exergy needed for chemical processes can be derived from the difference in exergy levels between outputs and inputs, it is worthwhile to have a brief look at how chemical exergy levels are calculated. For substances that do not occur in the reference states, specific chemical exergy is given by:

$$b_{chem} = G_{form} + \sum_{el} n_{el} b_{chem,el} \,. \tag{2.10}$$

In equation (2.10), G_{form} stands for the standard Gibbs free energy of formation of the substance, the n_{el} are the numbers of moles of the elements contained in the substance, and the $b_{chem,el}$ values denote the specific chemical exergies of these elements. It is the energy required for the reaction in which the substance is formed from the elements. G_{form} is the crucial quantity in this equation. It is positive if energy has to be provided to enable the formation. It is negative if the substance forms spontaneously, and the formation has a net energy output. For example, the G_{form} values of common metallic minerals are negative (Chapman and Roberts, 1983). Pure metals accordingly have higher chemical exergy than their minerals, which implies that exergy inputs are required for the reduction of the minerals. For combustible fuels, the respective combustion products are taken as reference species. The chemical exergy of fuels corresponds closely to their caloric value. It attains large values, because large quantities of work can be derived from the reactions in which these fuels are combusted. Processes in which fuels are burnt accordingly result in large exergy losses.

So far the discussion of chemical exergy has been limited to pure substances. Finally, exergy differences between pure and mixed substances have to be taken into account. The mixing of substances reduces the exergy of the total system because it eliminates a gradient in composition. (Whereas separation of substances, as the inverse operation, leads to an increased exergy, and accordingly requires that exergy be added to the system from the environment.) The effect of mixing is incorporated in the calculation of the chemical exergy measure B_{chem}. Using simplifying ideal gas assumptions, the chemical exergy of a mixed substance can be calculated as:

$$B_{chem} = \sum_i n_i b_{chem,i} + RT_0 \sum_i n_i \ln z_i \qquad (2.11)$$

where R is the gas constant, n_i gives the number of moles of the ith component of the solution, and z_i is the mol fraction of the ith component (Szargut et al., 1988). Since all $z_i < 1$, the second term in (2.11) is negative, and the exergy of the mixed substance is indeed smaller than that of its pure components.

Formula (2.11) for the exergy loss due to the mixing of substances can again be related to the analogous formulae used to study entropy changes in resource extraction. For instance, in Faber et al. (1995) the increase of entropy due to mixing is calculated by using the standard formula for the mixing of two ideal gases:

$$\Delta S = R \left(n_1 \ln \frac{V}{V_1} + n_2 \ln \frac{V}{V_2} \right) \qquad (2.12)$$

where V_1, V_2 are the volumes of the two substances, and n_1, n_2 stand for the respective numbers of moles. Since the ratio of volumes equals the ratio of the number of moles under ideal gas assumptions, the decrease in exergy due to mixing according to the second term of (2.11) equals T_0 times the increase in entropy given by (2.12) – which again indicates the inverse relation of entropy and exergy changes that was already seen in equation (2.9). In other words, entropy changes due to (un-)mixing are a special case of exergy changes.

The comparison made in the last paragraph demonstrates that the same processes can be expressed in terms of entropy and in terms of exergy. But why should the unfamiliar notion of exergy be used when there is the entropy concept as a much more familiar alternative? Thinking about energy issues in terms of exergy rather than entropy has several advantages. First, exergy is a general measure for the possibility of distinguishing a thermodynamic system from its environment, which is based on differences in terms of state of motion, temperature, pressure, chemical composition, etc. All these differences can be expressed as differences in exergy, and it follows from the second law of thermodynamics that they cannot increase in an isolated system. Exergy thus reflects the multidimensional character of energy. It is broad enough to capture aspects of energy use that may be overlooked if energy issues are restricted to the analysis of specific fuels (Lozada, 1999). Second, the relationship between entropy and (dis-)order, which has caused much confusion, can be given a precise meaning in terms of exergy. Gradients in physical exergy, differences in chemical composition and varying degrees of purity, all of which can in some way be interpreted as kinds of 'order,' can be summarized in a single exergy value. Third, exergy carries less mystical and controversial connotations than the entropy concept with its long history of heated debates, contested applications, and loose analogies. Fourth, there is a very pragmatic advantage of exergy. Changes in exergy are into the intuitive direction, with decreasing exergy meaning a reduced capacity of a system's energy to do work and vice versa. It is thus more intuitive than entropy, which increases with the 'unavailability' of energy.

2.3 OPEN SYSTEMS THERMODYNAMICS

Open Systems and the Self-Organization of Dissipative Structures

The second law of thermodynamics has often been interpreted as a general law of decay postulating the loss of order in any natural system. But how can such a general law of decay be squared with the observation that in the evolving biosphere, increasingly complex structures came into existence, and also with notions of progress and development in the social realm? This apparent paradox between thermodynamics and evolution has puzzled scientists for a long time. It is, however, easily resolved once two points are taken into consideration. First, the interpretation of increasing entropy as loss of order is correct, as was argued above, only under quite restrictive conditions. Second, the second law is defined only for isolated systems, whereas all real-world systems are open or at least closed, i.e. they exchange exergy (and in the case of open systems also matter) with their environment.

Starting at the most encompassing level, the planet earth is a closed thermodynamic system but not an isolated one. The earth receives a permanent inflow of exergy from the sun, and it emits heat of lower temperature (i.e. of lower exergy) into outer space. There is thus a net inflow of exergy from the sun to the earth. Whereas this exergy inflow is more or less steady over very long periods of time, it is not a priori clear whether it is higher or lower than the loss of exergy caused by internal processes within the system earth. For example, the 'exergy stores' of fossil fuels exploited today have accumulated over long periods of time. This suggests that during the accumulation process there was a 'surplus' of solar exergy. The present-day accumulation of biomass by organisms similarly means that they are, temporarily, able to increase their level of exergy. At the same time, the exergy of chemical and physical gradients existing on earth is permanently reduced in various geological, ecological and biological processes (such as erosion or wood fires).

Changes in the total exergy of the earth can be written as an exergy balance in the following way (the representation is analogous to the formulation in terms of entropy by Prigogine, 1976; the basic insight underlying the representation can already be found in Schrödinger, 1945):

$$dB = d_i B + d_e B . \qquad (2.13)$$

Equation (2.13) states that the total change of exergy dB of a non-isolated system can be broken down into changes $d_i B$ caused by internal processes that do not involve exergy flows from and to the environment, and changes $d_e B$ that are based on flows between system and environment. The change of exergy due to internal processes $d_i B$ cannot be positive. (This simply follows from (2.1) and (2.9).) For the system earth, it is clearly negative as real-world exergy conversions are not proceeding infinitely slowly and are therefore not reversible. On the other hand, $d_e B$, the net exergy inflow from the sun, is positive, and accordingly the sign of dB is not determined a priori. The change in the total exergy of the earth can in principle be positive or negative.

The aggregate of all anthropogenic processes may be defined as the economic subsystem of the system earth. The economic subsystem is a thermodynamically open system, i.e. it exchanges both energy and matter with the environment (which by definition encompasses all energy and matter that is not utilized for human purposes). For the economic system, the exergy balance of equation (2.13) holds as well. The internal change of the economic system's exergy is necessarily negative, and the total exergy of the economic system can increase only if the internal decrease is compensated by positive exergy flows from the non-economic environment. In other words, the thermodynamic system 'economy' requires exergy inputs in order to develop and maintain gradients in kinetic and potential exergy, temperature, pressure and chemical composition.

A separate branch of open systems thermodynamics has been developed during the past decades, which deals with open systems and their capacity to develop and maintain 'dissipative' structures of increasing complexity on the basis of energy exchanges with the environment (Prigogine and Stengers, 1984, ch. 5). Open systems thermodynamics distinguishes between three realms of thermodynamics. First, in the state of thermodynamic equilibrium, entropy is at its maximum (and exergy is zero). Second, within a certain distance from equilibrium, flows of entropy-producing processes can be represented as linear functions of the underlying forces (such as temperature gradients), and the system develops toward a stable stationary state. In this stationary state, entropy production (exergy loss) is at the minimal rate compatible with the boundary conditions. Sustained exergy flows from the environment are required to prevent the system from reaching the equilibrium state. Finally, if due to increasing exergy inflows from the environment, the system attains a critical distance from equilibrium, there may be processes that cannot be described by linear relationships between flows and forces, and stationary states need no longer be stable. In this far-from-equilibrium realm of thermodynamics, instabilities may occur in which random fluctuations are so amplified that they have a permanent effect on the system's development. Due to the possibility of bifurcations, the exact development of the system is not predictable in the far-from-equilibrium realm.

The states that far-from-equilibrium systems attain are qualitatively different from those close to equilibrium. The development of far-from-equilibrium systems has been referred to as the 'self-organization of dissipative structures' (Prigogine, 1976). This expression highlights that structures are developed 'from within,' without organizing forces from outside the system, and that the development depends on the dissipation of exergy. As all complex physical, chemical, biological and also economic systems exist in the far-from-equilibrium realm, the concept of dissipative structures provides a universal thermodynamic characterization of their development. On its basis, it has been argued that, in terms of thermodynamics, an economy is 'the 'same sort of thing' as an organism, a flame, or a convection cell' (Proops, 1983, p. 354).

On the Relationship between Self-Organization and Evolutionary Change

Prigogine's work on open systems thermodynamics can be utilized to derive some relationships between the self-organization of dissipative structures on the one hand and evolutionary processes on the other.[17] In doing so, I will

---

17. The argument of this section is developed in more detail in Buenstorf (2000). For a related, but somewhat different position, see Foster (1997).

understand self-organization as the emergence of system-level structures and properties brought about by the interaction of the system's components, in the absence of centralized control or coordination. Self-organization is driven by exogenous changes in the system's boundary conditions (changing exergy flows from the environment). Evolutionary processes, by contrast, are understood as processes that endogenously generate complex structures in the system, without any (exogenous) manipulation of the system's boundary conditions taking place.

It can first be noted that far-from-equilibrium conditions are necessary for evolution. This simply follows from the observation that close-to-equilibrium systems develop to a stable stationary state of minimal exergy loss. It is only far from equilibrium that the development of the system is not determined by the minimization of exergy loss. This indeterminacy is a prerequisite for the development of increasingly complex structures in evolutionary processes.

Second, the self-organization of dissipative structures is not sufficient for an evolutionary process. Numerous non-living systems (for example convection cells and autocatalytic chemical processes) develop dissipative structures, but do not evolve in the sense of generating endogenous complexity. Qualitative changes in the behavior of these systems are only caused by exogenous changes in boundary conditions.

Third, self-organization dynamics may underlie evolutionary processes. Self-organization is based on an interplay of non-linear relations of positive and negative feedback between the system's components. Prigogine emphasized that, in the self-organization of dissipative structures, order arises through fluctuation (Prigogine, 1976; Prigogine and Stengers, 1984, ch. 6). Positive feedback is necessary to amplify random fluctuations such that they can have a lasting effect on the system's development. Prigogine and his co-workers showed that if the boundary conditions of particular auto- and crosscatalytic chemical reactions are progressively modified, transitions between behavioral states occur at critical parameter values. At these transitions the system's further development is no longer predictable, but depends on the specific realization of random fluctuations. Negative feedback is required in self-organization in order to temporarily stabilize the system against further fluctuations, i.e. for the maintenance of structured states. These basic dynamics of self-organization as an interplay of positive and negative feedback can also be identified in evolutionary systems. Consider for example the evolution of biological systems. Mutations in individual organisms may change the relative fitness of a number of organisms interacting with them. These changes may trigger behavioral adaptations by other organisms and thus give rise to entirely new patterns of interaction. From the system perspective, then, mutations represent fluctuations from which a new structure of interaction and possibly a new 'order' at the system level may develop. In turn, the specifics of the new 'order' affect the chances of success for later mutations (an 'occupancy effect,' Witt, 1999), so that the system's development is historically contingent.

Finally, evolutionary processes are based on the self-organization of dissipative structures, combined with endogenous change in the boundary conditions. Prigogine et al. (1972; a similar point is made by Ebeling and Feistel, 1992) suggest that early organisms developed from non-living far-from-equilibrium structures in a process involving a series of bifurcations. For this process to result in increasing complexity, the presence of positive 'evolutionary feedback' (Prigogine et al., 1972, p. 25) was necessary. Evolutionary feedback is argued to operate whenever evolutionary changes result in increasing exergy flows into the evolving system, and therefore enhance the sytem's further evolutionary potential. The existence of evolutionary feedback fundamentally changes the conditions of the self-organization process: Boundary conditions are no longer exogenous (as for the simple chemical systems), but they are endogenously modified by the system's development itself. In the evolution of the biosphere, photosynthesis is a straightforward example of evolutionary feedback. Photosynthesis vastly expanded the range of exergy sources that could be exploited by organisms. It thus created the preconditions for countless further evolutionary changes. Similar positive evolutionary feedback can also be identified in economic evolution. Human creativity has drastically modified the energy-related boundary conditions of economic activities by making new exergy sources available to human agents. This feedback is even more direct than that present in the evolution of the biosphere, as it operates on deliberate behavioral modifications rather than random variations, with incentives for further evolutionary change resulting from the rewards and punishments of market competition (the dynamics of which can also be considered a form of self-organization; see Witt, 1985).

These considerations suggest that, although economic processes are far-from-equilibrium processes, open systems thermodynamics is not sufficient as a conceptual foundation for studying them. Because of human ingenuity, an economy, as an evolutionary system, is capable of generating endogenous novelty. This includes the capacity to modify the energy-related preconditions for its own further development. In this way, then, an economic system is more than a convection cell. The self-organization of dissipative structures is part of evolutionary processes, but evolution cannot be reduced to self-organization.

2.4   ECONOMIC IMPLICATIONS OF THERMODYNAMIC CONCEPTS

The Necessity of Exergy as an Input into Production

Based on the above discussion of thermodynamic concepts, a definition of production processes can now be given. The definition includes the physical level and takes into consideration the non-equilibrium character of the environment in which a variety of exergy-dissipating processes occur without human intervention. Human production activities intervene into these spontaneous processes to generate an output of useful goods. The *production of goods* can then be defined as:

> anthropogenic modification of spontaneous natural processes within a system of matter that aims at making the system of matter better suitable for fulfilling human wants.

On the basis of this definition, two basic types of production processes can be distinguished, which differ in the physical nature of their product (see Figure 2.1). This distinction is useful to clarify the relationship between exergy and the use value of goods. The first kind of production process (type 1 of production processes in Figure 2.1) aims at creating new local gradients of exergy, i.e. its desired products have higher exergy than the material inputs that went into their production. The second kind of production process (type 2 of Figure 2.1) aims at artificially eliminating exergy gradients. In these processes, the exergy of the desired products is lower than that of the material inputs.

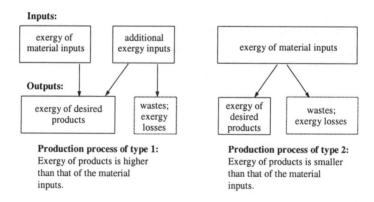

Figure 2.1 Inputs and outputs of two types of production processes

Some thermodynamic analyses of production have focused on the first kind of production processes and suggested increases in exergy (or, equivalently, reductions of entropy) from inputs to outputs as a general property of production. Such a position is consistent with Georgescu-Roegen's view (1979) that low entropy is a necessary (albeit not sufficient) condition for a thing to have value. Baumgärtner (2000, p. 76) takes the fact that desired products have lower specific entropy (per mass unit) than the inputs into their production as the defining characteristic of a class of processes, which he refers to as 'industrial production processes.' Many real-world production processes are indeed of such an exergy-increasing kind. For a simple example one might think of the construction of a wall of bricks, where the bricks in the wall attain additional exergy in the form of a gradient of potential energy relative to their environment. Similarly, increasing the concentration of a natural resource by means of physical processes increases its exergy as compared to the initial, diffused state. In traditional agriculture, solar energy is utilized to produce products that have higher exergy than the substances on which their growth is based.

It is, however, not necessarily the case that the desired outputs of production processes have higher exergy than the inputs into the process (this point is also made by Kaberger and Mansson, 2001). As an example with some industrial relevance consider machining. Turning a block of metal into, say, a camshaft, decreases the total exergy of the workpiece, because its mass (and therefore its exergy) is reduced, without any compensating increases in potential, kinetic, physical or chemical exergy being discernible. And the fact that the new shape is more useful for a specific human purpose than the original block of metal does not enter the calculation of exergy.[18] The 'specific' exergy per mass unit of the workpiece remains constant in this process, as long as its chemical composition is unaltered.

Industrial processes may also result in reductions of the 'specific' exergy of the end product vis-à-vis the raw materials. This is the case in processes that are primarily based on exothermic chemical reactions or the mixing of different materials. Goods made from composite materials (such as tires or processed foods) exemplify this kind of production processes. If in the above example of constructing a wall, the wall is made from concrete rather than

---

18. It may be objected that the exergy of the workpiece has been increased in earlier stages of the production process, particularly in the production of the metal. This objection is not generally valid, however. It would for example not hold for a stonemason's production of a sculpture from a stone. The difficulty involved in representing important production processes such as machining in thermodynamic terms may have provided the impetus for Ayres' (1994b) informational approach, which combines thermodynamic concepts with measures of morphological information.

from bricks, an exergy decrease stemming from mixing the concrete counteracts the exergy increase due to higher potential energy. Similarly, the hot air in a sauna is the output of a production process, since it stems from a modification of natural processes and some people have a desire to experience the heat transfer from the sauna to their body. In this case, the very existence of a heat transfer implies that some of the exergy of the fuel inputs into the production process has been dissipated (recall that exergy is defined as the availability of its energy to do work and that heat can only imperfectly be converted into work).

This distinction between exergy-increasing and exergy-decreasing kinds of production processes shows that there is no simple relationship between the usefulness of goods on the one hand and their exergy or entropy on the other. Moreover, due to the existence of these different kinds of production processes, it does not seem possible to give a physical definition of production which is less abstract than the one proposed above, and which nonetheless is of sufficient generality. Irrespective of their kind, however, one general physical regularity applies to all production processes. At the most encompassing level (i.e. taking into account both the economic system and its natural environment), they invariably accelerate the equilibration of gradients brought about by natural processes. Exergy is therefore a necessary input into both kinds of production processes. In processes of the first kind, the establishment of new local exergy gradients requires a compensating elimination of other exergy gradients, because otherwise these processes would violate the second law of thermodynamics. Since real-world processes are not infinitely slow and therefore are irreversible, the 'losses' of exergy gradients must be larger than the 'gains' in the desired product, so that there is a net exergy input into the process. In production processes of the second kind, accelerating the equilibration of gradients (through the reduction of the product's exergy) is the very purpose of the process. Accordingly, there is a net input of exergy into the process. In both kinds of production processes, then, exergy inputs are required. If one aims at a complete description of production processes at the physical level of analysis, exergy is a necessary input into any production process. Exergy enters either via the material resources themselves, or it has to be provided through additional exergy inputs.

One final point should be made in this context. Although the input of exergy is necessary for all modifications of natural processes, exergy inputs are not a sufficient condition for an actual modification to qualify as a *production* process – because the exergy input alone does not guarantee the usefulness of the product. The latter cannot be established on the basis of physical considerations alone.

The Output Side: on the Ubiquity of Joint Production

So far the argument has focused on the inputs into production processes. But the thermodynamic analysis of production also allows for useful insights into the output side of production. It shows that, as Faber et al. (1998) succinctly put it, 'All production is joint production.' In their thermodynamic analysis, which is further elaborated in Baumgärtner (2000, ch. 4) and embedded in a more conceptual discussion in Baumgärtner et al. (2001), they utilize the joint production concept to emphasize that external effects from production are not special cases, but rather the 'ubiquitous and inevitable consequences of the physical nature of producing goods' (Faber et al., 1998, p. 145).[19]

More specifically, these authors distinguish between three cases of joint production. First, joint production may be implied by the first law. This is the case if the mass balance of the first law requires more than a single product to be fulfilled. Put differently, only if all matter that enters the production process through the various inputs is contained in a single output is there no thermodynamic requirement for a joint product implied by the first law. For this condition to hold, all chemical elements have to be contained in this single output in exactly the same quantities as they were contained in the inputs. Second, joint production may be a consequence of the second law. All real-world processes are irreversible and produce heat as a joint product. In addition to this general case of heat production, a third class of joint production is distinguished for those production processes in which the specific entropy (entropy per mass unit) of the product is lower than that of the material inputs (the abovementioned class of 'industrial production processes'). For this reduction in specific entropy to be possible, a 'shifting of low specific entropy from fuels to desired products' (Faber et al., 1998, p. 142) has to occur. An additional high-entropy waste product is accordingly necessary in order for the process to be consistent with the second law. This argument for a third class of joint production depends on the use of the entropy concept, and on conceiving of entropy as a product. If alternatively (and equivalently) one thinks of the second law in terms of exergy, the increased exergy (per mass unit) of the end product relative to the low-exergy inputs obviously requires inputs providing this exergy. However, no by-products in addition to waste heat (captured by the second case of joint production in Faber et al., 1998) are necessarily produced. Of course, this observation does not alter the general result of the authors: At the level of

---

19. Although they did not discuss it as a phenomenon of joint production framework, the ubiquity of undesired outputs and external effects was already pointed out by Ayres and Kneese (1969).

thermodynamics, joint products (if only in the form of waste heat) result with necessity from all production processes.

Exergy as a Driving Force of Economic Evolution?

As I have argued in more detail in section 2.1, more sweeping claims are sometimes made about the economic significance of energy (more precisely, exergy) than that it is only necessary as an input in all production. Authors from various backgrounds have suggested that energy is a force driving economic or more broadly cultural evolution. Their arguments have been based on evidence suggesting both a close correlation of economic activity and energy use, and a significant role of new energy technologies in waves of technological innovation and economic development.

The above distinction between the self-organization of dissipative structures and evolutionary processes, combined with the necessity of exergy as an input into production processes, suggests a subtle yet significant shift in perspective. It implies both that the availability of new energy technologies is not exogenous to the activities of economic agents, and that additional energy inputs into the economic system are not sufficient for its development. If, first, exergy is required as an input into all production, and if, second, the competitive market process endogenously creates incentives for innovation, then the observable correlation of economic activity and exergy use can be explained without relying on exergy as an exogenous explanatory factor. Because of the necessity of exergy as an input, an expanding production volume simply requires increasing amounts of exergy, unless its increasingly efficient use 'liberates' sufficient exergy resources to allow for the expansion. Under competitive conditions, the need for exergy will be translated into an incentive for making new kinds and quantities of exergy available. If the search for new exergy sources is successful, aggregate exergy use will tend to increase. At the same time, a competitive advantage can also be gained by being able to use the existing exergy resources more efficiently than one's competitors, insofar and as much as the more efficient use translates into lower costs of production. Both increasing exergy use and increasing exergy efficiency in the process of economic evolution can thus be interpreted as *consequences* of the competitive economic process rather than as its driving forces. Moreover, the realization of both tendencies in an actual economic situation, and their relative importance, depends on the specific resource quantities, technologies and institutions available as well as on relative prices (Buenstorf, 2000). From this perspective, then, the driving force behind economic development is to be found in human ingenuity, shaped by economic competition, rather than in the amount of exergy 'pumped' through the economic system.[20]

2.5 CONCLUSIONS: THE NEED FOR A MORE ECONOMIC APPROACH

In this chapter I have dealt with two broad issues. First, I have reviewed the treatment of energy in economics. It emerged from the review that whereas energy plays only a marginal role in the economic mainstream, a long tradition of heterodox approaches exists in economic energetics that consider energy an important factor of economic production and development. The second aim pursued in this chapter was to derive some of the implications of thermodynamics for the study of production. The main finding of this endeavor was that, according to the laws of physics, exergy is a necessary input into all production processes. The exergy concept also proved useful for integrating the various aspects of thermodynamic considerations. Moreover, starting from concepts of open systems thermodynamics, the relationship between thermodynamics and evolution in general, and the energetic basis of economic evolution in particular, were discussed.

The discussion of this chapter aimed at clarifying the nature and limits of a physical analysis of economic processes. It indicated the rather general and abstract nature of the economic implications of thermodynamics. Thermodynamics is unsuitable for deriving detailed economic predictions. Its laws exclude some developments from the range of possible ones, but they cannot tell us which of the remaining ones are more or less likely to be realized. And the range of events that are compatible with the laws of thermodynamics is sufficiently large to render the constraints implied by these laws of little practical interest for most economic issues. A very notable exception is fundamental investigations into issues of resource availability and growth limitations. In these investigations, analysis of economic issues at the physical level is indispensable. They are not the subject of the present study, however.

At this point, it seems worthwhile to return to the distinction between physical and economic levels of analysis made in the introduction. In terms of that distinction, the various forms of economic energetics discussed in section 2.1 amount to reducing economics to the physical level. In their more

20. This is also suggested by the failure of Soviet-type socialist economies, which were grossly energy-inefficient but not particularly innovative.

extreme forms, energetic approaches deny the autonomous existence of an economic analysis, and reduce even the level of value to the physical concept of energy. By contrast, approaches using thermodynamic concepts to analyze specific economic issues tend to distinguish more clearly between the various levels of analysis (this is done most explicitly in Baumgärtner, 2000). What is less clear in these approaches is how the thermodynamic analysis links to the more genuinely economic issues of use and exchange value. And this missing link between the physical and the economic analysis may be the reason why many economists neglect the findings based on thermodynamic considerations. From the economist's perspective, the relevance of thermodynamic concepts is not as obvious as it may seem to physicists. For example, as long as heat can be emitted costlessly, and the accumulation of waste heat is not yet a pressing environmental problem, heat may well be a necessary joint product from a thermodynamic point of view, but it is none when seen from an economic perspective.

These considerations suggest that a more genuinely economic approach to the economics of energy in the production process may be useful: One that links the physical and economic levels of analysis, and that demonstrates the economic and 'not only' physical relevance of energy. In the chapters that follow I will develop the foundations of such an approach. The analysis will identify how the use of energy in production contributes to the use value of the produced goods. It will incorporate hypotheses on human wants, and it will ask why and how energy contributes to satisfying them. For this purpose, I will disaggregate the energy concept and specify the various services rendered by energy inputs into production. In the next chapter this alternative approach will be prepared by outlining an abstract framework for the representation of production processes.

2.6   A NOTE ON TERMINOLOGY

Before concluding this chapter, a note on terminology is necessary. As has been argued above, it is exergy rather than energy that is of interest economically. Strictly speaking, both in the title of the present volume and in the discussions of the following chapters, the term 'exergy' should be used wherever 'energy' is referred to. There is a simple reason why I will not do this. For most economists, as well as for most other non-physicists and non-engineers, exergy is not a familiar concept. It sounds awkward, particularly in contexts that are not intimately related to thermodynamics. The language of this volume will therefore stick to day-to-day usage of terms and use the imprecise notion of 'energy' instead of 'exergy.' This terminology is in line with most of the economic literature on energy.

3. Production as a sequential process

The previous chapter argued that physical approaches to economics alone are not sufficient to understand the role of energy in production. This volume aims at developing an alternative approach to this issue. It builds upon a variety of earlier contributions both in economics and in engineering. As a first ingredient to that approach, a conceptual framework for the analysis of production processes is developed in the present chapter. This framework has two characteristic features. First, it stresses the sequential character of production processes. Second, it allows for specifying the effects that the successive stages of the production process have on the product-in-processing. The argument of the chapter proceeds as follows: After outlining some characteristics of standard production models, I will sketch existing alternative ways of analyzing production. I then develop the conceptual framework on which the remainder of the study will be based. Finally, the chapter explores the implications that the present approach to studying production has for the concept of 'factors of production.'

3.1 ACTIVITY ANALYSIS: ABSTRACT MODELS OF INPUTS AND OUTPUTS

Activity analysis is the theoretical basis of present-day production modeling in economics. It was introduced to economic theory with the first applications of set-theoretic concepts and linear programming methods in the 1950s (Koopmans, 1951). The 'activity' concept is central to activity analysis. An activity is defined by a set of coefficients that describe the net flows of inputs and outputs generated by a production process. For example, the production of one unit of output x_3 by means of one input unit each of x_1 and x_2 is represented by the activity $(-1, -1, 1)$. Economists normally assume that a multitude of activities exist for producing a particular good. By contrast, substitutability of inputs is not explicitly assumed in activity analysis, although it follows from two assumptions that are commonly made: divisibility and additivity of activities. Activities are divisible if they are capable of proportional contraction or expansion by any non-negative scalar quantity. They are additive if the inputs and outputs of jointly performing two activities are equal to the sums of inputs and outputs of performing the same activities separately; i.e. if neither synergies nor productivity losses result from joint use of activities. Divisibility and additivity imply constant returns to scale and convexity of the production possibility set (Koopmans, 1951).

Activity analysis was introduced in the context of general equilibrium models to identify efficient production programs in the economy (i.e. lists of efficient net outputs for all commodities in the economy) as well as the price vectors giving rise to these programs. In this context, the empirical validity of the divisibility and additivity assumptions can be justified by the fact that the scale of individual production activities tends to be small relative to total output (Arrow and Hahn, 1971). Moreover, neither the technical specifics of production processes nor the nature of inputs and outputs are of particular importance for general equilibrium models, but the interest is rather in issues of allocation and pricing.

Textbook examples and applied production models frequently make use of production functions rather than activity analysis. Economic theory treats production functions merely as approximations of the production possibility set (Varian, 1992). If a large number of alternative activities exist for a given production process, the commonly utilized smooth production functions (such as Cobb–Douglas and CES production functions) are good approximations of the piecewise linear convex production possibility sets that follow from the assumptions made on activities. There is a fundamental difference between production function models and activity analysis, however, in that the substitutability of inputs explicitly enters as an assumption by specifying continuous differentiable production functions rather than being implied by the possibility of combining multiple processes.

In spite of its proven usefulness in addressing many important economic issues, the stylized representation of production processes in terms of their input and output coefficients precludes the analysis of some interesting questions related to production. Accordingly, I will extend it in two dimensions below. The first extension is related to the *process* of production. The representation of production adopted in this volume is a sequential one. It captures the fact that production processes usually consist of more than one single stage. These stages are often not independent of one another, so that changes introduced at one stage of the process may affect the feasibility and the costs of executing other stages. The second extension is related to the *nature of outputs and inputs*. As regards outputs, the effects of the individual stages of production on the product-in-process are taken into account. Moreover, it is argued that material statements can be made on the generic functions performed in production processes. These arguments provide the point of departure for a reinterpretation of the production factor concept on the input side of production. The conceptual framework to be developed below draws on a variety of earlier approaches. These will be discussed next.

3.2 SEQUENTIAL PRODUCTION IN ENGINEERING AND ECONOMICS

Classifications of Production Operations in Engineering

The engineering literature is a straightforward place to look for production models that go beyond the traditional economic ones. In designing and supervising actual production processes and facilities, engineers are forced to deal with the technical specifics of production. As opposed to economists, they cannot afford to treat the production process as a 'black box' and to restrict their attention to the quantities of inputs and outputs. I will argue in this section that the engineering literature is helpful in illustrating the sequential character of production, and that it can be used as a point of departure for material statements on the 'content' of production processes.

A basic distinction related to the sequence of production is the subdivision made in engineering between materials processing on the one hand and manufacturing on the other. Materials processing (also known as primary processing) refers to the manipulation of bulk materials in continuous flow and batch production. Its output consists of bulk liquids and gaseous substances, or of solids in standard forms that are typically not yet suitable for end consumption (so-called 'standard industrial stock' (DuVall, 1996, p. 25) such as granulates, steel bars, or pure chemicals). By contrast, manufacturing (or secondary processing) consists of the operations used in unit production of geometrically defined solid objects.

Production processes quite generally involve both materials processing and manufacturing operations, and there is a regular sequence in which the operations have to be executed (see Figure 3.1). The first stages of production tend to be materials processing operations, since most materials are not found in nature in the state required for manufacturing processes. This holds for all synthetic materials and most metals, but even for a natural material such as wood, which has to harvested and cut before it can be used in manufacturing. Some production processes (for example, those of consumable liquids) end with these material transformations. For most solid products, however, manufacturing operations to change their shape are required after the materials processing stage. As a third stage of the production process, surfaces and physical properties of objects are further modified. Frequently these further operations are required precisely because of the effects of the earlier shaping processes. Metalworking is a case in point. The grinding of hardened steel, for example, creates internal stress in the metal. Subsequent heat treatment is used to reduce the stress and thus to increase the durability of the final product (Todd et al., 1994, ch. 8). This third stage of manipulating physical properties and surfaces is subsumed under the category of manufacturing processes in the engineering literature, although some of the utilized processes are identical to those used in primary materials processing.

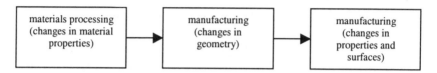

Figure 3.1 Typical sequence of industrial production processes

In addition to this basic distinction between three stages of processes, there are usually numerous operations required at each of the stages. To distinguish and systematize the different operations of materials processing and manufacturing, various classifications have been developed in the engineering literature. Although they differ in their details, these classifications are remarkably similar in their major categories. In terms of economics, operations of the different categories are both complements and substitutes. They are complements insofar as most actual production processes will require operations from multiple categories to be executed. At the same time, particular classes of operations can also be substitutes, because many modifications of the object of production can be realized by several alternative operations. Typically, the substitutability of alternative operations is imperfect, since they use different principles and tools, and since they also tend to differ in their specific effects on the object of production and in their costs. In the following paragraphs, some broad categories of materials processing and manufacturing operations are outlined.

Classes of materials processing operations

Operations of materials processing can be classified according to the dominant kind of change effected in the material (Vauck and Müller, 2000, ch. 1). At the most general level, physical and physico-chemical materials processing on the one hand (the subject of chemical engineering) is distinguished from chemical materials processing on the other (on which the field of reaction kinetics focuses). In many industrial production processes, operations from the two classes follow a typical sequence. Physical processing is required to prepare the materials before the actual chemical processing in controlled chemical reactions can take place. After the chemical reaction is finished, further physical processing is normally necessary to separate and purify the reaction products (ibid.; McCabe et al., 2001).

In both categories of materials processing, a variety of different operations can be identified and classified. The classification of physical and physico-chemical materials processing operations is worth dwelling on in some detail because of its central role for the field of chemical engineering. Early chemical engineering was lacking a clear conceptual foundation. This foundation was provided by the notion of 'unit operations' first proposed by Arthur D. Little in 1915. Little argued that:

> [a]ny chemical process, on whatever scale conducted, may be resolved into a coordinate series of what may be termed 'Unit Operations,' as pulverizing, dyeing, roasting, crystallizing, filtering, evaporation, electrolyzing, and so on. The number of these basic units is not large and relatively few of them are involved in any particular process. (quoted in Reynolds, 1983, p. 12)

Starting from Little's original suggestion, the unit operation concept has been further developed and refined. Unit operations constitute the basic theoretical building blocks of chemical engineering. They can be analyzed in terms of the same scientific principles, independent of the specific production process under consideration, even though the different substances and conditions of actual production processes may require different practical constructive measures. The unit operations concept moreover allows for the standardized combination of operations into various constellations for different production processes. Unit operations can thus be used as modules in the design of a plant layout (Reynolds, 1986; Rosenberg, 1998).

The unit operations of physical and physico-chemical materials processing can be further classified. Vauck and Müller (2000, p. 32, see also Table 3.1) propose a two-dimensional classification. Along the first dimension, operations are subdivided into those that separate materials versus those that associate and mix materials. The second dimension of classification proceeds according to the primary kind of energy transfer on which the operation is based. It distinguishes between mechanical, electric/electric-magnetic and thermal unit operations. Mechanical and electric-magnetic unit operations utilize mechanical tools or fields of mechanic, fluid-dynamic, electric or magnetic forces for the separation or mixing of materials. Their effect on the material is based on mechanical and electrical work rather than on heat transfers, even though some heat is necessarily produced by the dissipation of energy. Thermal operations, by contrast, are characterized by the generation of molecular forces through gradients in temperature and concentration. These forces drive transfers of heat, matter or impulse.

Table 3.1 Classification and examples of unit operations for physical and physico-chemical materials processing

Class of operation	Mechanical	Electric / electric-magnetic	Thermal
Unit operations for separation of materials	Sedimenting Cyclone scrubbing Filtering Extruding Centrifuging Crushing Grading by sifting Separating Flotation	Electroprecipitation Magnetic separation Electro-osmosis Electrophoresis Electrodialysis	Condensing Evaporizing Crystallizing Drying Distilling Extracting Absorption Permeation Dialysis
Unit operations for association and mixing of materials	Spraying Fumigation Stirring Homogenizing Kneading Blending Dosing Compacting	—	Solution Adsorption Extracting

Source: Vauck and Müller, 2000, p. 14; my translation based on De Vries and Kolb, 1978

Table 3.2 Categories and examples of operations in chemical materials processing

Thermal processes	Electrolytic processes	Catalytic processes	High pressure processes	Photochemical processes
Baking Roasting Calcining Causticizing	Solution electrolysis Smelting flux eletrolysis	Alkylating Hydrogenating Oxidizing Isomerizing Polymerizing Cyclization Vinylation	Synthesizing Carbonylation Oil-hydrogenating	Chloridization Sulfo-chloridization Vitamin enrich-ment

Source: Hemming, 1998, p. 11; my translation based on De Vries and Kolb, 1978

In analogy to unit operations, the operations of chemical materials processing have been systematized into 27 groups, which are also known as 'unit processes.' (Note that in Little's original proposal, chemical reactions were still part of the unit operations concept.) As opposed to the operations of physical materials processing, however, no systematic classification according to unambiguous criteria could be established for unit processes

(Vauck and Müller, 2000). Accordingly, existing classifications are based on a variety of criteria, including boundary conditions, the kind of reaction, or the reaction vessel used. They cannot be used as general building blocks of chemical materials processing capable of recombination in the same way as the unit operations of physical processes (Hemming, 1998). To illustrate the approach, Table 3.2 reproduces a classification based on the type of reaction.

Classes of manufacturing operations

Manufacturing technologies are utilized to manipulate solid workpieces. Like those of materials processing, the operations of manufacturing can be classified into a small number of groups. Such a classification can achieve a high level of generality. For example, the authors of the German industrial norm DIN 8580, which codifies the classification of manufacturing operations, are confident that they succeeded in establishing a universal and time-invariant classification. The norm states that all existing and conceivable (*'alle existierenden und denkbaren'*; Deutsches Institut für Normung, 1985, p. 3) manufacturing operations can be subsumed under their categories.

The following exposition follows a taxonomy proposed by Todd et al. (1994, ch. 1). This taxonomy classifies some 300 different manufacturing operations and has been adopted by the members of the US Manufacturing Consortium. It is based on the classification principles developed in Alting's (1994, ch. 1) 'morphological process model.' The highest levels of the taxonomy specify the kind of effect that the operation has on the object of production. Shaping and non-shaping manufacturing processes are subdivided into five major categories (see also Kazanas et al., 1981):

- mass-reducing processes (also called separating or material-removal processes)
- mass-conserving processes (also called forming processes)
- joining processes (also called assembling or fabricating processes)
- manipulation of material properties (also called conditioning)
- surface finishing.

A variety of operations exist within these classes. Operations are grouped into 14 major families according to their physical operating principles and the major kind of change effected in the workpiece. Figure 3.2 reproduces the top three levels of the taxonomy of Todd et al. (1994).

Mass-reducing processes 'include all processes in which the desired geometry is created by removing excess material from a solid workpiece' (Todd et al., 1994, p. 17). They are further distinguished according to the form of energy operating on the workpiece ('process energy,' ibid., p. 3) into

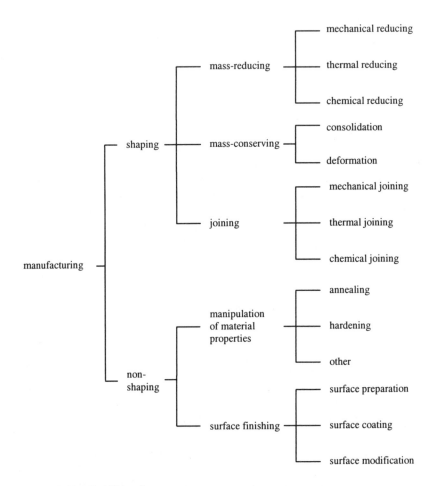

Source: Todd et al., 1994, p. 7

Figure 3.2 Classification of manufacturing processes

the families of mechanical, thermal and chemical mass-reducing processes. *Mass-conserving processes* can be of the consolidation or of the deformation type. Consolidation processes create solid objects from unformed substances. Deformation processes such as forging, rolling and forming exert mechanical work on a solid workpiece to effect a plastic change in its shape. The classification of *joining processes* again follows the process energy of the operation. Joining operations can be further distinguished into permanent and non-permanent ones. *Manipulation of material properties* is the summary heading used for various operations modifying physical properties of the workpiece that affect its usefulness, such as toughness, hardness or resistance to deformation. They generally change the material at the atomic level and include magnetizing, heat treatment, as well as chemical and physical (radiation, magnetism) treatments. Finally, *surface finishing* affects the outer appearance and the surface properties of the workpiece.

Why are these engineering classifications of interest in an economic context? They demonstrate two points that will be emphasized below. First, the engineering classifications highlight the sequential character of production processes, which usually involve a number of different stages before the product is finished. As has already been noted, there is a typical sequence of operations of materials processing and manufacturing operations. Specific technologies moreover require specific sequences of operations within these broad categories. The issue of sequentiality will be taken up in section 3.3; it will figure prominently in Chapter 6 below. Second, the engineering classifications demonstrate that material statements on the 'content' of production processes can indeed be made with a high level of generality. In spite of the variety of goods that are generated in production processes, the operations of these processes can be grouped into meaningful categories along abstract criteria. This classification of processes has been the very purpose of developing the unit operations concept of chemical engineering. The possibility of making general material statements on production processes will be drawn upon in section 3.4.

It seems important also to note the limitations of the engineering concepts discussed in this section. One potential limitation derives from their origin in traditional engineering fields. This may cause problems if operations to modify new kinds of materials, or operations based on fundamentally new technological principles (for example in biotechnology), are to be classified. It will emerge from the discussion in Chapter 5, however, that many new operations can indeed be handled within the established concepts and categories. Perhaps more importantly, the engineering concepts deal only with the production of material objects but do not include information processing activities. Although it is also possible to classify such processes (this is done for example in theoretical approaches to the process of product design, see Baldwin and Clark, 2000), such a classification would have to proceed along different lines of distinctions.

Economics meets Engineering: Engineering Production Functions

The engineering production function approach to modeling production was pioneered by Hollis Chenery (1949, 1953; see also Wibe, 1984; Forsund,

1999).[21] This approach is a hybrid between engineering and economic concepts. It stands in the engineering tradition because of its interest in the technical detail of production, and also because of the way in which the production process is conceived. The influence of chemical engineering concepts on the engineering production function approach is clearly discernible. At the same time, applications of the approach have focused on traditional economic issues such as the scale properties of production processes and the elasticity of substitution between inputs.

The general principle underlying the engineering production function is that parameters of production models are derived from theoretical considerations rather than from empirical data or a priori considerations. To this purpose an elaborate theoretical framework has been developed (Chenery, 1953). In line with the engineering theories outlined in the previous section, production processes are first subdivided into stages or 'industrial processes' (ibid., p. 299), which correspond to the unit operations and unit processes of engineering. The input–output relations of the individual stages are then represented by analytical 'design laws' (ibid., p. 302). The design laws are based on theoretical laws of physics and chemistry. To allow for the analytical representation of industrial processes, they involve idealizations such as ideal gas assumptions, the neglect of friction, etc.

The theoretical framework suggested by Chenery (1953) interprets production as the application of energy to materials. Following this basic conceptualization, Chenery differentiates between two kinds of input factors: materials (which enter the product) and processing factors (which do not). The latter are further subdivided according to their function in the production process into energy supply, energy transformation (including machinery and vehicles), and control factors (humans and instruments).

Based on the distinction between materials and processing factors, Chenery uses three kinds of equations to describe an industrial process. The 'material transformation function' develops an analytical model of how the material is modified, which expresses physical output quantities in terms of energy inputs and the physical characteristics of materials. In the simple example of steam production given by Chenery, the material transformation function would specify the amount of steam generated as a function of the amount of heat provided and the initial temperature of the water. The second set of equations ('energy supply functions') expresses the services provided

21. Predecessors of the engineering production function include George Stigler and Ragnar Frisch (Forsund, 1999). Stigler (1940) suggested constructing production functions from technical data. Frisch used an approach similar to the engineering production function in a 1935 case study of factor substitutability (see Forsund, 1999).

by the processing factors (measured in energy terms) as functions of the processing factors' physical characteristics. In the steam generation example, the amount of heat generated by a boiler would be related to its power rating. Finally, a set of 'input functions' relates the physical variables to tradable economic variables. In the example, an input function would express the boiler's electricity input as a function of its power rating and operating conditions, from which the costs of the boiler can be derived.

To arrive at the engineering production function for an individual stage or industrial process, the energy supply functions are substituted into the material transformation function. The engineering production function accordingly expresses the material output of the process as a function of the technical properties of materials and processing factors. It is transformed into an economic production function by use of the input functions. Finally, a production function for the entire process is developed by aggregating the functions for the individual stages. Chenery acknowledges that the aggregation may be complicated by interdependencies between the individual stages, but he does not investigate in detail the potential implications of such interdependencies.

Ideally, the engineering production function approach is capable of expressing the output quantities of a production process in terms of tradable inputs in the same way as a traditional production function. The crucial difference to standard production functions consists in how this functional relationship is developed, namely by use of engineering knowledge. It was recognized from the beginning (Chenery, 1949) that the approach is applicable only to production processes for which a complete analytical model can be developed. Strictly speaking, this limits its applicability to automated processes such as the transport of gases and liquids in pipelines or electricity generation in power plants. But even for these cases the usefulness of the engineering production function approach has been questioned. It has been criticized that the idealizations involved in deriving design laws may often be inappropriate for handling real-world engineering problems. According to Mirowski (1989, p. 330) the idealizations amount to 'ignor[ing] almost everything that distinguishes the engineer from the physicist.' In practice, using the engineering production function approach frequently requires the use of complementary empirical data, because no analytical model can be specified for the entire process. In these cases, the difference between engineering production functions and econometric methods of coefficient estimation is diminished. [22]

---

22. The disaggregation of sequential production processes on the basis of engineering principles is also discussed in Ayres (1978, ch. 3). Ayres' discussion is part of his broader endeavor to

The engineering production function concept had little success among economists (Wibe, 1984). In addition, most empirical studies using engineering data have not made use of the theoretical framework proposed by Chenery (1953) as it was found to be too abstract to be operational. These practical considerations notwithstanding, the engineering production function approach helps to highlight two points for the present discussion. First, its representation of production as a sequential process is noteworthy. As with the engineering approaches discussed above, the black box of production is opened, and technical information is utilized to arrive at a more realistic representation of production. Yet although the multiplicity of stages is indicated by the notion of industrial processes, the issue of their mutual relationship is not explored in much detail within the engineering production function approach. Second, the engineering production function concept indicates the difficulties involved in the attempt to describe actual production processes in all their technical specifics. The generality of a production model diminishes rapidly with an increasing degree of technical detail. In addition, the representation of the production process may easily be rendered obsolete by technological progress.[23] These problems suggest that for a general conceptual framework like the one envisioned here, too much technical detail may not be desirable.

Sequential Production Models in Economics and Management

So far the discussion of sequential representations of production processes was limited to concepts that had their origin in engineering considerations. However, sequential production models have also been developed in economics and management. In this section, I sketch some pertinent examples. I do this to show in what sense the conceptual framework that will be developed below differs from earlier models.

Nicholas Georgescu-Roegen (1970, 1971, ch. 9; see also Morroni 1992, 1999 for an elaboration) introduced a sequential production model that is well-known in economics. It focuses on the temporal structure of processes

develop a framework for modeling and measuring economy–environment interactions. In this context, Ayres dismisses the practicability of splitting up production processes into separate stages. He accordingly adopts the level of the individual firm, which he refers to as the 'economic unit process' (ibid., p. 66), as the smallest unit of analysis. Ayres' 'economic unit process' is a more aggregate concept than the 'unit processes' and 'unit operations' of engineering (or the 'industrial processes' in Chenery's framework). It is also more aggregate than the notion of 'operations' defined in the next section.

23. This problem is illustrated by Forsund's (1999) finding that in today's execution of the production process that Frisch had studied in 1935 (see note 21), the substitution problem analyzed by Frisch no longer exists, because the process has been automated since then.

where multiple units of the same kind of output are produced, and studies how different ways of organizing the production process affect the productivity of input factors.[24] In particular, Georgescu-Roegen emphasizes the dramatic productivity effect caused by the factory system.

Georgescu-Roegen's analysis is based on a distinction between flow factors and fund factors. Inputs of flow factors are consumed in the production process, whereas fund factors (for example, machines or human workers) are not consumed but utilized in the process. The notion of fund factors requires the inclusion of a temporal dimension in the modeling of production, since the utilization of fund factors can only proceed at a particular rate per unit time. Moreover, the time during which a particular fund factor is utilized in the production of an individual unit of output (called an 'elementary process'; Georgescu-Roegen, 1971, p. 235) is frequently much shorter than the total time required for producing that unit of output. In other words, fund factors are idle for most of the time in any single elementary process. Georgescu-Roegen then proceeds to discuss how elementary processes are best organized to minimize idleness of fund factors. He identifies the factory system, which arranges the elementary processes in line, as the most important organizational innovation in this context. On a more theoretical note, his discussion exposes implicit assumptions underlying standard production models.

Georgescu-Roegens's production model provided the foundation of the 'task-process theory of production' developed by Roberto Scazzieri (Scazzieri, 1993; see also Landesmann and Scazzieri, 1996). This approach aims at integrating three dimensions of production processes: the tasks to be executed, the available factors and their capabilities, and the stages of material processing. Scazzieri's (1993) principal interest is in the interdependence between the scale of production and the technique adopted. Landesmann and Scazzieri (1996) explore the implications of the multidimensional character of production for the temporal structure of the production process. As in Georgescu-Roegen's model, differences in fund factor utilization under alternative organizational forms of production, and their importance on the cost structure of the production process, are emphasized.

Production models of management theory show the pervasive influence of economic modeling approaches. Both activity analysis and production

---

24. Although Georgescu-Roegen's production model was published at the same time as his thermodynamics-inspired work (see Chapter 2 above), there is little common ground between both lines of reasoning. Notably, the distinction between energy and materials that figures so prominently in the latter is absent from the production model.

functions are commonly applied in that discipline. However, management theorists have frequently found the actual production models from economics wanting, and have used them as building blocks to develop their own models. For example, German management scholars have over the past decades developed an entire tradition of alternative production models (so-called *Produktionsfunktionen Typ A–Typ F*), and they have introduced a variety of different production factor categorizations (for reviews see for example May, 1992; Ellinger and Haupt, 1996). Arguably due to the underlying interest in planning and controlling the production process, these models frequently exhibit more interest in the details of production processes than those used by economists.

Management theorists have moreover proposed concepts that distinguish between the stages of the production process. Such discussions of the sequential character of production can be traced back at least to the prominent German business economist, Erich Gutenberg ([1951] 1983). A sequential perspective also underlies the influential value chain concept proposed by US management theorist Michael Porter (1985, ch. 2). The value chain is not a technical concept, however, but a managerial one that was developed with a focus on improving a firm's performance. Porter's contribution subsumes the entire production process under a single category of 'operations,' which he does not discuss in any further detail. From the present perspective, the importance of Porter's approach is in indicating that the sequential character of firm activities even goes beyond the production process proper.

More closely related to both the production sphere and to economic modeling concepts is another sequential approach in management theory: the input–output approach (Kloock, 1975). It applies macroeconomic input–output modeling techniques to firm-level production problems. The principal interest is in representing the intra-firm structure of flows of inputs, intermediate products, and outputs. Using linear algebraic methods, it is possible to derive aggregate input–output-relations for the entire production process from knowledge of the direct input uses at the individual stages. The firm-level input–output approach is therefore helpful for the analysis of processes with complex patterns of flows between stages and possibly products. The major drawback of conventional input–output models is their limitation to technologies with constant and fixed coefficients. Due to these limitations, they cannot accommodate the presence of multiple and changing technological alternatives.

3.3 PROPERTY VECTORS, OPERATIONS AND TECHNIQUES

A Sequential Framework for Analyzing Production Processes

With the preparatory groundwork having been laid in the earlier sections of this chapter, it is now time to develop the conceptual framework for the subsequent discussion of production processes. This framework is related to the engineering approaches outlined earlier in that it highlights the sequential character of production and allows for material statements on how the production of useful goods actually proceeds. As opposed to the engineering and management concepts sketched above, it is not meant to reproduce production processes in detail, however. Furthermore, the approach taken here differs fundamentally from the sequential models developed in economics by Georgescu-Roegen and his followers, because I am interested in an entirely different set of issues. The sequential models of economics have focused on the implications of alternative ways of organizing the production of multiple units of output. The present framework, by contrast, is restricted to the level of individual units of output (Georgescu-Roegen's 'elementary processes').

The Workpiece as the Object of Production

The first building block of the present framework is the notion of a 'workpiece.' This term has been borrowed from the engineering literature, but it is to be understood in an abstract, comprehensive way to apply to all objects of production processes. The term 'workpiece' may refer to a workpiece in the literal sense of a geometrically defined material object of production that is being worked upon in a manufacturing process. It will also be applied, however, to bulk materials manipulated in materials processing. Furthermore, even immaterial informational objects of production processes (for example in the service industries) can be referred to as workpieces. As an example of an immaterial workpiece, consider an electronic document that is successively modified by a number of authors.

I will assume in the following that the workpiece can be described by a set of properties, and that production processes successively modify the properties of the workpiece in order to transform it into a useful good. The workpiece can then be defined in a slightly more formal way by a vector

$$x = \begin{pmatrix} x_1 \\ x_2 \\ ... \\ x_n \end{pmatrix}.$$

This vector is called the 'vector of relevant properties' or simply 'property vector' of the workpiece. Each of its elements x_i characterizes a property of the workpiece. I assume that the alternative states taken by the workpiece's properties can be meaningfully expressed as numerical values ($x_i \in \mathbb{R}$). This assumption is straightforward with regard to basic physical properties such as size, mass, temperature, etc. Many other dimensions characterizing a workpiece, for example its material or color, can easily be encoded in numerical values. In this notation, n is the total number of relevant properties over the entire production process. I assume that this number is known in advance, and that a start value can be assigned to each property.

A key characteristic of the present approach is that the elements of the property vector fall into two (potentially overlapping) categories. As a first set of elements, the property vector includes all those dimensions of the workpiece that are relevant for the consumer of the end product; i.e. the product dimensions which are desired by consumers or which are contrary to their tastes. Obviously, these are the dimensions that determine the product's use value. Changing the 'user-relevant' elements of the property vector from their initial values to the desired end values is the very purpose of the production process. Second, the present framework is intended to capture potential interdependencies among the stages of the production process. As a second set of elements, the property vector therefore includes all dimensions of the workpiece that are significant *within* the production process, because the value they take at a specific stage of the process affects the possibilities and the cost of executing that stage. By contrast, these 'production-relevant' dimensions of the workpiece need not affect the use value of the final product. If a workpiece property is exclusively production-relevant, but not user-relevant, end product users are indifferent between all possible values that this property can take. Consider as an example the sound insulation material used in the production of an automobile. For the end consumer it may be a matter of indifference whether the sound insulation is made of plastic or of cardboard. Nonetheless, the choice of material used for the sound insulation makes a difference at those stages of the process where the sound insulation is formed and fixed to the car body.

For the sake of simplicity, it is assumed in the following that each production process has only one single workpiece. This simplification is of course not intended as a realistic representation of actual production processes, as production often involves the joining or assembly of different objects. (Recall that joining processes constituted one of the main groups of manufacturing processes in the engineering classification of section 3.2.) Moreover, complications in joining different objects are an important source of interdependencies in production, and they have received much attention in innovation studies. (Some of the relevant literature will be discussed in Chapter 6.) For a realistic sequential representation of production processes in general, one would therefore have to analyze the various stages of production for all of the involved objects of production, and to account for potential interdependencies both among the stages of production and among the components of a product. However, for the present purposes a more stylized representation is sufficient, which focuses on the process dimension and neglects all interdependencies arising from the interactions of components. In what follows, the joining of two objects will therefore be treated as the addition of a component to the single workpiece of the process. The addition will cause changes in workpiece properties, some of which may affect properties that had no well-defined value before the component was added, but only a (arbitrary) start value. Think for example of the assembly of engine and body of an automobile. If the car body is interpreted as the workpiece, those elements of the property vector that relate to the characteristics of the engine have an arbitrary value before the engine is actually mounted to the body.

The present concept of a property vector is closely related to the characteristics concepts developed by Lancaster (1966) and by Saviotti and Metcalfe (1984). Lancaster analyzed consumer behavior in terms of the objective characteristics of the available goods. In his framework, only those characteristics are relevant which affect consumers' choice between alternative goods – in other words its user-relevant properties. Saviotti and Metcalfe distinguish between three kinds of vectors of technical, service and process characteristics, respectively. A mapping is assumed to exist between these vectors: A product's technical characteristics translate into its service characteristics, and also into process characteristics of the production process. Saviotti and Metcalfe (1984) suggest the distinction between different kinds of characteristics as a conceptual framework for output indicators of technological change. It allows classifying innovations according to how they affect the technical and service characteristics of the finished product. By contrast, the development of the characteristics vectors during the production process itself is not analyzed.

The distinction between technical and service characteristics is useful to clarify the nature of the property vector concept developed above. In terms of this distinction, the elements of the property vector are technical characteristics. Only technical characteristics can be meaningfully defined during the production process (before the product is finished), and they alone are relevant for the relationships between the stages of the production process. The property vector concept is more encompassing than that of technical characteristics, however, because of the inclusion of properties which are not relevant for the use value of the final product, but which are of importance during the production process. They correspond to the process characteristics of Saviotti and Metcalfe (1984).

Moreover, the property vector concept is intended to capture the multifaceted character of a product's use value, which is also highlighted in the notion of service characteristics, as well as in Lancaster's original concept. For this double use of the property vector (as a representation of both technical and user-relevant properties) to be meaningful, two simplifying assumptions have to be made. There has to be an unambiguous mapping from technical to service characteristics of the final product, and this mapping has to be constant over time. Put more simply, the present concept abstracts from innovative uses of commodities that do not alter the technical characteristics of the respective commodity (for examples of such innovations see Metcalfe, 2001).

Operations: Input Combinations Change the Properties of the Workpiece

The second key concept of the present framework is the notion of an 'operation.' An operation is defined as any separable stage of the production process in which the property vector of the workpiece is changed in one or several of its dimensions. The present usage of 'operation' accordingly refers to the same level of processes as, for example, the 'unit operations' of chemical engineering, the 'industrial processes' of the engineering production function concept, or the 'stages of material transformations' in Landesmann and Scazzieri (1996).

An operation is characterized, first, by its effect on the workpiece. This 'output' dimension of the operation can be expressed at two levels. On the one hand, as will be stressed in the following section, it is possible to specify the operations required for the production of particular kinds of goods in terms of specific *functions* that they perform in these production processes. Starting from the functions, the required input factors can then be identified. On the other hand, the 'output' of the operation can be described in terms of its effect on the *property vector* of the workpiece, i.e. the way in which the properties of the workpiece leaving the operation differ from those that the workpiece had when it entered the operation. The effect on the properties of the workpiece thus provides a detailed description of the operation. However, different operations may be suitable to fulfill the same function. These alternative operations may differ with regard to their precise effect on the property vector. It is possible, for example, that one operation has a side effect on a property that would not be required to fulfill the function. The internal stress created by the grinding of hardened steel (mentioned earlier in this chapter) is an instance of such a side effect. Alternative operations may have different side effects. The extent to which such differences are allowable is limited by the proper fulfillment of the operation's function. In spite of all being compatible with the function of the operation, differences in the operations' precise effect on the workpiece may give rise to interdependence problems if one of the alternatives is replaced by another one.

Executing an operation requires the use of inputs. The description of an operation therefore needs to specify its 'input' side as well. It is assumed that each input needed to execute the function of the operation can be measured quantitatively so that the use of inputs can be represented in a vector of quantities. The nature of these inputs will be discussed in more detail in the following section.

The complete representation of a single operation that is part of a production process accordingly includes as inputs (1) the property vector of the workpiece entering the operation and (2) the quantities of other inputs required to execute the operation. The output of the operation is given by (1) the property vector of the workpiece leaving the operation and (2) any by-products or wastes that are generated in the operation. In essence, then, the present framework treats each operation of the production process as an activity (in the sense of section 3.2) whose output is multidimensional.

Production Processes as Sequences of Operations

Production processes are interpreted in the present framework as sequences of operations in which the workpiece is successively changed. Over the sequence of operations making up the entire production process, the property vector is modified in its dimensions until all user-relevant dimensions have the desired values (at which stage the production process is completed). Yet another simplification is made here to keep the argument tractable: I will assume below that production processes are strictly sequential, i.e. that no operations proceed at the same time, but a new operation begins only after the previous one has been finished. Albeit stylized, the sequential representation of production processes seems an appropriate description for numerous real-world production processes. As was seen in the review of engineering concepts above, stages in manufacturing may be strictly sequential simply because an earlier stage is the prerequisite for the execution of later stages.

Before moving on, one final concept needs to be introduced. In what follows, a distinction is made between techniques and production processes. I will use the term *technique* to denote a specific sequence of operations used in the production of a particular kind of good (which can be defined in terms of its user-relevant properties). Often, several techniques are available for producing the same kind of good. By contrast, I will refer to the production of different kinds of goods as different *production processes*. For a clarification of this terminology, see Figure 3.3:

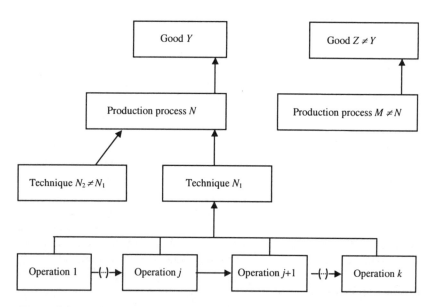

Figure 3.3 Levels of production technology

As the figure illustrates, a sequence of operations $(1 \ldots k)$ makes up a technique (N_1). This technique constitutes one specific way of executing the production process (N) turning out the product (Y), which is defined by the user-relevant elements of the property vector. There exist two alternative techniques $(N_1$ and $N_2)$ for the production of product (Y); both are therefore instances of the production process (N). And there exist, of course, different production processes (here: N and M), which turn out different goods (here: Y and Z).

3.4 FROM OPERATIONS TO FACTORS OF PRODUCTION

Factor Services as Inputs into Operations

The stylized framework of the previous section provides a basis for making material statements on production processes. To this purpose, the functions of operations are discussed in more detail in the present section. What does the function of an operation consist in? How can it be fulfilled? In comparison to the traditional economic approach to the study of production processes, answering these questions implies a significant shift in perspective. From the answers to these questions, a new interpretation of the notion of factors of production can moreover be derived.

To identify the function of a concrete operation one has to adopt the perspective of the engineering approaches to production and ask what the operation actually 'does.' It may be helpful to consider the stylized production process of a simple good to illustrate the approach. Assume that a knife is manufactured in no more than three stages. First, a block of steel is forged into the form of the knife. Second, the knife's blade is sharpened by grinding. And finally, the knife is heat-treated. Each of the three operations fulfills a specific function in the production of the knife, which is related to the properties of the workpiece. Forging and grinding are shaping operations that modify the geometry of the knife. Forging (according to the classification of Figure 3.2, a deformation operation) defines the overall shape of the knife, which affects such properties as handling and versatility. Grinding (a mechanical mass-reducing operation) serves to increase the sharpness of the knife. Sharpness constitutes another property that presumably is relevant to the end consumer. Finally, the heat treatment serves to harden the knife and to render it more resistant to wear and tear, also a property that can safely be assumed to be of importance to the end consumer.

It is thus possible in the simple example to identify the functions of the individual operations and the user-relevant properties of the workpiece that they modify. From the engineering concepts it can be learned that there are only a limited number of suitable operations to fulfill any given function, and that it is possible to characterize these operations in terms of their operating principle. Furthermore, each particular operation requires a specific combination of inputs. To execute the forging operation, the workpiece has to be heated, and a strong impact has to be exerted on it to do the deformation work. This presupposes that both a suitable tool (a hammer) and a source of heat are available, and also sufficient kinetic energy for an impact that yields the desired forming effect. Similarly, sharpening the knife requires both a grinder made from suitable material and the availability of kinetic energy to drive it, so that it can do work on the workpiece. Heat treatment requires a source of heat and a medium for the subsequent cooling. Moreover, in all three operations the tool has to be operated, the workpiece has to be handled, and the operation must be controlled.

In each of the three operations, a set of complementary inputs is thus required, which each makes a specific and identifiable contribution to the production process. I will refer to these contributions as the inputs' 'factor services.' The requirement that factor services be specific is perhaps most evident in the case of tools. A hammer cannot substitute for a grinder. As can be learned from the engineering literature, an abstract description of the services provided by different kinds of tools can be achieved with any degree of precision. Based on these abstract descriptions, a system of factor services of tools can be developed that is independent of the actual production process under investigation. For example, engineers define the tools used in the various mechanical mass-reducing operations (such as turning, boring, drilling and sawing) in terms of criteria such as their number of cutting edges (single-point cutting, multi-point cutting and abrasive machining) and the direction of movement of the tool relative to the workpiece (translational versus rotational; see Todd et al., 1994, ch. 2). Classifications of this kind thus denote the 'generic' factor service provided by a given kind of tool. A lathe used for turning can be characterized as a single-point cutting tool to cut a rotating workpiece with translational feed (see also Alting, 1994, ch. 7).

More generally, from the function to be fulfilled (say, deformation of a metal workpiece) and the known operations suitable to fulfill it (for example, forging and extruding), the required combination of factor services can be derived. There may be several such combinations. Given a set of factor services for the execution of the operation (such that its function is fulfilled), the suitable agents, objects and flows can be specified that are capable of providing these services. These are then the factors of production for the respective operation. If there are several suitable sets of inputs to provide the factor services, all of them are factors of production for the operation. Factors of production are thus defined by their capacity to provide factor services in operations fulfilling desired functions in production processes.

In summary, the present argument amounts to characterizing each operation in the production process by means of a function such as mechanical mass-reducing, deformation or information processing. This function is (1) related to a user-relevant property of a good (which is capable of fulfilling a human want; a point that will be taken up in the next chapter) and (2) requires the provision of services by one or several factors of production. The relationship between these concepts is illustrated in Figure 3.4.

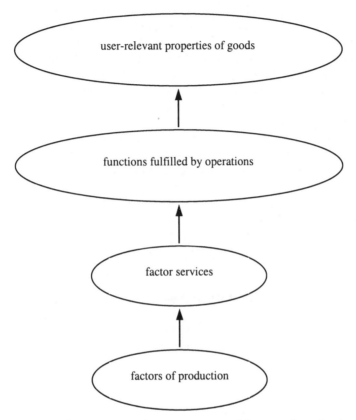

Figure 3.4 Goods, operations, factor services and factors of production

The distinction of functions, operations and factor services suggests the existence of two levels of substitution in production. Substitution is possible, first, at the level of factor services. Some of the services used in operations can be provided by different factors. This holds for example for tool operation. If a simple hand-held hammer is used for forging, the hammering person operates the tool. By contrast, with use of a drop forging hammer, the tool operation service is performed by a specific piece of machinery (a tool-operating tool, as it were) rather than by a human being. Similarly, the input of mechanical energy for doing the mechanical work can be provided by different factors. In forging with a hand-held hammer, the person who operates the hammer provides at the same time the input of energy. If a drop forging hammer is utilized, the energy is provided by some non-human source of energy. Various sources of energy and kinds of engines exist that can be used.

Substitution is also possible at the level of operations. There are frequently multiple operations that are capable of fulfilling a given function. These alternative operations can be substituted for each other in production processes that require the respective modification of the workpiece. Often, they are only imperfect substitutes in that even though all of them fulfill the desired function, their precise effect on the workpiece properties is not identical. For example, instead of being forged, the knives of the above example might also be cast in the first operation. Casting would turn out raw knives with a molecular structure and surface different from that of the forged ones, however. These differences may affect the user-relevant properties of the knives, they may affect production-relevant properties such that accompanying changes in subsequent operations are required, or the changes may not be economically relevant. In the latter case, the two alternatives of executing the operation are perfect substitutes economically even though they are not technically equivalent. In any case, the substitution of one alternative execution by another one may require the use of an entirely different set of services.

The Categories of Factors of Production

The sequential production framework can now be used for reinterpreting the notion of factors of production. From the perspective of this framework, *factors of production* are:

> agents, objects and flows that are capable of providing factor services in production operations.

In principle, this way of characterizing factors of production allows for an arbitrary number of different factors. Indeed, the heterogeneity of factors will play an important role in the subsequent discussion of energy and innovations in energy use. The number of factors capable of providing a service moreover increases over time because of innovations in production technologies. Nonetheless, just as a meaningful classification of operations and factor services is possible, broad categories of factors of production can be identified that are characterized by their capacity to provide certain kinds of factor services. It is proposed here to distinguish between four categories of factors of production: tools, human labor, energy and materials.

The notion of 'tools' is chosen as a collective term for all non-human inputs that are not used up in the production process of an individual unit of output, but are utilized for the production of multiple units of output. The category of tools thus includes inputs such as coolants and lubricants, provided they are used in the production of more than a single unit of output.

How factor services can be identified for the production factor 'tools' has already been sketched in the previous section: The service provided by a tool can be described in an abstract way in terms of its operating principle, direction of motion, etc. Although such a description may often be complex, the engineering literature demonstrates that it is feasible in principle. At the same time, the aggregation of all kinds of tools into the notion of 'capital' is not useful at the present level of analysis. As I have argued in the introduction, many production models in economic theory deal with the 'price-theoretic' level of production, i.e. with issues of allocating scarce resources to production processes and the pricing of inputs to production. For such purposes, the aggregate concept 'capital' is appropriate. By contrast, if one is interested in material statements on production processes, a more disaggregated perspective is required. At the level of use value, different categories of tools are typically not commensurable.

The productive services provided by human labor inputs can be identified in a similar way by making use of classifications developed in labor economics. According to one such classification, labor inputs are at the highest level of differentiation classified into the categories of physical labor, mental work and the application of social and affective skills (Cordes, 2003). Physical labor can be further subdivided into the service of executing mechanical work (for example in powering the hammer) and the application of specific psychomotoric skills (as in the services of tool operation and workpiece handling). Services based on human mental work include the control of processes, the collection, processing, storage and transmission of information, problem solving, and creative mental work.

The services provided by energy can be classified according to the different forms of energy. The factor services of energy, and how they relate for example to the services of human labor, will be dealt with in more detail in the following two chapters. They are therefore not discussed further here.

Finally, materials are all inputs that are used up in the production of one unit of output, with the exception of fuels (energy inputs). From the 'factor service' perspective adopted here, the factor status of materials is not controversial. Materials are required as 'carriers' of workpiece properties such as a geometry and defined surface. Moreover, materials differ in their physical and chemical characteristics, so that specific materials provide specific services such as hardness, capacity of thermal insulation, machinability or electrical conductivity. Extensive lists of materials and their characteristic properties can be found in Ayres (1978, ch. 3).

Two final remarks have to be made at this point. The first remark is related to Georgescu-Roegen's distinction between fund and flow factors. This distinction is not explicitly reproduced in the different factor services distinguished here. Factor services can be provided both by flow factors (energy and materials) and by fund factors (tools and human labor). In addition, flow and fund factors may be substitutes in the provision of a specific factor service, as was indicated by the above example of mechanical energy required to drive a hammer. It can either be provided by a human worker or by a non-human source of energy. To that extent, the distinction between flows and funds is reflected in the present framework, but it is mediated by the additional level of factor services.

The second remark is related to 'auxiliary' factor services. Not all factor services into an operation are directly modifying a property of the workpiece. Some 'auxiliary' factor services are required to help in the provision of 'primary' factor services. An example would be the inputs into the maintenance of tools. (They affect, as it were, the properties of the factors affecting the properties of the workpiece.) For these factors providing auxiliary services, the argument has to be extended analogously. They can be classified, however, into the same broad categories.

On Knowledge as a Factor of Production

Numerous authors have argued that knowledge is a factor of production (see for instance Boulding, 1981; Weissmahr, 1992; Witt, 1997, 2003a). Indeed, it seems beyond doubt that knowledge is crucial for production activities, and that economic growth is to a large extent driven by advances in knowledge. In the present framework, however, some intricate problems would result from treating the broad aggregate of knowledge as a factor of production. Although these problems cannot be dealt with in depth here, briefly discussing them is warranted in the light of the existing proposals for treating knowledge as a factor of production.

A first problem with knowledge as an analytical concept derives from its non-additivity. Different items of knowledge cannot simply be added up. There is no universal metric of knowledge, and new knowledge may consist in no more than the insight that what was previously thought to be known can no longer be relied upon. This incommensurability problem is essentially in the same way faced by the capital concept. In the case of capital, it is typically dealt with by imputing the value of capital from the discounted expected payoffs.[25] This 'solution' is problematic for knowledge because of its peculiar characteristics. As early contributions to the economics of knowledge have stressed, knowledge may possess public good characteristics, i.e. non-excludability and non-rivalry in use (Nelson, 1959;

---

25. Note that this is a value-level argument. As I have argued above, the capital concept is not useful at the level of use value at which the present analysis is located.

Arrow, 1962a). Insofar as this is an adequate characterization, knowledge faces the pricing problems known from other kinds of public goods.

During the past decades, however, analysts have increasingly realized that this characterization is not valid universally, and that knowledge is highly heterogeneous also with regard to the extent it exhibits public goods properties (Pavitt, 2002). One aspect of heterogeneity stems from the fact that agents cannot articulate some of their knowledge. This 'tacit knowledge' (Polanyi, 1966) is not a public good that can be freely accessed and used by others. Rather, it is 'embodied' in individuals or organizations, and it is difficult for others to learn and imitate, unless it is codified into explicit, verbally expressed knowledge (Cowan and Foray, 1997). As another complicating aspect, not even all explicit knowledge can be understood equally well by an agent. Learning, remembering and communicating items is dependent on the availability of context knowledge (for an overview, see Buenstorf, 2003, and the literature cited therein). These differences in how various kinds of knowledge can be shared and diffused among agents have been argued to underlie the pronounced differences in economic performance among firms, regions and nations. As a consequence of these differences, a distinction is moreover made in the literature between information (codified knowledge, which has public good characteristics) and knowledge more generally (which does not necessarily have them).

The heterogeneity of different kinds of knowledge might be taken to suggest, in analogy to the approach adopted above, a disaggregation of the production factor knowledge into various different factor services. But in the case of knowledge, even that disaggregated treatment seems inappropriate, since knowledge cannot be analyzed independently of the other factors of production. This lack of independence has different implications for 'disembodied' social knowledge (information in the sense of the past paragraph) and for the knowledge 'embodied' in individual human beings.

As regards 'disembodied' codified knowledge, there is a fundamental problem involved in interpreting it as a factor of production. Knowledge cannot be represented at the same level as the other factors, because the service-providing capacity of all the above-mentioned categories of factors is dependent on the state of technological knowledge. Knowledge underlies the available set of tools, the available forms of energy, the range of usable materials, and even the services that human labor can provide in production. Changes in the state of technological knowledge open up new factor services and entirely new operations, and they enhance the capabilities to use the existing ones. The only level at which the availability of energy and materials is independent of the state of knowledge is the fundamental physical level of thermodynamic analyses where energy (exergy) and matter are indeed treated as broad aggregates (see Chapter 2), but there is no place for knowledge as a factor of production at that level.

The notion of knowledge may alternatively refer to the subjective knowledge held by the individual workers who provide the human labor inputs into production. Most factor services provided by human labor require knowledge on behalf of the worker; some are little more than the application of previously acquired knowledge to a particular situation (think of routine supervisory or problem-solving activities). In turn, processes for making the societal fund of knowledge available to the production process by educating agents are important parts of present-day economic activities (Witt, 2003a). For this 'embodied' knowledge of workers, there is again a problem caused by the lack of independence of categories. If labor inputs are based on knowledge, then labor clearly cannot be independent of knowledge. Separate consideration of knowledge and labor is then possible only by subdividing human labor inputs into separate categories, which is frequently done in practical modeling by distinguishing between skilled and unskilled labor, or by treating 'human capital' inputs separately from labor inputs. In the present framework, the consideration of different services provided by labor inputs allows for a more detailed representation of their knowledge-dependent character and of the heterogeneity of knowledge held by agents. The solution to managerial problems, for example, will often depend on acquired social and affective skills as much as on factual knowledge. The kind of knowledge required for developing new products and technologies, or for supervision of a production process, is of an entirely different kind. To capture the role of individual knowledge and skills in production processes, a closer investigation into the various factor services provided by human agents would therefore appear more promising than an undifferentiated endorsement of treating knowledge as a factor of production, or a distinction between skilled and unskilled labor.

Finally, it has already been argued in Chapter 2 that the generation of new knowledge by human ingenuity can be considered the primary driving force of economic evolution. Each input is a function of knowledge, and so is the output that can be generated with the use of these inputs. Increases in the societal fund of knowledge underlie the differences over time in the feasible combinations of inputs and outputs in production processes. This knowledge-dependence of output is reflected by the standard economic measure of factor productivity, although the productivity measure is located at the price-theoretic level (at least with regard to output), rather than the present level of use value.

3.5 CONCLUSIONS

In this chapter I have outlined an alternative conceptual framework for studying production processes. This framework is inspired by contributions developed outside the core of economic theory. It stresses two characteristics of production processes. First, their sequential character is reflected by interpreting production as a process of several interdependent stages that have been referred to as operations. Second, the economic aim of production – to generate an output of useful goods – is captured by allowing for a multidimensional output characterized by a vector of user-relevant technical properties. The individual operations making up the production process have been characterized by their function in modifying the workpiece such that its usefulness is increased, and factors of production have been defined on the basis of their contributions (factor services) to the functions of the operation. The chapter has moreover suggested ways to specify functions and factor services of actual production processes and to classify factors of production into the broad categories of tools, labor, energy and materials. Finally, I have discussed why an aggregate factor 'knowledge' cannot, in the present conceptual framework, be included at the same level as the other four proposed categories.

4. More than heat and light: the services provided by energy use in production

On the basis of the conceptual framework developed in the previous chapter, this chapter will study in more detail the production factor energy and the factor services provided by it. As an initial step, energy is, in accordance with the distinctions made in physics, subdivided into its various forms. I then discuss two ways of identifying the factor services of the individual forms of energy. On the one hand, there are cases in which useful properties of goods are directly dependent on energy inputs of specific forms. On the other hand, the necessity of energy inputs of specific forms may be caused by the characteristics of operations performed in the production process, even though the workpiece properties modified in those operations are not directly related to energy. In concluding the chapter, I discuss some of the implications of the present approach of identifying factor services provided by energy.

4.1 FORMS OF ENERGY AND THE FACTOR SERVICES PROVIDED BY THEM

At the macroscopic level, physicists distinguish between various forms of energy. The principal forms of energy are nuclear energy, chemical energy, mechanical energy (potential energy, kinetic energy and pressure), thermal energy, light, and electric energy (Alting, 1994; Erdmann, 1995). This distinction between energy forms is taken over for the present purposes. It will be investigated in the following whether all these forms can provide factor services in production processes.[26]

---

26. The distinction made here is a phenomenological one that is not perfectly discriminating. For example, at the microscopic level thermal energy would be regarded as kinetic and potential energy of atoms. Likewise, radiation of electromagnetic waves is one of the three forms of heat transfer. It is not fundamentally different from light, except for its different wavelength. Recall moreover from the argument of Chapter 2 that only a part of the total energy of a particular

The perspective on energy adopted in the present chapter is fundamentally different from that in Chapter 2. It was demonstrated there how the various forms of exergy of a given system of matter can be aggregated into a single quantity which yields a general measure for the amount of work that the system's energy can theoretically perform. The approach of Chapter 2 was valuable in deriving the necessity of energy as a factor of production and other fundamental regularities at the physical level of production. By contrast, the aggregate exergy value is not very helpful for studying the role of energy in the production of useful goods. Quite the contrary: The present chapter will stress the central role played by the heterogeneity of energy forms in determining their factor quality in production processes.

A particular form of energy can only provide a service in the production of a particular good if, in addition to its being available in the physical sense, there exists a known way of utilizing it in useful operations, and if this utilization is economically viable (i.e. it is not prohibitively expensive). Particular operations of particular production processes require specific forms of energy inputs, so that the degree to which these conditions are fulfilled differs between the various forms of energy. Accordingly, all energy forms are not equal in their factor service quality for specific operations. The energy of the bonds in the atomic nucleus, for example, cannot be used for most economic purposes, even that part which is physically available.

Differences in the service qualities of different energy forms are only imperfectly equilibrated by the possibility of converting energy from one form into another. Although all energy forms can theoretically be converted into one another, not all actual conversions are technologically feasible or economically viable. In Figure 4.1, those conversions for which no viable direct conversion technology exists today have been denoted with 'N.A.'. Moreover, all real-world energy conversions are imperfect (see again the argument of Chapter 2) so that indirect conversions necessitated by the lack of direct ones come with additional conversion losses. A different way to express this makes use of the concepts of work and heat. These concepts have a precise meaning in physics: Whereas energy is a property of a body, work and heat are energy transfers between two bodies. The conversions in Figure 4.1 involve transfers of work and heat. Conversion losses in a combustion engine, for example, mean that not all of the chemical energy of the fuel is converted into mechanical energy that can do work, but some of it is

system of matter can be used in production processes: its exergy (available energy; corresponding to the system's ability to do work on its environment) which is determined by the existence of gradients in the various forms of energy between that system and its environment. Strictly speaking, the following discussion applies only to exergy.

converted into a heat transfer to the environment, which will eventually cause an increase in the environment's thermal energy.

A further source of complexity stems from the fact that the above forms of energy are found in different fuels or, more generally, sources of energy. (I prefer to use the term 'sources of energy' because of the connotations of the term 'fuel,' which is normally used for substances with a high content of chemical energy. These, however, constitute only a fraction of all sources of energy.) Wood, coal and oil, for example, are all sources of chemical energy. Energy provided by different sources may be differently suited for a particular economic application, even though it is of the same form. Such differences may result in difficulties if one source of energy is to be replaced by another one in an operation. One concrete instance of such difficulties, the historical transition from wood to coal, is reviewed in detail in Chapter 7. The more abstract discussion of the present chapter, by contrast, will focus on the level of energy forms.

Finally, all three dimensions of service quality – usefulness of an energy form, feasibility of energy conversions, and the actual usefulness of various sources of a particular energy form – are knowledge-dependent and subject to technological change. They are different at different points in time; an issue that will be the focus of the following Chapter 5.

From \ Into	Chemical energy	Thermal energy	Mechanical energy	Light	Electric energy
Nuclear energy	N.A.	Fission reactor	N.A.	N.A.	N.A.
Chemical energy		Combustion (exothermic)	Combustion engine	Fire Gas light	Battery Fuel cell
Thermal energy	Endothermic reactions		Thermal expansion (heat engine)	N.A.	N.A.
Mechanical energy	N.A.	Friction		N.A.	Generator
Light	Photosynthesis Photochemistry	Laser Solar heating	N.A.		Photovoltaic cell
Electric energy	Electrolysis	Electric heater and furnace	Electric motor	Electric light	

Source: Own compilation based on Alting, 1994; Smil, 1994; Erdmann, 1995

Figure 4.1 Economically important direct conversions between energy forms

The capacity of a particular energy form to provide factor services can be identified in three ways. First, one could argue that all energy inputs into production processes provide factor services because they would not be used otherwise. On the basis of such an argument, the service quality of a form of energy would then be deduced from its actual use. There are two problems involved in this method of identifying the, as it were, 'revealed factor services' provided by energy forms. The fact *that* a form of energy is used in production processes does not yield any information about *what* it is used *for*, for example in what kind of operation it is used. In addition, the use of the various energy forms in production cannot be determined empirically. Energy statistics measure the inputs of the various energy forms at the levels of economies and sectors, but they do not show which services these forms actually provide, as the user may (and typically does) convert the purchased energy into another form in the production process. Electricity, for example, is almost completely converted into mechanical energy (to do mechanical work), chemical energy, heat, and light in the production process. As an energy form, electricity itself has become capable of providing direct services (in various electronic devices) only quite recently. Its economic attractiveness is to a large extent caused by the very fact that it can be converted into other forms of energy with high rates of efficiency. (As Ayres and Warr (2001, p. 8) put it: 'electricity can be defined as "pure" work.') Since electricity accounts for roughly one-quarter of total industrial energy use in the OECD (IEA, 2002, table II.17), however, the lack of data on factor services provided by purchased inputs of electricity alone makes quantitative estimates of the services of energy forms problematic. This approach to finding the factor services of energy forms will not be considered further in the present study.

Instead, two alternative ways of identifying the factor services of energy forms will be explored in the following. First, section 4.2 will inquire to what extent the use of specific forms of energy in production can be related directly to the satisfaction of the wants of consumers. To answer this question, I study whether user-relevant properties of goods are directly energy-based, and if so, what forms of energy can be used to modify these user-relevant properties. This method of identifying 'direct' factor services of energy forms will turn out to be limited to specific classes of goods. Section 4.3 subsequently investigates a more indirect form in which user-relevant properties of goods can be energy-dependent. It argues that the execution of operations to modify properties of goods may require specific forms of energy inputs even though these properties are not related to specific energy forms. Because of the dependence of operations on specific energy inputs, these energy forms can be considered factors of production for the respective operations.

4.2   REGULARITIES IN HUMAN WANTS AND DIRECT SERVICES OF ENERGY

To make material statements about directly energy-dependent properties of goods presupposes that the nature of human wants is accessible to an investigation by external observers. The possibility of such an investigation is the fundamental proposition made in Ulrich Witt's (1991, 1999, 2001) work on consumer behavior. Witt aspires to develop material hypotheses on what humans want, how different wants may differ in their satiability, and what directions the long-term development of wants (and accordingly demand) can therefore be expected to take.

Witt suggests that, as a result of natural selection during human phylogeny, all humans share (as with all genetic traits, within some range of inter-individual variation) a set of common, genetically fixed basic wants. These basic wants are present in the genetic repertoire, because they were conducive to having surviving offspring in times of intense selection pressure. According to Witt (1991, p. 567; 1999, p. 29), the objects of these basic wants include air, water, sleep, warmth, nutrition, sexual activity, affection, physical activity, safe living space, status, mobility and entertainment ('cognitive arousal'). These items are closely related to the primary reinforcers that have been identified empirically by behavioral psychologists. They can be further distinguished into two categories. Some wants can be satisfied by direct inputs (flows of goods that are used up in the act of consumption), whereas others require the services of durable consumer goods or consumption 'tools' (Witt, 2001, p. 27) in order to be satisfied.

In learning processes that start from the genetically fixed basic wants, humans acquire new wants, and also new knowledge on how to satisfy the existing ones through the consumption of goods. The observable variety of individual consumption patterns reflects the contingencies and idiosyncrasies of individual learning histories. Moreover, due to the sophistication of human learning capacities, some parts of a person's consumption may only loosely be related to the innate basic wants. On the other hand, inter-individual variety of wants is limited by the social character of learning. Members of interacting groups and cultures are likely to share similarities in their acquired wants. In spite of individual variations, Witt accordingly suggests that inter-individual commonalities in wants and consumption patterns exist, which can be explained by reference to genetic and cultural influences. This argument for common elements of human consumption behavior implies a partial rejection of the 'radical' subjectivism prevalent in most of economic theory (Witt, 1999, p. 29).

If one accepts that there is sufficient inter-individual regularity in consumer behavior to make material statements regarding its actual content (be it because of shared innate wants or because of shared cultural influences on learning histories), then the above argument can be extended into the production sphere. Both direct inputs into consumption and 'consumption tools' are useful goods. The existence of inter-individually shared wants then allows for statements on the nature of their user-relevant properties. Except for properties that are already present in objects as they are found in nature, these properties are the result of operations in production processes. Some user-relevant properties are directly dependent on inputs of energy in the production process. I call this provision of energy for modifications of energy-dependent properties of goods the 'direct' factor services of energy. Depending on the specific nature of the energy-dependent property, factor services of particular energy forms are required. In the following, four kinds of energy-dependent properties of goods and the factor services required for their modification are discussed: the chemical energy of food, the temperature of objects, light, and the state of motion of devices for personal transportation.

Provision of Chemical Energy for Nutrition

The usefulness of food depends with necessity on the energy it contains. Chemical energy content is one of food's several user-relevant properties; since only particular kinds of organic matter are digestible for humans, it is a necessary but not sufficient condition of an adequate diet. The production of food accordingly requires an input of energy that can be converted into chemical energy. To date, the only form of energy that can provide this service is the radiant energy of light, which is converted into the chemical energy content of plants in photosynthetic reactions.

Provision of Thermal Energy

As homoeothermic animals, humans depend for survival on the maintenance of their body temperature. This physiological need is reflected by the innate want for warmth, i.e. a range of temperatures that is experienced as comfortable. The temperature of spaces (as consumption 'tools') and of direct inputs into consumption (food is an obvious example) is therefore one of their user-relevant properties. If this temperature is manipulated by humans, the modification is part of a production process that is directly dependent on energy inputs in the form of heat transfers. The heat transfers are factor services provided by energy inputs into the respective operations. As can be seen from Figure 4.1, heat can in principle be derived from conversions of all forms of energy. In most cases, however, only a limited range of energy forms are practically usable as heat sources.[27]

Obtaining the desirable range of temperatures for spaces and objects often requires cooling rather than heating them, i.e. heat has to be transferred from them to the environment. A temperature gradient between the object and its environment is artificially created in this way, which requires an input of energy. The most important practical applications of cooling, air conditioning and refrigeration, are based on heat transfers in processes of evaporation and condensation. They are realized by the circular flow of a medium which is driven by a pump.

Maintenance of a particular level of temperature is a product of major economic importance. Space and water heating and cooling account for the major part of residential energy use. Moreover, there is a tendency both to reduce the range of tolerated temperature variation and to extend the space that is kept at the desired temperature. This tendency to increase the temperature-controlled space can be related to the genetically fixed want for safe living space, which apparently is not easily satiated. It moreover indicates that the thermal insulation of the body (by means of clothing) is not a perfect substitute for modifications of the environmental temperature.

Provision of Light

In addition to its significance as a source of heat, the use of fire also provided prehistoric humans with a first source of light that was independent of the sun. Illumination of spaces (as consumption 'tools') allowed our ancestors to increase their range of activities both temporally (activities at night) and spatially (activities underground). Similar to the want for heat, humans seem to have a universal want for the availability of light. That such a want evolved under selection pressure is plausible since artificial light offsets the disadvantages that humans as diurnal animals have with regard to nocturnal predators. Moreover, although the range of intensity within which light is experienced as comfortable limits per capita energy use for lighting purposes, applications of artificial lighting are far from reaching the intensity of sunlight. This suggests that the want for artificial light is unlikely to be satiated soon in terms of intensity. Per capita light consumption has moreover been increasing over time because of increases in the quantity of space that is lit. Again, these increases can be related to the basic want for safe living

---

27. This difference between theoretically and practically usable energy forms for provision of heat indicates the need to distinguish between the physical and the economic levels of analyzing energy that has been argued for above.

space. In terms of physics, artificial light is radiant energy of a particular wavelength emitted by hot objects. Generating the radiation requires inputs of chemical or electrical energy.

Mechanical Work for Personal Mobility

Humans depend on their personal mobility for the maintenance of basic vital functions (for example in collecting food), and also to escape from dangers. Mobility moreover allows for exploring one's environment. Given these functions of personal mobility, it is straightforward to assume that humans have in their phylogeny developed an innate want for it. This assumption is also consistent with the apparently insatiable demand for personal mobility observable in today's developed economies, even though the latter may in part be due to cultural learning processes.

The want for personal mobility can be satisfied by the body's own activity or by using a self-propelled vehicle. The state of motion (kinetic energy) of the human body and of the vehicle is an energy-dependent property.[28] It must be changed in transportation, and to do so a factor service of mechanical work is required. The production of personal transportation services is therefore dependent on inputs of mechanical energy, which can be provided by the human body itself (on the basis of earlier intake of chemical energy), or by a variety of fuels powering the vehicle.

The use value of a transportation system (again, conceived of as a consumption 'tool') increases with the speed it can attain. Speed determines the distance that can be traveled per unit of time, and thus the possible range of its user's mobility. Speed is directly related to the energy requirements of the transportation system. In addition, the use value of a system of transportation also depends on whether or not it requires human physical activity, because humans dislike physical activity once it exceeds a certain level. Again, independence of human physical activity presupposes factor services of non-human energy inputs.

Implications

The energy-dependence of nutrition, heat, light and personal mobility indicates that direct factor services in the production of goods and services are provided by energy forms, which can be identified by exploring the consequences of regularities in consumer behavior in the production sphere.

---

28. Even though this terminology is somewhat awkward, both the human body and the vehicle can be considered workpieces in this case, which are the objects of a production process.

From knowledge on basic wants shared by humans, some of the uses of energy inputs into can be deduced. Knowledge on the uses of energy allows for specifying the suitable forms of energy.

This method of identifying factor services is faced with two inherent limitations, however. First, material statements about wants, and by extension about the factor services required to satisfy them, can only be made for those parts of consumer behavior that are common to a large number of people. Second, and more importantly, an additional degree of freedom is introduced by the shift from consumption to production. Even for sufficiently universal wants, the goods required to satisfy them may be produced by a variety of different techniques, which may be based on entirely different factor services. This problem seems particularly pronounced for consumption 'tools.' Insofar as consumption depends on direct inputs, the range of alternative production processes is rather limited. Food, heat, and light can only be produced in quite specific ways. By contrast, a wider range of techniques exists for the production of most consumption 'tools.' Accordingly, it is hard to find regularities in factor use between the various different techniques, so that the identification of factor services on the basis of the goods produced is restricted to a relatively small part of the spectrum of goods. In the following section, an alternative way of identifying factor services is therefore discussed.

4.3   INDIRECT FACTOR SERVICES OF ENERGY USE

The previous section identified direct factor services of energy on the basis of energy-dependent modifications in the user-relevant properties of goods. In the present section, a second, indirect, form of factor services is analyzed. These factor services do not result from the energy-dependence of a *property* of the *good*, but from the energy-dependence of an *operation* used in the production *process*. As opposed to direct factor services, the kind of good produced need not be known to specify indirect factor services. The present method of identifying factor services is therefore more generally applicable than the one discussed above. The necessary information can be derived from the descriptions and classifications of production operations found in engineering. The identification of indirect factor services starts from the functions to be fulfilled in a production process. Due to physical, technological and economic factors, there are only a limited number of operations capable of fulfilling a particular function. For these operations the required factor services of energy can then be derived, along with the forms of energy that can provide these services.

In this section, this approach to the specification of factor services and suitable energy forms will be applied to the broad classes of operations that fulfill four generic functions: the processing of materials, the manufacturing of objects, the transport of materials and objects, and the processing of information. In addition, the category of process control is introduced. Process control is not a separate class of operations, but a necessary element of all operations. It determines part of their factor service requirements.

Materials Processing

Most goods are made from materials that are not found in nature. Materials processing operations are required to bring the materials from their natural state into one that humans find more useful. All changes in materials that do not occur spontaneously require the services of energy inputs.

A large variety of materials processing operations exist. It was shown in Chapter 3 how these different kinds of operations are classified in engineering. The present chapter will not reproduce these conventions in detail. Instead, a broad distinction between the various kinds of operations will be adopted. It is based on the notion of 'process energy' proposed by Todd et al. (1994, p. 3, see also Chapter 3 of this volume). The process energy of an operation specifies the form of energy to which the material is subjected in the operation, or in other words, the kind of work or heat transfer exerted on the material. According to their process energy, mechanical, thermal and chemical operations of materials processing can be distinguished. Two aspects of the process energy concept make it well suited for the present purposes: It focuses attention on the useful effect of energy use in an operation (i.e., the desired output, which due to conversion losses may be much smaller than the total energy input into the operation), and it determines the kind of energy required as factor service in the operation. For energy inputs to be useful in that operation, they must be of a form that allows for converting them into the required process energy (in an economically viable way).

In mechanical materials processing operations, mechanical work is done on the material by means of relative motions between the material and a transfer medium, pressure differences across the material or mass forces generated within the material (Alting, 1994, p. 17). In this way, a mass flow is created that associates, joins or separates different kinds of materials, or larger chunks of material are separated into smaller pieces. Two forms of energy can be used to do this work: mechanical energy and, for the separation of materials having different magnetic properties, (electro-)magnetic fields. Of course, both may be derived from prior conversions of other forms of energy, for example in a combustion engine.

In materials processing based on thermal process energy, the material is subjected to gradients of temperature, concentration or velocity which induce heat transfers (conduction, convection, or radiation) or molecular transfer of matter (ibid., p. 25). Thermal materials processing operations often involve changes in the state of aggregation (melting and evaporation) to associate or separate materials. The necessary inputs of thermal energy can be derived from chemical energy (combustion), from electric energy, from a heat reservoir, or in particular cases from mechanical energy (friction).

Chemical materials processing is based on chemical reactions taking place in the material, i.e. on chemical process energy. They can be further subdivided into exothermic and endothermic reactions. Exothermic reactions require in principle no energy inputs other than the chemical energy of the reagents themselves. In practice, additional energy inputs are often necessary in exothermic chemical reactions, because boundary conditions have to be created artificially. These exothermic reactions may require inputs of mechanical energy (pressure) or of thermal energy (high temperatures) for their initiation. In biotechnological operations based on the growth and metabolic activity of microorganisms (for example fermentation), the chemical energy of a substrate is required for the working of the organisms' metabolisms. Finally, some chemical materials processing operations utilize radioactive radiation to modify organic matter in a desired way.

The reaction products of endothermic reactions have a higher chemical energy content than the reagents. Endothermic reactions accordingly require a permanent input of energy from the environment for the reaction to take place. This energy may be provided as thermal energy, as electricity or in the form of light. Endothermic chemical reactions are of particular economic significance in the reduction of metal ores to metals, i.e. the production of metals. In iron smelting an input of thermal energy is partially converted into heat and partially into the higher chemical energy of iron as compared to iron ore. The production of aluminum through the electrolytic reduction of aluminum oxide (which first has to be produced from bauxite, the aluminum-containing ore found in nature) is based on electric energy inputs. From the total energy requirement of aluminum production, almost 60 per cent is reaction enthalpy, i.e. chemical energy of the reaction products in excess of that of the reagents. As an example of endothermic reactions used for the chemical processing of materials outside metallurgy, consider the production of chlorine, on which a large share of the modern chemical industry is based. It is another instance of an electrolytic process requiring an input of electric energy.

Manufacturing of Solid Objects

As was outlined in Chapter 3, the distinction between materials processing and manufacturing is based on the nature of the workpiece rather than the operations used. Manufacturing operations effect changes in geometrically defined objects rather than in unstructured material flows. The basic subdivision of manufacturing operations is between shaping operations that modify the geometry of the object and operations that affect the material properties of the workpiece at the chemical level. As with the operations of materials processing, manufacturing operations can be differentiated in terms of their process energy, i.e. the kind of work done on the workpiece. Again, mechanical, thermal and chemical operations are distinguished.

Mechanical shaping operations include mass-reducing separation of parts of the workpiece through inducing local fracture, mass-conserving consolidation and deformation operations, as well as joining based on material flow. Mechanical energy inputs, and in some cases electric energy inputs, are used to do the required mechanical work. Thermal shaping applies heat transfers to the workpiece to cause local melting and/or evaporation. Finally, chemical shaping operations induce local chemical reactions in the workpiece. Some of them require only chemical energy (exothermic etching reactions), others also need additional inputs of thermal or of electrical energy (electrochemical machining).

Non-shaping operations modifying properties of the workpiece are of importance for example in the production of goods from metal and from ceramics. Ceramic products have to be fired after shaping. To this purpose, the workpiece is exposed to heat flows that induce thermochemical reactions to render the shape permanent. Thermal operations are also used in annealing and in the heat treatment of metals. These operations consist in controlled heating and cooling to modify the workpiece properties. Both thermal and chemical processes are moreover utilized for treating surfaces of the shaped product.

Transportation of Materials and Objects

That the use value of goods has a spatial dimension is probably too evident a fact to draw much attention. It implies that an object's location is one of its relevant properties. Changing this location requires a factor service of mechanical work and accordingly, in addition to a suitable means of transportation, an input of mechanical energy. Transportation of materials and objects is thus an energy-dependent operation. As opposed to personal mobility, however, it is the location that is valued and not the process of transportation itself. For example, the use value of a bundle of two-by-fours bought in Maine does not depend on whether the wood was harvested in Maine or imported from Sweden (provided the product is homogeneous otherwise).

Transportation operations may involve movements of finished materials and objects, but transportation is also necessary within the sequence of a technique and as part of operations fulfilling other functions. Manufacturing operations necessitate 'control movements' (Devine, 1990a, p. 44) for the handling of workpieces, the feeding of workpieces into the tool, and/or the operation of the tool into or across the workpiece. These short-distance movements of the workpiece and/or tool require in principle the same factor services of mechanical energy, as do operations dedicated to transportation. In practice, the necessary factor services for control movements are often provided in special ways, because of the small distance of movements, the required precision and/or the number of times the movement is repeated.

Information Processing

A large and increasing part of economic production activity is related to the processing of information (where information is, as in the previous chapter, understood as codified knowledge). Similar to transportation, information processing tasks may be required as parts of materials processing and manufacturing operations, but information processing itself may also be the function of operations, with material processes only being executed as auxiliary processes. And although the energetic aspects of information processing are less obvious that those of the classes of operations discussed before, the present framework can fruitfully be applied to information processing operations.

As with the processing of materials and objects, the physical necessity of energy for information processing is at a fundamental level established by the laws of physics. Physicists have shown the equivalence of energy and information (in the technical sense of information theory), and the minimum energy requirements of information processing have been calculated (Tribus and McIrvine, 1971, and see the discussion of thermodynamics and information theory in section 2.2). More significant in practical terms are the energy needs, and the restrictions in the energy forms suitable for information processing, that result from technological limitations. Information processing can broadly be subdivided into communication and manipulation of information. The latter includes the transformation of information into another form, and the modification of its content through logical and mathematical operations.

Process Control

The final category of 'process control' does not refer to the function of a class of operations. It rather provides a generic label for a set of factor services needed to execute all kinds of operations. Irrespective of its function, some of the factor service requirements of an operation derive from the need for process control, which is based on a specific kind of information processing.

Factor services for the supervision of the operation's proper execution are a first component of process control. Supervision involves detecting errors and equipment breakdowns, and either correcting them or interrupting execution of the operation. As a second component, process control includes the adaptation of the operation to changes that are made necessary by changing output requirements, variations in the nature of inputs, or variable equipment performance (wear of tools). Both supervision and adaptation tasks have long been the domain of human labor inputs, but factor services based on non-human energy inputs have become available over the past century. They will be discussed in Chapter 5.

Implications

What follows from these considerations on the indirect factor services of energy? The answer to this question has several aspects. At the conceptual level, the discussion indicates how the factor services of energy required for broad classes of production operations can be derived from technical considerations and engineering concepts. Distinguishing operations according to their process energy is helpful to identify the required factor services, which in turn allows for specifying the forms of energy that are suitable as inputs into the respective class of operations. This analysis proceeds, as it were, at the 'phenomenological' level of production processes. It is based on actual technologies employed in the production of useful goods. Neither is it necessary to specify the nature of the produced goods, nor is the role of energy inputs traced back to first principles of physics. The generic capacity of operations to increase the use value of the processed workpieces is taken to follow from the fact of their actual use.

The discussion of indirect factor services moreover highlights the heterogeneity of energy. Different forms of energy are not perfect substitutes in production. For example, inputs of mechanical energy cannot provide the factor services required for chemical materials processing. Iron cannot be made on the basis of mechanical energy alone. In turn, chemical shaping operations in manufacturing are not suitable substitutes for many mechanical and thermal shaping operations. Further limits to substitution exist within the above categories of operations. Although mechanical energy can be used as an energetic factor service for friction welding, it cannot be used as an input into arc cutting, although both operations fall into the category of thermal manufacturing operations. In this respect, the broad categories distinguished in this section still tend to overstate the possible substitutability between different energy forms.

There is an important caveat to the argument of the previous paragraph. The specificity of energy forms in operations has been demonstrated at the level of process energies. It is mediated insofar as other forms of energy can be converted into the required process energy. This is quite often the case. The energy required for the mechanical work done in turning, for instance, is in practice converted from various forms of energy, including the mechanical energy of falling water, the chemical energy of fuels, or electricity powering an electric motor. Because of their capacity to alleviate the specificity of energy inputs, mastering energy conversions is important both technologically and economically. Innovations in energy conversions have indeed been, as will emerge from the discussion in the following chapters, among the most significant energy innovations in human history. The flip side of the coin is that energy conversions which are not feasible technologically, or not viable economically, for example the conversion from mechanical into chemical energy, constitute important restrictions of energy use.

4.4 CONCLUSIONS

This chapter has argued that energy is a factor of production to the extent that, in addition to being physically available, it can provide a useful service in the production of goods. To identify the factor services provided by energy, I started from the physical distinction between different forms of energy and studied their usefulness in various types of production operations. Two types of factor services were distinguished: first, services used to change directly energy-dependent properties of the workpiece, and second, services required in energy-dependent operations of the production process.

The above discussion emphasized the heterogeneity of energy forms. It showed that different forms of energy differ in their capacity to provide the factor services required in the various operations of production processes. These differences do not simply follow the distinction made in physics between (inferior) heat and all other forms of energy, which is based on the fact that heat cannot be completely converted into mechanical work. From the present perspective, the factor quality of an energy form depends on its practical usefulness in production. It is determined at the economic level, not at the physical one, and varies with both the kinds of goods produced and with the available conversion technologies. For example, given the existence of combustion engines and the lack of an economically viable large-scale technology to generate useful thermal energy from mechanical energy, thermal energy may in many situations be more useful than mechanical energy. The service quality of different energy forms is thus not given a priori but changes with the state of technological knowledge. This issue will be taken up in the following chapter.

Finally, there is also a difference between the direct and indirect services of energy in terms of their substitutability. Direct services of energy can only be provided by specific energy forms. If other forms of energy are to provide these services, they have to be converted first, which entails technical problems and by necessity conversion losses. In indirect services, on the other hand, the specific form of energy input is not essential for the final service, as the relevant properties of the object of production are not in energetic terms. For example, in manufacturing, machining operations can often be replaced by casting, because the physical differences in workpiece qualities that are caused by the substitution do not affect the usefulness of the object. This implies that there is a greater variety of ways to perform indirect services, and also a higher potential for innovation.

5. Changing power relations: the long-term development of energy use in production

The physical forms in which energy occurs do not change over time. Their usefulness for economic purposes does. As a result of changes in the state of technological knowledge, the history of human energy use is characterized by an increasing number of energy forms, conversion technologies and particular energy sources (fuels). The first part of this chapter discusses the major qualitative changes in energy use, which I call 'energy innovations.' In addition to the major energy innovations studied here, the history of human energy use is a history of quantitative increases in energy use for all of the services distinguished above. Furthermore, a multitude of incremental innovations have improved existing energy technologies, both with regard to their qualitative performance and with regard to their energetic efficiency (i.e. the fraction of energy input that is converted into useful work). The second part of the chapter discusses the macro-level pattern resulting from these three developmental trends in energy use.

5.1 QUALITATIVE CHANGES IN ENERGY USE

A Taxonomy of Historical Energy Innovations

The major energy innovations of human history are summarized in Table 5.1. The table classifies energy innovations according to several criteria. The first column indicates the kind of good or production operation for which the new energy technology is used. This classification follows the discussion of the previous chapter. The second column gives the form of energy provided by the energy technology, as given by the 'process energy' or the kind of work/heat transfer derived from it. The next columns list the energy innovation and its (approximate) date of introduction. In the fifth column, energy innovations are subdivided into those that introduced the use of a new source of energy (fuel), those based on a new conversion between forms of energy, and those which modified both source of energy and conversion technology. Finally, the table indicates the effect of the energy innovation on earlier technologies by distinguishing between 'partial' and 'universal' adoption. Universal adoption of a new technology means that earlier technologies were replaced in (practically) all their uses. Partial adoption denotes innovations that substituted for pre-existing technologies only in some applications, whereas the earlier technologies remained prevalent in other ones. Differences in the degree of adoption are in part determined by physical and technological factors, but the use patterns of energy technologies also depend on relative prices, in particular where alternative technologies are based on different sources of energy. Moreover, as is well known in the literature on innovations, the success of a new technology may also be affected by the context of its introduction (for example, the need for complementary infrastructures and the presence of network effects) and by historical contingencies. The distinction between partial and universal adoption therefore is entirely descriptive; it does not argue in favor of an inherent superiority of one technology or another, or suggest a deterministic pattern in the characteristics of newly adopted technologies.

In the following, the major energy innovations are discussed according to the kind of workpiece properties or operations affected by them.

Innovations in the Provision of Chemical Energy for Nutrition

At the fundamental energetic level of the present analysis, there has not been a single energy innovation in how nutrition is procured by humans. From prehistoric times to the present day, all food is organic matter whose chemical energy content can be traced back to the photosynthesis in plants, which converts the radiant energy of solar light into chemical energy of biomass. The chemical energy stored in the biomass of plants is consumed by humans either directly or via intermediate stages. From the beginning of agriculture and animal husbandry some 9000 years ago to the high-yield crops, chemical fertilizers, and mechanized agriculture of our days, there has been pervasive change in agriculture. It has helped both to relax some limitations of growth processes in plants (for example by fertilizers), and to reduce the inputs of human labor into agricultural production. These changes have at the same time drastically increased the overall energy requirements in agriculture (Pimentel and Pimentel, 1996). None of these changes, however, have modified the basic biochemical processes of photosynthesis (as a conversion technology), nor have they eliminated its dependence on light as a source of energy. Genetic engineering may eventually bring about the first energy innovations in the human production of food by introducing changes to photosynthetic processes, but so far this has not yet been achieved.

Table 5.1 Major innovations in energy use

Affected good or operation	Energy form (process energy)	Energy innovation	Year of intro-duction (approx.)	Type of innovation	Adoption
Nutrition	Chemical	N.A.	–	–	–
Heat	Thermal	Combustion of wood	400 000 BC	Conversion + Source	Universal
		Combustion of coal	1200	Source	Partial
		Combustion of oil and natural gas	1859	Source	Partial
		Electric heating (various sources + forms)	1910	Conversion	Partial
Light	Radiant	Lamp (wick) burning animal and vegetable fats	38 000 BC	Conversion + Source	Universal
		Lamp (wick) burning coal gas	1792	Source	Universal
		Incandescent electric light (various energy sources)	1882	Conversion	Universal
		Fluorescent electric light (various sources)	1930s	Conversion	Partial
		Light emitting diodes (various sources)	1990s	Conversion	Partial
Personal mobility and transport of objects	Mechanical	Riding and draft animals	4000 BC	Source	Partial
		Sail and raft (wind and water)	3000 BC	Conversion + Source	Partial
		Steam engine (wood and coal)	1807	Conversion + Source	Partial
		Internal combustion engine (Otto/Diesel; oil)	1876	Conversion + Source	Partial
		Electricity (energy sources: as in materials processing)	1888	Conversion	Partial
		Internal combustion engine (gas turbine)	1928	Conversion	Partial

Affected good or operation	Energy form (process energy)	Energy innovation	Year of intro-duction (approx.)	Type of innovation	Adoption
Materials processing and manu-facturing	Mechanical	Animals	4000 BC	Source	Partial
		Wind and water wheel/turbine	100 BC	Conversion + Source	Partial
		Steam engine (wood and coal)	1712	Conversion + Source	Partial
		Electricity (water and steam power)	1873	Conversion	Universal
		Electricity (gas turbine)	1950	Conversion	Partial
		Electricity (nuclear fission)	1956	Conversion + Source	Partial
	Thermal	Combustion of wood	12 000 BC	Conversion + Source	Universal
		Combustion of coal	1200	Source	Universal
		Combustion of oil and natural gas	1859	Source	Partial
		Electric furnaces	1878	Conversion	Partial
		Electric machining	1950	Conversion	Partial
		Laser machining	1960	Conversion	Partial
	Chemical	Exothermic reactions (fermentation)	6000 BC	Conversion	Universal
		Wood in endothermic reactions (iron)	1300 BC	Conversion + Source	Universal
		Coal in endothermic reactions (iron)	1750	Source	Universal
		Electrolysis; electrochemical machining	1886	Conversion	Partial
Infor-mation processing	Mechanical	Mechanical sorting and calculating	1873	Conversion + Source	Partial
	Electrical	Telegraph (communication)	1837	Conversion + Source	Partial
		Digital computer	1959	Conversion	Partial
Process control	Mechanical	Jacquard loom (programmable)	1804	Conversion + Source	Partial
	Electrical	Electrical servomechanisms (supervision)	1930	Conversion + Source	Partial
		CNC machine tools (programmable)	1970	Conversion + Source	Partial

Source: Own compilation; data on years taken from Ayres, 1990; Nye, 1990; Cameron, 1993; Smil, 1994; Islas, 1997; Nordhaus, 1997; Mokyr, 2000

Innovations in Heat Generation

Humans began to use fire for the generation of heat through the combustion of fuels (i.e. for converting chemical energy into thermal energy) several hundreds of thousand years ago. Fire had a profound effect on early human development, because it enabled humans to settle in regions that would otherwise have been too cold to survive, and to expand the range of their diet by cooking food that would not have been digestible in a raw state. The change from wood- to coal-based heat generation (in Europe beginning in the thirteenth century, and after an interruption, again in the sixteenth century) was an innovation in the source of energy. It constituted the first human use of a fossil fuel. The transition from wood to coal has received considerable treatment in the literature, and will be discussed in more detail in Chapter 7. Although burning coal has replaced wood in most applications in the industrialized economies, fuel wood is still used in some marginal applications. This is largely due to the fact that some fuel wood grows as a 'by-product' of forestry that is primarily carried out for other reasons, and to the existence of some specific niche uses of fuel wood. The relative importance of wood firing is small in today's industrialized economies. By contrast, fuel wood still plays a more significant role in the energy supply of less developed countries.

The use of mineral oil and natural gas for the generation of thermal energy constituted another innovation in sources of energy, whereas the conversion technology (combustion) remained the same. A major advantage of oil and gas lies in the easier automation of fuel input with liquid or gaseous fuels as compared to solid fuels. Although coal can be, and indeed was, processed into coal gas (used for gas lighting) and coal oil, this conversion was more expensive than using mineral oil and natural gas. Part of the initial success of oil was moreover due to dissimilar regional supply patterns of coal and oil. As a consequence of these differences, oil had drastically lower costs of transport in some regions (see Pratt, 1981, for the role of regional factors in the ascent of oil in US energy supply in the early twentieth century). Oil and gas only partially replaced coal in heat generation, but the share of coal seems to be continuously decreasing at least in domestic uses. Electric heaters were an innovation in conversion technology, as electricity can be produced from the same fuels (coal, oil) that can also be directly utilized for heat generation. The principal advantage of electric heating is its flexibility, as it needs little additional equipment where the basic electricity supply infrastructure is present. Its major drawback lies in its energy inefficiency. Electric heaters gained only a fraction of the market for heating technologies.

Innovations in Lighting

In addition to the light emitted by open fires, wick-equipped lamps burning vegetable and animal fats were the first sources of artificial light that humans controlled. They remained the most sophisticated and effective means of lighting from prehistoric times to the late eighteenth century (Nordhaus, 1997). The introduction of gas lighting beginning after 1792 constituted the first major innovation in lighting technology in modern times. Gas lighting used town gas produced from coal, and its diffusion was limited to the urban distribution networks for this fuel. In the second half of the nineteenth century, the remaining market for liquid lighting fuels (outside these networks) was taken over by petroleum, which replaced whale oil and coal-based kerosene. Both gas and petroleum lamps were based on new fuels, while keeping to the established conversion technology of combustion with use of a wick.

Various forms of electric lighting were introduced in the late nineteenth century. Electric arc lamps for illumination of public spaces were first installed in 1867, and incandescent lighting using light bulbs began in 1882. Electric lighting is an innovation in conversion technology. When compared to the direct use of combustible material for lighting, it seems to involve a paradoxical detour. Combustible materials such as oil can be directly used for lighting, or alternatively they can be used to generate electricity, which is then used for lighting. In spite of the double conversion (and in contrast to the use of electricity for the generation of thermal and mechanical energy), early electric lighting had a higher thermal efficiency than contemporary gas and petroleum lamps.[29] Fluorescent electric light and light emitting diodes (LEDs) are the most recent major innovation in lighting. Both are innovations in conversion. Fluorescent light further increased the thermal efficiency of electric light, but it has only partially replaced incandescent light. LEDs promise to combine efficiency with durability. As LED-based white light has only in the past decade become technologically feasible, it is not yet clear whether it will find significant use in the future.

---

29. However, as David Gugerli (1996) has shown for Switzerland, early electric lighting systems were more expensive to construct than gas lighting, and electric current was expensive for private consumers. Gugerli accordingly suggests that early uses of electric light were not (primarily) governed by cost considerations.

Innovations in Personal Mobility and Transportation

Inputs of mechanical energy are needed to do physical work (changes in the state of motion) in transporting people and objects. The first source of this energy were human labor inputs. The domestication of animals for use as riding and draft animals shifted some of the work burden in transportation from humans to animals, but it remained muscle work that was done. Sailing and rafting on rivers were the first ways that humans found to reduce their dependence on muscle work in transportation. As both these forms of transportation were restricted to waterways, they could not completely substitute for animate energy sources. They strongly affected geographic patterns of economic activity, however.

In the early nineteenth century steam power became practical for powering ships and for inland transportation with railways. Steamships soon began to replace sailing ships completely. By contrast, railways with their need for an expensive infrastructure were less a substitute for animate energy sources than a complementary new technology that made long-distance transport viable. The major advantage of internal combustion engines (Otto and Diesel) over the steam engine lies in smaller weight and size, and in easier handling. They have become predominant in small-scale applications, in particular in transportation. Early automobiles powered by Otto engines replaced inanimate energy inputs in transportation for all but the shortest distances, but like muscle work before they initially complemented rather than replaced the railway.[30] Although automobiles and trucks eventually did become a substitute for most rail travel and transport, Otto and Diesel engines still do not provide all of the mechanical energy for transportation, as electric railways continue to be in widespread use.

Otto and Diesel engines are innovations in conversion technology that were closely related to a new source of energy. Although the first Otto engines were powered by coal gas, their diffusion was based on the use of mineral oil, which had not been utilized for driving motors before. The gas turbine, also a form of internal combustion engine, is another innovation in conversion technology. It differs from Otto and Diesel engines in that it directly generates rotary motion rather than first powering reciprocating pistons, and was first utilized in the 1930s to power jet airplanes.

---

30. In the early days of the automobile, there was technological competition among steam power, electric motors and the internal combustion engine. Arthur (1984, 1989) has argued that the eventual success of the internal combustion engine was only caused by first-mover advantages, and not by the superiority of that engine. This view is not borne out by more recent research, however (Cowan and Hultén, 1996; Foreman-Peck, 1996).

As was argued in Chapter 4, short-range transportation is also required as a factor service in production operations. Replacing human muscle work for these control movements became feasible in the Industrial Revolution when inanimate energy sources, most importantly water and steam, were combined to mechanize workpiece handling and tool operation in machines such as the spinning jenny and the water frame. In the twentieth century, electric and hydraulic systems allowed for pervasive replacement of muscle work in workpiece handling (epitomized by the conveyor belt introduced in 1913) and tool operation.

Innovations in Materials Processing and Manufacturing

The overlap in the physical principles of materials processing and manufacturing operations has already been noted in Chapter 4. Historical changes in the energy technologies used in these two categories of industrial processes are sufficiently similar to allow for a joint discussion. As in Chapter 4, factor services of energy required in industrial processes are distinguished according to the process energy criterion into mechanical, thermal and chemical energy. This classification implies that electric energy is studied in its applications for generating mechanical, thermal and chemical process energy rather than as a separate category. This is consistent with the observation that electric energy itself does not provide factor services in materials processing and manufacturing operations, but has to be converted into other forms of energy first.

Mechanical energy for industrial use was, over most of human history, provided by the muscle work of humans and animals. The reliance on muscle work ended only with the widespread availability of electricity. Even in the late nineteenth century, long after invention and diffusion of the steam engine, physical work done by humans and animals accounted for most of the small-scale mechanical energy inputs into US manufacturing – which in turn made up the larger part of all US manufacturing. Not only large animals such as horses and oxen but even dogs were utilized as energy sources of nineteenth century materials processing and manufacturing (Hunter and Bryant, 1991, ch. 1).

As in transportation, the first inanimate sources of mechanical energy in industry were made available through the introduction of water and wind wheels (beginning around 100 BC; see Cameron, 1993). Wind and water power were innovations in both the sources of energy and the conversion technology. Their utilization was limited by transmission and control problems and also by local supply restrictions. As water and wind wheels are restricted to stationary use, they could not replace animate power for example in plowing. Within the history of water and wind power, the water turbine was the most significant innovation. It uses a jet that increases the pressure of the water hitting the blade. The water turbine is more efficient than the water wheel and started to replace it after 1830. Although it is still in widespread use in electricity generation, new ways of obtaining physical work from fossil fuels became predominant in the nineteenth century so that water and wind power were never adopted universally.

The steam engine converts chemical energy into mechanical energy (which is used to do mechanical work) via a prior conversion into thermal energy. When it was introduced in the eighteenth century, the innovative part of the process was the second conversion, i.e. the heat engine that converted thermal into mechanical energy by means of steam driving a piston. By contrast, the first conversion (combustion of wood and coal) had been used ever since humans had started to use fire. The steam engine represents an innovation in both energy sources and conversion technology. It was the first engine that enabled humans to derive mechanical work from the chemical energy of indigestible materials. Moreover, although many steam engines were fired with wood even in the nineteenth century US (Melosi, 1982), it was in combination with coal that the steam engine became economically most significant. Coal-based steam power made it possible to use the chemical energy of fossil fuels to generate mechanical energy. It thus drastically increased the amount of energy over which humans had command, which was a prerequisite for the subsequent increase in production volume after the Industrial Revolution. Nonetheless, alternative power sources were available for most of the steam engine's applications, and the engine competed with water power throughout its entire history. It never was the unique technology in use for the generation of mechanical energy. After 1888, steam turbines began to be substituted for reciprocating steam engines. They use steam to generate a rotary motion directly instead of first driving a piston, and they are lighter and more efficient at high speeds than reciprocating steam engines (Smil, 1994). Internal combustion engines were, as opposed to their dominant role in transportation, of relatively minor importance for the generation of mechanical energy in industrial operations.

Today, the bulk of all mechanical energy for materials processing and manufacturing operations is generated by electric motors. Electricity is moreover used in mechanical shaping operations that take place directly within an electromagnetic field without using a motor. The electric motor, an innovation in conversion technology, has completely replaced the direct use of steam and waterpower. Since most electricity is generated from mechanical energy that drives a generator, the use of electric motors to provide mechanical energy (to do mechanical work) is an energetic 'detour.' Under identical boundary conditions, the thermal efficiency of converting mechanical energy into electricity and back into mechanical energy can never match that of directly using the mechanical energy to do the work. The widespread use of electric motors in spite of this principal disadvantage is owed to two characteristics. Electricity can comparatively well be transmitted over long distances, and even small electric motors are reasonably energy efficient. The availability of small motors allowed for their use in many applications where only human muscle work could be used before (see the more detailed discussion of section 7.3). Electricity to drive electric motors and other equipment is mostly generated in steam power plants. In addition to coal and water, oil and natural gas have been used for large-scale electricity generation in the twentieth century. These new fuels have only partially replaced coal in the generation of electricity. Finally, gas turbines and nuclear fission have been introduced for the generation of electricity. The gas turbine as an internal combustion engine constitutes a innovation in conversion technology. By contrast, the use of uranium in fission reactors combines a new energy source (and in this case also a new energy form, nuclear energy) with a new conversion technology.

Heat transfers for thermal materials processing and manufacturing operations can in principle be generated in the same ways as those used for direct factor services of heat. The historical pattern of change in heat sources for industrial uses accordingly reflects the general developments in heat generation. However, for industrial processes, electricity-based generation of thermal energy has attracted more attention than in space and water heating, because it has some desirable characteristics for industrial use (Burwell, 1990; Devine, 1990b; Alting, 1994): Electric furnaces reach higher temperatures than those heated with conventional fuels; they thus created new technological possibilities for the processing of materials. At the same time, electric furnaces can be more energy efficient than conventionally fuelled ones for the generation of high temperatures, since technologies such as electric arc and induction furnaces allow for directly heating the workpiece. Electric arc furnaces have been widely adopted in steel making.[31] Other innovations in thermal manufacturing operations include several forms of welding, brazing and soldering. In electrical discharge machining, the heat of numerous small sparks is utilized to local heating and evaporation of the workpiece. Finally, laser machining uses coherent light to heat, melt or evaporate small sections of the workpiece. It can be used for cutting, boring and surface treatment.

The transition from wood and charcoal to coal and coke was the first important innovation in the provision of energy for (endothermic) operations

---

31. Electric steel making is treated as a thermal process since it is primarily a re-melting process of scrap metal rather than the production of a metal from an ore.

of chemical materials processing and manufacturing operations. Coal was later replaced by oil and natural gas in numerous operations that change materials and objects at the chemical level. Finally, since the 1880s electricity has become increasingly important in chemical and metallurgical processes. Electrolysis made the large-scale, continuous process production of materials such as aluminum and chlorine economically viable. More recently, this technology has also found applications in manufacturing, for example in electrochemical machining, where electrolytic reactions are used for locally dissolving the workpiece (Alting, 1994).

Innovations in Information Processing

For most of the humankind's history, only human labor inputs could execute the various information processing operations. Progress in the communication and manipulation of information was unrelated to energy innovations. It rather consisted in improved mental techniques to deal with the information (for example through innovations in language, writing, mathematics, logics and the like, but also by means of new artifacts such as the slide-rule). To the degree that technological change in information processing was of a physical kind, it did not change its energetic base. It was largely restricted to the technology by which information was communicated. Copying was revolutionized by the printing press. Spatial information transmission remained dependent on human messengers and the transport of documents until the semaphore visual telegraph was invented in 1794. It allowed communicating 'pure' information (without a physical medium) by means of a chain of visual signals, which still had to be sent and read by human operators.

It was only in the nineteenth century that innovations in information technologies had a significant energetic component. The electric telegraph, being the first of a sequence of electricity-based communication technologies, was invented in 1837 (Dudley, 1999). The first machines for the manipulation of information became available even later. Practical mechanical calculating machines were developed around 1880. Punch card sorting, tabulating and calculating machines were invented around the same time. They quickly became important for statistical applications such as censuses (Ayres, 1990). These early advances notwithstanding, a large-scale adoption of automatic information processing took place only after the invention of electronic computers in the 1950s. The electronic computer is based on the successive development of vacuum tubes, transistors and microprocessors allowing for increasingly cheap and energy-efficient electronic data processing. After the introduction of the microcomputer in the 1970s, computers quickly replaced all earlier information-processing machines. Recent experiments in DNA computing demonstrate the possibility of using biochemical processes for information processing, but this technology has no practical applications yet. Since human labor is still used for a large fraction of information processing operations, adoption of the various innovations in information processing has not been universal.

There is a significant difference between electronic information processing technologies and the earlier uses of electric energy to provide factor services. In electronic information processing, electric current is used to transmit signals and to perform logical operations. In these applications electricity itself is applied; there is no need for a conversion of electricity into other forms of energy to make it useful for human purposes. By contrast, all of the above-mentioned uses of electricity required its conversion into other forms of energy to provide factor services. Because of this difference, for innovations based on electronic information processing, electricity is indicated in Table 5.1 as the energy form on which the factor service is based, whereas in the other uses of electricity (except for process control, for which the same argument holds), that form of energy is listed in the table into which the electricity is converted.

Innovations in Process Control

The automation of supervision and error detection tasks in process control is a recent development for which the availability of electric equipment was instrumental. Automated process supervision is closely related to the development of servomechanisms capable of automatically controlling the position of machine elements or tools. Servomechanisms are based on a feedback mechanism: Sensors transmit signals on the actual position of the tool, these are then compared to the desired position, and the actual position is corrected according to the deviations measured before. Process control through servomechanisms is thus based on electronic information processing technology. Servomechanisms were first adopted in the 1930s for specific metalworking and materials processing operations. Electronic controllers based on vacuum tube amplifiers were crucial for the practical use of servomechanisms after World War II. Transistors and microprocessors have subsequently replaced vacuum tubes (Devine, 1990a).

Adaptation of an operation's execution to changing conditions and requirements was introduced as the second component of process control in Chapter 4. It is another domain where factor services of human labor have been indispensable for most of history. Operations with mechanized tool operation and workpiece handling are adaptable to changing conditions if the sequence of motions is not predetermined but can be varied (programmed). Where programmable tool operation is used, humans are no longer required for the actual adaptation. The need for human labor inputs is restricted to the programming task. Probably the first machine that allowed for programming the mechanized tool operation was the Jacquard loom of 1804 used in silk weaving. Several generations of programmable machine tools were developed after 1930 (Devine, 1990a). The first generation operated on a mechanical basis. It used cams that transmitted information on the necessary tool movements from a physical model of the workpiece to the machine tool. Later programmable machines incorporated electro-mechanic control, using first physical sensors, then punch cards and numerical models of the required tool movements. Computer-numerically-controlled (CNC) machine tools based on electronic information processing were introduced around 1970.

Implications

This overview of important energy innovations was given to illustrate three points. First, the pervasiveness of energy innovations can be noted. Except for nutrition, for all classes of factor services provided by energy, new sources of energy and/or new conversion technologies have been introduced over the course of economic history. These energy innovations caused dramatic qualitative change in how energy is used in economic processes. They may have been more significant for the evolution of production processes than both quantitative increases and efficiency improvements. Accordingly, an encompassing analysis of the historical development of human energy use has to account for their role; it cannot restrict itself to a purely quantitative analysis.

Second, the above overview shows that new energy sources and conversion technologies frequently did not result in the complete replacement of older sources and conversion technologies, but were substitutes only in a subset of the various applications, while the older technologies continued to be used in other applications. As a consequence of partial replacement, the variety of energy sources and technologies in use increased over time, as did the 'specialization' of particular sources and technologies. This ever more differentiated use of energy forms as factors of production reflects the 'Smithian' (Mokyr, 1990) mode of economic development through division of labor and specialization. Its implications for the development of macroeconomic energy use patterns are highlighted in the next section.

Third, the history of human energy utilization is often interpreted as a gradual replacement of human physical work through inanimate sources of energy. If one takes into account the entire range of energy forms utilized in production processes, a somewhat more complex picture of this substitution process emerges. Again, the distinction between the different factor services provided by energy is helpful to make this point. The only form of energy that human labor inputs can provide in substantial amounts is mechanical energy. It provides important factor services in materials processing, manufacturing and transportation, and in these uses of energy the physical work of human labor inputs has indeed been largely replaced by other sources of energy. In addition, humans are capable of information processing and of executing process control tasks, both of which do not require large quantities of energy to be provided. In these activities, the successive replacement of human labor by other inputs is under way.

By contrast, human labor cannot provide heat, light and chemical energy in substantial amounts. Increasing use of non-human inputs of these forms of energy is not directly due to the replacement of human labor, but may be caused by two kinds of developments. One is increasing consumption of goods with energy-dependent properties and of goods that require energy inputs into the operations of their production. The other is the indirect substitution of human labor inputs. Instances of indirect substitution of human labor can be observed in materials processing and manufacturing, for example when mechanical assembly operations based on screws and bolts are replaced by less labor-intensive chemical joining through adhesive bonding. Since it requires changes in the basic execution of the operation, rather than merely the replacement of a factor service, the indirect substitution of human labor is a more complex technological change than the direct one.

5.2 THE MACRO PICTURE: INCREASING VARIETY RATHER THAN STAGES OF DEVELOPMENT

Human use of energy has increased dramatically over time. From hunter-gatherer times to present-day industrial economies, growing demand for energy has resulted in a more than twentyfold increase in per capita use (Kümmel, 1998, ch. 2). And even from Renaissance times to today, the amount of energy used by each individual in Western Europe has gone up by a factor of four to five (ibid.). As was argued above, these increases came with major changes in humans' ability to use energy forms and particular sources of energy (fuels), and with the development of new conversion technologies.

Some authors (e.g. Marchetti, 1987; Fritsch, 1992) have described the development of energy use after the Industrial Revolution as a series of stages in which energy innovations resulted in the successive replacement of earlier technologies by newer ones, which was linked to a parallel replacement process in the use of fuels. This interpretation is supported by long-term developments in the shares of total energy use accounted for by the various primary energy sources. Changes in relative shares suggest a succession of 'dominating' sources of energy from wood, coal, oil and gas to nuclear energy. This interpretation is in striking contrast, however, to the pattern of partial replacement of older by newer energy technologies and their fuels that was emphasized above. It hinges on the focus on relative shares. If instead one looks at the development of absolute use of the various sources, a different picture emerges, which is consistent with the above arguments (see Figures 5.1 and 5.2 for the development in the US and worldwide, respectively).

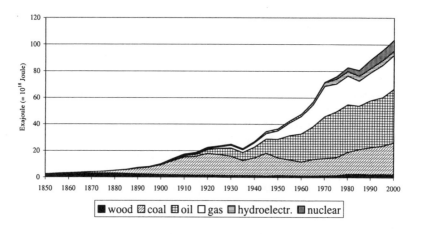

Source: Energy Information Administration, 2002

Figure 5.1 US energy use, 1850–2000

In absolute terms, wood is the only primary energy whose use may have been going down during the past 150 years. But in spite of its drastically diminished relative share in today's total energy use, the absolute decline in fuel wood consumption has not been that spectacular. In relative terms, the share of fuel wood in US energy use fell from 90 per cent to 2.6 per cent from 1850 to 1955, and further decreased to 0.7 per cent in 1995. In comparison, the absolute amount of fuel wood (measured by its caloric content) went down from 2200 Petajoule (PJ = 10^{15} Joule) to 1100 PJ in 1955 and 650 PJ (or 30 per cent of its 1855 value) in 1995 (US Bureau of the Census, 1997; IEA, 1999). Moreover, the decline in wood energy use vanishes completely if the use of wood products such as black liquor and wood waste as fuels is taken into consideration, as is done in Figure 5.1. In this more inclusive demarcation, US wood energy use in 2000 was even slightly higher than in 1850 (Energy Information Administration, 2002). The absolute level of coal consumption, as another traditional source of energy, has not decreased either over the last 200 years. US coal consumption in 2000 was 40 per cent higher than in 1945, when it had peaked before temporarily falling in the 1950s (ibid., see also Figure 5.1).

On the global scale as well, coal has not been replaced by oil and gas, even though worldwide oil and natural gas production has increased faster during the twentieth century than has coal production (Smil, 1994; see also Figure 5.2). Moreover, if the comparison is limited to the period following the oil price shocks of the 1970s, increases in coal use are even larger than those of oil. In the OECD, total supply of coal (including imports, excluding exports) has grown by 33 per cent from 1971 to 2000, whereas oil supply has only increased by 25 per cent. The total supply of natural gas went up more than 75 per cent in the same time period (IEA, 2002).

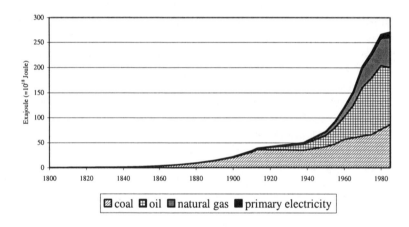

Source: Etemad and Luciani, 1991

Figure 5.2 World production of coal, oil, natural gas, and primary electricity (hydro and nuclear), 1800–1985

To make sense of these patterns of changes in energy use, one has to distinguish between three overlapping trends whose interaction produced the overall development. The first trend is the immense quantitative growth in energy use that shows both in per-capita energy use and in the aggregate figures for national economies and at the global level. It is reflected by the rapid increase of total energy use in Figures 5.1 and 5.2, interrupted (in the US case) only by brief periods of decreases during the Depression years and after the 1970s oil price shocks. This secular trend of growing energy use is due both to the availability of new energy technologies and to increases in the use of existing ones.

The second development is related to the heterogeneity of energy use. As has been argued above, energy provides quite different factor services in production, and these require that different forms of energy be used. The primary sources of energy included in the macro-level figures are all used in several applications. They were subject to the pattern of only partial replacement of earlier energy technologies that has been stressed above. This pattern suggests a change in the basic heuristic for interpreting the history of energy use. Rather than seeing it as a series of successive stages, possibly even one in which 'higher-quality' sources of energy are continually replacing 'lower-quality' sources of energy (measured, for example, in terms of energy density, see Fritsch, 1992), it seems more appropriate to liken the various uses of energy in production processes to niches in an ecosystem that are filled by different technologies at different points of time. Niche boundaries may be of varying rigidity. On the one hand, the different categories of energetic factor services identified above establish clear-cut boundaries between niches. On the other hand, subdivisions exist within these categories in which different technologies are in use, and these subdivisions can be shifted by technological change that affects the competitive advantages of the respective technologies. A new source of energy or a new conversion technology may then be able to capture a part of an older technology's niche, as oil and gas captured most of coal's niche in the domain of space heating. Unless it captures the entire niche of the earlier technology, however, both technologies will coexist in the market, and the variety of energy technologies in use will increase. It is also possible, as in the case of oil as a fuel for the automobile used in personal transportation, that the rise of a particular source of energy is primarily caused by an entirely new use – which creates a new niche, as it were – rather than by replacing other sources in existing uses.

The combination of growing total energy use and increasingly specialized use in individual applications allows for constant or even increasing use of an energy source even though its relative importance is going down, as its use is discontinued in some of the applications. Again, coal is a good case in point. Coal is no longer used in mobile applications, it has largely been replaced in space heating, and even in the generation of electricity it has been challenged by various new technologies. Nonetheless, the absolute use of coal is still rising.

A third development concerns the efficiency with which energy is converted into useful work. Increasing energy efficiency of technologies is a robust characteristic of their developmental life cycle, which can clearly be identified for individual technologies. (It is shown for the steam engine in

Chapter 7.) At the macroeconomic level, it is reflected by the declining energy intensity of the social product of industrial economies. The increasingly specialized use of energy technologies is one factor that underlies rising energy efficiency, since it reduces the likelihood that a particular technology is used in an application for which it is grossly inefficient. Moreover, the increase in energy efficiency implies that absolute decreases in the use of 'older' energy technologies could arise even if there were neither replacements by newer ones nor decreases in demand, but simply because of increasing efficiency of its use (less input is required to do the same amount of useful work). In the light of this argument, the observable increases in coal consumption suggest that both the partial replacement of coal and the rising efficiency of its use have been overcompensated by quantitative increases in the remaining specialization of coal.

To conclude these observations on macro-level developments in energy use, a finally remark is necessary. The above argument of specialization and prolonged coexistence holds only for primary sources of energy. It is in striking contrast with continual increases in electricity generation (Schurr et al., 1990) and the proliferation of new technologies based on electricity that was also documented in the above review. Electricity is clearly gaining in absolute and relative importance. It is not a primary source of energy, however, so that it cannot replace primary sources of energy, but its generation actually requires inputs of one of them. The attractiveness of electricity as an energy form is caused by the fact that its conversion into other energy forms is both feasible and highly efficient, by its particular characteristics, and also by its unique capacity to provide factor services in information processing.

5.3 CONCLUSIONS

In the present chapter, the distinction of different energy forms and the factor services provided by them has been applied to a review of historical changes in energy use. The review showed that in all the direct and indirect categories of factor services (except for the provision of chemical energy for nutrition), energy innovations made it possible to use new energy forms, conversion technologies and/or sources of energy (fuels) for the production of useful goods. The new technologies have often been unable to replace earlier technologies completely, and there has rather been a pattern of increasingly specialized use of the various available forms and sources of energy. In addition, new conversion technologies led to increased substitution possibilities among energy forms. They thus lifted some of the restrictions arising from the heterogeneity of energy forms. In spite of these advances, different forms of energy still tend to be imperfect substitutes in their particular applications.

The final section of the chapter suggested a reinterpretation of the long-term development of human energy use, emphasizing the increasing specialization of energy use. It showed that also at the aggregate level, older sources of energy such as wood and coal have only partially been replaced, and even keep growing in use. The complex development of energy use has been explained as an interplay of increasing absolute energy use, increasing specialization, and increasing energy efficiency within existing applications.

6. Process innovations in sequential production

The previous two chapters dealt with the factor services of energy in the individual operations of a production process, and with long-term changes in the way they are provided. In the present chapter, the analysis is broadened with regard to two dimensions: First, it is investigated more generally how technological change affects the execution of operations. I argue that process innovations modify both inputs and outputs of operations, and that they may be related to individual operations or longer sequences of operations. Second, this chapter studies what consequences for the innovation process result from the sequential character of production. It is suggested that innovations in individual operations may affect other operations in various ways and at various levels. The chapter moreover explores parallels between technological change in sequential production processes and the concepts of modularity and decomposability, which figure prominently in recent work on innovation and in complex systems theory more generally. Building on these parallels, I finally suggest that the decomposability of techniques varies over time and that it is partly endogenous to the production process.

6.1 KINDS OF CHANGES IN PRODUCTION OPERATIONS

Changes in Individual Operations

Technological change affecting production operations can be classified along several dimensions. In what follows, three dimensions are discussed: the origins of technological change, its effect on the input requirements of the operation, and the way it alters the operation's output in terms of modifying workpiece properties.

The sources of technological change
Process innovations often have origins that are external to the operation. Prominent among these are deliberate research and development efforts.

They may be motivated by the search for improvements, often in response to competitive pressure. Other changes to the production process are forced upon the producer by changing economic conditions, which may include shortages (or significant price changes) of crucial inputs, variations in demand and also changes in legislative regulation. In addition, new possibilities of executing an operation may be suggested by analogous changes in other operations – in this case, process innovations are the result of 'spillovers' or complementarities between operations. Complementarities are at the center of the following section of this chapter.

Alternatively, some technological change has its origins in the operation itself, as it results from learning processes that take place in executing the operation. The effects of such practical learning are captured by the notions of 'learning by doing' (Arrow, 1962b) and 'learning by using' (Rosenberg, 1982a), and ample empirical evidence for their significance has been established (Argote and Epple, 1990; Bahk and Gort, 1993). Learning by doing may cause improvements in the performance of individual workers and of entire workgroups, and with regard to a variety of tasks. Learning by using denotes performance effects stemming from increasing familiarity with pieces of equipment. They result from more proficient tool use, from reductions in equipment down time that are made possible by fewer breakdowns and longer maintenance intervals, and also from improvements made to the equipment itself that are suggested by its use ('embodied' learning by using; Rosenberg, 1982a, p. 123). As an example of embodied learning by using, Rosenberg refers to modifications to aircraft designs during the production runs of given models, which result in the 'stretching' of the aircraft body. He argues that these changes are made possible by the accumulation of experience of airlines and manufacturers with the flight performance characteristics of the respective model. As can be seen from this example, the effects of practical learning are by no means limited to experience-based improvements in simple manual tasks.

Learning by doing and using has potentially far-reaching implications for technological dynamics. Where learning effects are substantial, they may give rise to frequency dependence effects in the adoption of alternative techniques, even if no network externalities are present otherwise. If producers can benefit from the learning-based improvements made by other producers, and if this learning from others is stronger among producers that have adopted the same one of the alternative techniques, dynamic increasing returns caused by learning effects may result. The more a technique has been adopted in the past, the more learning will then focus upon it, and the faster it will be improved. As a consequence of learning and imitation, the relative productivity of the alternative techniques will no longer be given exogenously, and the adoption of a technique may become more dependent on the prior history of the industry than on the inherent 'goodness' of the alternatives (Cowan, 1987; Arthur, 1989). Implicitly underlying these hypotheses on dynamic increasing returns based on learning is the assumption that knowledge can 'flow' among the producers that use the same technique. As was argued in Chapter 3, this view of technological knowledge as freely accessible to others is too simplistic. And both theoretical and empirical considerations suggest that firms possess proprietary knowledge, which cannot easily be replicated by their competitors, and which plays an important role in shaping the evolution of industries (Klepper, 1996; Klepper and Simons, 1997). These qualifications do not rule out dynamic increasing returns from learning, however, for which it is only necessary that producers learn *something* from other users of the same technique, and that they learn *more* from users of the same technique than from users of other techniques.

Effects on factor requirements
Their effects on the input use of operations constitute the second dimension along which different forms of technological change in operations can be distinguished. In terms of the framework developed in Chapter 3, there are several levels at which changes in operations can have an effect on input use. The changes may, first, consist of the gradual improvement of the productivity of one or several factors. Learning by doing in manual skills would typically be expected to result in this kind of change. Second, the set of inputs may be modified by replacements of one or several factors by other factors that are capable of providing the same factor service. This is the case for example if one kind of fuel is substituted by another one, or if workpiece handling in a manufacturing operation is mechanized, so that a human labor input is replaced by a suitable tool and an input of mechanical energy. Third, the operation may be changed completely, and an entire set of new factor services may be utilized. As an example from manufacturing, consider the replacement of machining a metal part by molding an analogous part from a plastic material. Changes of the latter kind are more likely to originate from deliberate research and development activities than endogenously from learning by doing.

Effects on the output of the operation
A third dimension along which technological change in production operations can be distinguished is in terms of the output of the affected operation. In the remainder of this chapter I will focus on this distinction. To do so, it is useful to return to the sequential framework developed in Chapter 3. In that framework, operations have been characterized by their function, i.e. by the way in which they modify the workpiece. I have moreover argued that the function of an operation may be fulfilled in different ways, and that

operations may differ in their precise effect on the property vector of the
workpiece, and may nonetheless all be suitable to fulfill the required
function.

In terms of their effects on the output of operations, only a basic
distinction between two kinds of technological changes is made here. It
distinguishes between changes to an operation after which the output of the
operation is the *same* as before, and changes after which the output of the
operation result is *different* from before. The output of an operation is
specified in terms of its effect on the workpiece properties (both user-relevant
and production-relevant ones).

Since this distinction is central to the argument of this chapter, it seems
justified to express it in terms of the abstract formulations of section 3.3. For
example, assume that the second operation ($o2$) in a production process is
modified. If $x_{(o1)}$ denotes the property vector before the operation under
consideration, and $x_{(o2)}$ and $x_{(o2)}*$ denote the property vectors of the
workpiece after the old and the new operations, respectively, then the
operations can be represented by:

$$\text{old }(o2): x_{(o1)} = \begin{pmatrix}1\\2\\4\\5\end{pmatrix} \rightarrow x_{(o2)} = \begin{pmatrix}1\\2\\7\\5\end{pmatrix} \qquad \text{new }(o2)^*: x_{(o1)} = \begin{pmatrix}1\\2\\4\\5\end{pmatrix} \rightarrow x_{(o2)}^* = \begin{pmatrix}1\\2\\7\\5\end{pmatrix}$$

This kind of change in a single operation, which is not visible in the
operation's effect on the property vector of the workpiece, will below be
called a *change within the operation*.

By contrast, the new way of executing an operation may modify the
workpiece properties in a different way to the older alternative of execution.
For example, using the same notation as above:

$$\text{old }(o2): x_{(o1)} = \begin{pmatrix}1\\2\\4\\5\end{pmatrix} \rightarrow x_{(o2)} = \begin{pmatrix}1\\2\\7\\5\end{pmatrix} \qquad \text{new }(o2)^{**}: x_{(o1)} = \begin{pmatrix}1\\2\\4\\5\end{pmatrix} \rightarrow x_{(o2)}^{**} = \begin{pmatrix}2\\2\\9\\5\end{pmatrix}$$

This second kind of change will below be referred to as a *replacement of
operation* ($o2$) by ($o2$)**. It may result in a different property vector of the
workpiece leaving the operation (as in the example) and/or it may require a
different property vector of the workpiece as it enters the operation.
Moreover, old and new operations may differ both in *what* properties they

affect and in *how* they affect them. In the above example, $(o2)$** differs from $(o2)$ both in the affected properties (first and third versus only third before) and in the kind of change made to the third property.

The distinction between changes within operations and replacements of operations is relevant because replacements of operations, through their different effect on the workpiece, may have repercussions on other stages of the technique in use. If replacing one operation by another one affects production-relevant properties, various kinds of effects on other operations may arise. The replacement may make the execution of other operations more difficult, it may facilitate the execution of other operations or it may change the opportunities for changes in other operations. These possible forms of interdependencies between operations will be further explored in section 6.2. By contrast, a change within an operation cannot (by definition) in this way result in repercussions on other operations (otherwise, the vector of relevant properties is incomplete).

Changes Affecting Multiple Operations

In the above discussion, technological changes were restricted to changes in a single operation. It is possible, however, that a process innovation affects not only a single operation but several operations in the technique. In some cases, such changes in the interplay of the various operations are the primary effect of process innovations.

All of the three dimensions of classifying process innovations discussed above are also applicable to innovations that affect more than a single operation. First, the technological changes may be caused either by external factors or by endogenous learning processes. As an external factor affecting several operations, one might think of a new factor service becoming available that is applicable in various operations of the same technique. Examples of above-operation-level learning effects include improved matching of individuals and tasks, changes in the spatial layout of the plant, and modifications in the organization of materials handling and routing (Bahk and Gort, 1993). With regard to inputs, technological change affecting several operations may increase the productivity of otherwise unmodified factor sets, it may replace some of the factors providing the required factor services, or it may completely change the operation.

Finally, technological changes affecting multiple operations also differ as to whether or not they change the way the workpiece is modified. For changes that affect continuous sub-sequences of operations, a distinction can be made that is entirely analogous to the one introduced above for single-operation changes. Again, there are two principal alternatives. First, the change may be such that a sequence of operations is modified, whereas the aggregate effect of the sequence on the workpiece properties is unchanged. In other words, the property vectors of the workpiece entering and leaving the sequence are the same for the old and the new sequence of operations. I refer to this case as a *change within a sequence of operations*. For example, let there be the following sets of property vectors:

$$\text{old: } x_{(o3)} = \begin{pmatrix} 5 \\ 4 \\ 7 \\ 0 \\ 9 \end{pmatrix} \rightarrow x_{(o7)} = \begin{pmatrix} 7 \\ 2 \\ 5 \\ 0 \\ 8 \end{pmatrix} \quad \text{new: } x_{(o3)} = \begin{pmatrix} 5 \\ 4 \\ 7 \\ 0 \\ 9 \end{pmatrix} \rightarrow x_{(o5)}{}^* = \begin{pmatrix} 7 \\ 2 \\ 5 \\ 0 \\ 8 \end{pmatrix}$$

Obviously, the old sequence of operations (*o*4) to (*o*7), which changes the property vector $x_{(o3)}$ into $x_{(o7)}$, and the new sequence (*o*4)* to (*o*5)*, which changes $x_{(o3)}{}^*$ into $x_{(o5)}{}^*$, have exactly the same effect on the workpiece. It is thus possible to replace the old sequence by the new one, which consists of a smaller number of operations, without modifying the output of the sequence. In general, the new sequence may be shorter, longer, or of the same length as the old one.

- A *shortening of a sequence of operations* is caused by a process innovation that renders one or several stages superfluous. As an example, consider high-precision casting of metals, which requires less machining in later stages than traditional processes do.
- An innovation resulting in a new sequence with the same length as the old one is called *a length-invariant change within a sequence of operations*.
- Alternatively, the changes in the technique may result in the *lengthening of a sequence of operations*. This kind of change may for example be caused by a subdivision of operations introduced to trigger productivity increases, or if standardized equipment becomes available for an operation, which requires an auxiliary operation before it can be fit into the existing process.

The alternative possibility – which is analogous to the replacement of a single operation – is that a process innovation modifies the technique in such a way that the affected sequence of operations modifies the workpiece in a different way than the one it replaced. In other words, the interfaces between operations (in terms of workpiece properties) are different in the old and new sequences. As in the case of replacing a single operation, such a *replacement of a sequence of operations* will give rise to changes elsewhere in the technique, insofar as it affects production-relevant properties. A further subdivision according to the length of the old and new sequences can be made in the same way as for changes within a sequence of operations.

6.2 INCOMPATIBILITIES AND COMPLEMENTARITIES OF OPERATIONS

The previous section introduced a distinction between changes within (sequences of) operations on the one hand and replacements of (sequences of) operations on the other. I argued that these two kinds of technological changes differ in their capacity to cause repercussions to other operations. The replacement of single or multiple operations alters the way in which the workpiece is modified. This may result in various kinds of consequences to other operations and production processes. The present section explores these repercussions and relates them to current discussions in the literature on production, growth and technological change.

Forms of Interdependencies among Operations

Modified operations can affect other operations in one of three different ways. First, the effect on other operations may be adverse: Changing an operation may give rise to an incompatibility problem by making it impossible or more expensive to execute another operation. Incompatibility problems primarily arise between operations of the same technique. They tend to prevent the changes to the first operation as long as the second operation is not modified in a way that solves the incompatibility problem (otherwise, an adoption will only make sense if the cost increases due to the incompatibility are smaller than the benefits from the changes in the originating operation).

By contrast, it is also possible that changes in one operation have favorable effects on another operation, either by increasing the productivity of executing the affected operation or by creating new opportunities for increasing this productivity (which require further modifications to the affected operation before they materialize).[32] Both possibilities will be referred to below as complementarities between operations.

---

32. Logically there should also exist a fourth kind of effect that is symmetric to the creation of new opportunities: changes that have no direct effect on other operations, but that reduce the opportunities of innovation in these operations. This kind of effect does not seem very plausible, however.

Complementarities can be characterized as follows (this follows a similar definition proposed by Carlaw and Lipsey (2002) in a growth-theoretic context):

> Complementarities between two operations exist in any situation in which changes made to one operation (the originating operation) increase the productivity of executing the other operation (the receiving operation) and/or the opportunities for increasing this productivity. The two operations may be part of the same technique, they may be part of different techniques of the same production process, or they may belong to two different production processes.

Again following Carlaw and Lipsey (2002), the two types of complementarities covered in the definition can be called 'static' complementarities (resulting in direct productivity increases) and 'dynamic' complementarities (creating new opportunities for innovations in the receiving operation). Dynamic complementarities have also been referred to as 'innovational' or 'enabling' complementarities. In terms of the above framework of workpiece properties, one may express dynamic complementarities in a probabilistic way. Dynamic complementarities between changes in the operations (*oi*) and (*oj*) are present if:

$$P\left\{(oj) \to (oj)* \middle| \Pi\left[(oi^*);(oj^*)\right] > \Pi\left[(oi^*);(oj)\right]\right\}$$
$$> P\left\{(oj) \to (oj)* \middle| \Pi\left[(oi);(oj^*)\right] > \Pi\left[(oi);(oj)\right]\right\} \tag{6.1}$$

where Π stands for the profit realized in using the technique and the asterisks denote changed operations. The probability of finding profit-increasing alterations in (*oj*) is higher after (*oi*) has been changed.[33]

---

33. The present definition of complementarities is broader than the oft-cited one developed by Milgrom and Roberts (1990) in their analysis of flexible manufacturing. These authors focus on dynamic complementarities, which they define by the supermodularity of a profit function. The profit function is defined over a set of cost and decision variables. In general, a function is supermodular if separate increases in the arguments change its value less than an equally large joint increase of the same variables. Milgrom and Roberts show that for a continuous and twice differentiable profit function f, this condition is equivalent to the condition that marginal increases in one argument increase the marginal productivity of increasing another one, or $\partial f^2 (v_i, v_j) / \partial v_i\, \partial v_j \geq 0$ (where v_i, v_j are cost and decision variables and $\partial f / \partial v_k > 0$, $k = i, j$). The formal definition of Milgrom and Roberts cannot be adopted in the present context since workpiece properties are not necessarily defined as continuous variables and profit need not be increasing in the absolute value of a property.

Levels of Interdependencies among Operations

Part of the definition of complementarities was that they may arise between operations of the same technique, between operations of different techniques for producing the same good and between operations of different production processes. As an example of complementarities between operations of the same technique, consider the introduction of computer aided design (CAD) in a manufacturing company. If the data generated by this system can be fed directly into numerically controlled (NC) machine tools, then a static complementarity is present since the costs of programming the NC machine tools are reduced. By contrast, if there are no NC machines available or if the data from the CAD system are in a format that the NC machines cannot read, then there is an opportunity for a cost-reducing innovation, but it cannot be exploited without further effort – thus there is a dynamic complementarity between the design and manufacturing stages.

Complementarities between different techniques for producing the same good can be expected if techniques are in part identical, i.e. they contain some identical operations, and if technological change affects these operations. Given that the alternative techniques produce the same end products, their operations will often fulfill the same functions, so that the existence of identical operations would not be surprising. Nonetheless, the differences between the various techniques, for example with regard to specific inputs providing factor services, may cause the interfaces between the operations to vary between the techniques, so that the existence of complementarities cannot be taken for granted. Moreover, even if complementarities do exist between the operations of alternative techniques, the differences between the techniques may cause them to be of the dynamic rather than the static kind. In this case, further modifications are needed before the changes in one technique can be taken over for use in the other one. [34]

The notion of complementarities between techniques can be related to standard ways of modeling technological change. It is common microeconomic practice to represent technological change as an inward movement of the entire isoquant. Doing so implicitly assumes perfect static

34. Although the present discussion is located at the technological rather than the organizational level, it should be noted that boundaries between organizations – typically business firms – can be important obstacles of complementarities among techniques and production processes used by different producers. It was suggested above that significant parts of technological knowledge may be firm-specific. Similarly, organization theorists have emphasized the difficulties of firms in absorbing new knowledge that has been developed outside the firm (Cohen and Levinthal, 1990; Langlois, 1992).

complementarity between all techniques of the production process. Within the same microeconomic modeling tradition, this implicit assumption has been challenged by the notion of localized technological change (Atkinson and Stiglitz, 1969; David, 1975; Antonelli, 1995). Localized technological change implies that learning effects are technique-specific, i.e. that no complementarities exist between the alternative techniques (where techniques are defined by their ratio of factor inputs).[35] Although this way of modeling production does not specify the nature of production processes in detail, localized technological change has been related to the sequential character of production (David, 1975, ch. 1). David suggests that localized technological change may result from dynamic complementarities between operations of the same technique, which generate 'compulsive sequences' (Rosenberg, 1969) of innovations in the technique. As an example, David refers to the introduction of 'high-speed steel' (high-alloy steel that is particularly strong and wear-resistant) for cutting tools in manufacturing. The new material for tools gave rise to a dynamic complementarity, because stronger machines were required before the potential of the improved tools could be exploited. In this way, they shaped the further direction of innovations in the machine tool industry. Moreover, by inducing different kinds of further innovations, slight initial differences between alternative techniques potentially give rise to the progressive divergence of their development and thus lead to localized technological change.

Complementarities between the operations of different production processes may generate interdependencies even between seemingly remote processes and industries. This phenomenon has for a long time been known to economic historians (Rosenberg, 1979). It has also been referred to as 'technical interrelatedness' (Frankel, 1955; Landes, 1969; David, 1975, ch. 5) or 'technological networks' (Wright, 1997). From the sequential perspective on production assumed here, interrelations between production processes are not surprising: Some operations fulfill generic functions that are required in quite different production processes, and similarly some factor services are in widespread use throughout the economy. If innovations in one production process make available new operations suitable to fulfill a generic function, or new factor services that can be broadly used, then these innovations are likely to have repercussions in a variety of other processes.

---

35. Empirical evidence supporting the hypothesis of localized technological change has been established by Cantner, Hanusch and Westermann (1996). Analyzing the production techniques used by German manufacturing firms, they find that techniques cluster into a small number of technology fields (defined by input ratios), that the efficiency of production differs between firms, and that switches between technology fields are relatively infrequent (over a period of seven years, roughly one third of the firms changed their technology field).

The notion of 'general purpose technologies' has recently brought the issue of technical interrelatedness caused by common technological 'components' of production processes to the attention of growth theorists (Bresnahan and Trajtenberg, 1995; Helpman, 1998). According to the inventors of the concept, general purpose technologies are characterized by their 'potential for pervasive use in a wide range of sectors' (Bresnahan and Trajtenberg, 1995, p. 84), which stems from their capacity to fulfill a generic function. Typical examples of general purpose technologies include the steam engine and the semiconductor. Although there is some controversy about which technologies actually qualify as general purpose technologies (Lipsey et al., 1998), the concept of general purpose technologies goes beyond the usual restraint practiced by economic theorists in making material statements on the 'content' of production. It is closely related to the sequential framework developed above. Another characteristic of general purpose technologies is identical to the present notion of dynamic complementarity. According to Bresnahan and Trajtenberg (ibid.), general purpose technologies exhibit 'technological dynamism' that causes their productivity to increase over time, and an 'enabling' character that, rather than directly increasing the productivity of production processes, creates 'innovative complementarities' in application sectors.

The sequential perspective provides a conceptual framework into which general purpose technologies can be integrated. In terms of this framework, general purpose technologies appear as a particular form of the general phenomenon of complementarities. More specifically, they create new operations to fulfill generic functions, which are made possible by the availability of new factor services and which generate dynamic complementarities between production processes. This interpretation is consistent with the discussion in Carlaw and Lipsey (2002).

The present perspective moreover suggests a closer investigation into the nature of factor services and operations that are discussed under the heading of general purpose technologies. By identifying the function of the operations affected by a new general purpose technology, its economic effects can be identified in more detail. A new way of generating mechanical energy (such as the steam engine) affects other operations than a new electronic device (such as the semiconductor). Because of these differences, the direction of growth stemming from broadly used new factor services depends on their nature. For example, if instead of the steam engine an (similarly pervasive) information processing technology had been developed during the Industrial Revolution, modern economic growth would have developed quite differently. Finally, it can even be argued that the present perspective is more congenial to the concept of general purpose technologies than the standard framework of modeling production. General purpose technologies presuppose that it is possible to specify a subset of technologies (and the capital assets that are utilized by them) in terms of their technical characteristics. This does not fit easily into the standard framework where the concrete nature of both technologies and goods normally remain unspecified. By contrast, making material statements on how useful goods are actually produced is the primary purpose of the present framework.

6.3   INCOMPATIBILITY IN TECHNIQUES AND MODULARITY IN PRODUCT DESIGNS

Up to now this chapter has argued that technological change may affect sequential production processes in multiple ways. I have stressed the potential of changes in single operations to cause repercussions at other stages of the technique. In addition, the discussion indicated the possibilities for changes to spread between techniques and processes. In the remainder of the chapter, the perspective of the argument is changed in two ways. First, the focus will be on interdependencies among the operations of an individual technique rather than on the effects on other techniques and production processes. And second, whereas the above discussion took individual operations as its points of departure, the following discussion will study the characteristics of whole sequences rather than those of individual operations. In terms of the above framework, the degree of interdependence among operations finds its expression in the number of production-relevant properties of the workpiece. The greater the interdependence, the more aspects of the workpiece have to be considered as production-relevant. A corollary of this consideration is that with an increasing degree of interdependence, changes to the technique become more likely to be replacements of operations rather than changes within operations (or sequences thereof).

The issue of interdependence is not unique to production processes. It has previously been discussed in other contexts and disciplines. Before studying the innovational dynamics of sequential production processes in more detail, in this and the following section a brief digression is therefore made into product innovation and complex systems theory. I do this to explore whether findings on the dynamics of multi-component products in particular, and complex systems in general, can provide indications for the dynamics of sequential production processes.

The discussion of innovation in multi-component products starts from the notion of product 'architecture.' A product's architecture describes how the individual components are interrelated in order to bring about the function of the product. More precisely, product architecture can be defined by in terms of three relationships: '(1) the arrangement of *functional elements*; (2) the mapping from *functional elements* to *physical components*; (3) the specification of the *interfaces* among interacting physical components' (Ulrich, 1995, p. 420; emphasis in original). In this definition, functional elements correspond to the present notion of user-relevant properties. The mapping between functional elements and physical components denotes how many functions are allocated to a single component; Ulrich further distinguishes between one-to-one, one-to-many and many-to-one mappings. Finally, interfaces are the physical connections between the components of the product. The specification of interfaces describes how that connection is made (for example, by determining the surface size and characteristics of a geometrically defined interface, and the way in which the components are joined).

The architecture of a multi-component product may itself be subject to innovation. This kind of innovation was first studied by Henderson and Clark (1990). They developed the notion of 'architectural innovations' to denote innovations that modify multi-component products at the level of interfaces between their components, whereas the components themselves are not fundamentally affected (their 'core design principles' are not overturned) by the innovation. In addition, Henderson and Clark analyze the knowledge requirements of architectural innovations and suggest that they are particularly difficult to generate for established producers.

	Core concepts reinforced	Core concepts overturned
Component linkages unchanged	Incremental innovations	Modular innovations
Component linkages changed	Architectural innovations	Radical innovations

Source: Henderson and Clark, 1990, p. 12

Figure 6.1 A classification of product innovations

More generally, Henderson and Clark distinguish four different kinds of product innovations along the two dimensions of changes in individual components and changes in their linkages (see Figure 6.1). Incremental innovations change neither the basic design principles of individual components nor the linkages between them. Modular innovations fundamentally change a single component yet do not alter the linkages. The symmetric case of unchanged design principles of components and changed links between components is given by architectural innovations, whereas radical innovations change both the basic design principles of individual components and the way they are linked.

The 'modular product architecture' (Ulrich, 1995) concept extends this line of thought. Ulrich defines product architectures as modular if two conditions are fulfilled: First, there is a one-to-one mapping between functional elements and physical components, and second the interfaces between interrelated components are specified and decoupled (ibid.). An interface between two components is decoupled if each of the components can be varied at will (in the range of changes that are potentially useful) without this variation requiring further changes in the other component in order for the product to work correctly. In a modular design, then, all potentially useful variations in individual components can be realized by changing them separately, i.e. by modular innovations.

The modularity concept has recently gained much academic interest. Some management scholars have suggested modular product designs as a generally advantageous design strategy (Langlois and Robertson, 1992; Baldwin and Clark, 1997, 2000). Drawing on the successful use of modular product designs in the computer industry and elsewhere, these authors emphasize the potential of modularity to increase the speed of product innovations. The major advantage seen in modular products is that they allow for parallel problem solving, since the development of the product's separate components can proceed independently of changes in other components. It is moreover suggested that, because of the specialization made possible by modularity, high levels of product complexity can be handled in the design process. Further benefits from modularity include the feasibility of subsequent replacements of modules for which an improved design has been developed, and also the facilitated standardization of components: Because each function of the product is allocated to a separate physical component, modular designs increase the likelihood that components can be integrated into a variety of different products. Standardization may in turn allow for longer production runs and lower unit costs (Ulrich, 1995). Frequently, in addition to these technological issues, authors also explore the implications of product modularity on the vertical organization of industries (Langlois and Robertson, 1992; Brusoni and Prencipe, 2001; Frenken, 2001b; Langlois, 2003).

Product modularity comes at a cost, however. Most importantly, the *ex ante* specification of the product architecture and of the interfaces between components restricts the scope of allowable innovation. Architectural and radical innovations (in the sense of Figure 6.1) are not compatible with a modular product design because they would require changes in the interfaces between components. Further restrictions may arise if modifications of components turn out to exceed the range of change that the architecture can accommodate (Brusoni and Prencipe, 2001). Most importantly, whereas modular designs allow for the optimization of the individual modules, they prevent the optimization of 'global performance characteristics' (Ulrich, 1995, p. 432) of products. Global characteristics (such as minimal size and mass of a product) depend on the interplay between several or all components. Standardized components may moreover carry excess capacity (quantitatively and/or qualitatively) in some or even most of their applications. As a consequence, the decision for or against a modular design – presuming that this is a matter of decision making at all and not one determined by technological factors – involves a trade-off between product performance and facilitated change within the modules on the one hand, and the potential for architectural and radical innovation on the other.

Furthermore, as is acknowledged by the proponents of modular product designs, perfect modularity is an ideal that cannot normally be attained in practice. Limits to modularity arise in several ways. First, products are modular only at particular levels. Computer components and peripheral hardware, which are frequently mentioned as examples of modular products, are modular only at the level of their specified interfaces, whereas the components of the modules themselves are not. Second, the decoupling of interfaces tends to be imperfect. Perfect modularity would in any case invite the question why the product is marketed as a whole and not in its individual components (as may indeed be the consequence of increased modularity, see Langlois and Robertson, 1992). The existence of some degree of interdependence between components is reflected in the notion of 'loosely coupled' systems (Brusoni and Prencipe, 2001, p. 183). In the same vein, Baldwin and Clark (2000, p. 63) define modules as units whose 'elements are powerfully connected among themselves and relatively weakly connected to elements in other units;' they note that there are 'gradations of modularity.'

6.4   THE BROADER CONTEXT: COMPLEX SYSTEMS, DECOMPOSABILITY AND EVOLUTION

At a general, abstract level, the implications of interdependence and (non-) modularity for the development of evolutionary systems have been investigated in complex systems theory. The line of thought underlying the modularity concept can be traced back to Simon's ([1962] 1996) concept of nearly decomposable systems. More recently, Kauffman (1993) has used computer simulations to study abstract problems of evolutionary adaptation, in particular with regard to the genetic evolution of organisms. In his '*NK* models,' adaptive complex systems are modeled as strings of *N* interdependent elements, which are each expressed as a binary variable. Kauffman assumes that each element in the string makes a contribution to the overall fitness of the organism, which is dependent on the value taken by the binary variable. He then analyzes the consequences that changes in individual elements have on the string's overall 'fitness,' given different assumptions on how the individual elements' fitness contributions are mutually interdependent.

The key variable in Kauffman's models is K, which denotes the number of other elements that a given element is directly interdependent with. For $K = 0$, the fitness contribution of each element depends only on its own value. In systems of maximal complexity, $K = N - 1$, i.e. the fitness contribution of each element in the string is affected by the value of all other elements. With increasing K, the fitness values of similar strings become increasingly dissimilar (the correlation between fitness values of neighboring strings decreases). Each change in a single element results in a large variation of overall fitness. In Kauffman's (1993, ch. 2) terminology, this is expressed as increasing 'ruggedness' of the 'fitness landscape' with increasing K, where fitness maxima are likened to 'peaks' and low fitness values correspond to 'valleys.' Increases in K also increase the number of local maxima in the landscape (with $K = 0$, there is only a single maximum).

By means of simulations, Kauffman was able to derive some general findings on the dynamic properties of *NK* models. These properties are suggestive of the effects that interdependencies have on the adaptability of complex systems. Specifically, Kauffman found that local search in weakly interdependent systems (systems in which the fitness contribution of each element depends only on a small number of other elements) is more effective than search in both entirely independent and strongly interdependent ones. Local maxima of weakly interdependent systems have higher average fitness than those of other kinds of systems. Their basins of attraction are larger than those of strongly interdependent systems. With binary variables as elements, the size of basins of attraction is moreover correlated with their fitness values (i.e. the 'fitter' a local maximum, the larger the number of initial states from which it is reached). These findings suggest that systems with low degrees of interdependence among their elements are more adaptive than both strongly interdependent systems and systems whose elements are completely independent from one another (global fitness maxima of the latter tend to be lower than those of weakly interdependent ones).

In a recent economic application, a group of authors including Kauffman (Auerswald et al., 2000) has used a variant of the *NK* model to analyze the effect of random variations (interpreted as trial-and-error learning) in a sequential production context that is similar to the present one. In their model, there are several alternatives for performing each operation, and the costs of these alternatives follow a random distribution. K corresponds to the number of operations affected by the replacement of an individual operation (changes within operations would be equivalent to $K = 0$). It is then shown that changing the technique by randomly adopting a new alternative for one of the operations becomes less effective when the range of cost interdependencies among the operations increases. In other words, random attempts at improvements tend to be less successful in highly interdependent contexts.[36]

The *NK* model has some properties, however, that limit its usefulness for modeling process innovation in the way suggested by Auerswald et al. (2000). First, interpreting the *NK* model as a model of human learning means accepting two assumptions. One of them is that innovation involves random variations that are insensitive to the known properties of the fitness landscape. For example, even if in a landscape with maximal correlation between the fitness values of neighboring strings, the past five variations showed that improvements can be made by variations in a particular direction, this experience will not affect the way in which the next variation is made, but variations remain random. This clearly does not do justice to the human capacity of forming hypotheses and expectations to deal with uncertainty. The *NK* model moreover assumes local search by variation of only one element at a time. Again, this representation of human learning is too simplistic (even though it can be justified more easily than the random character of search, for example by reference to increasing costs of more far-reaching variations). The second shortcoming of *NK* models is their rather simple structure of interdependence between elements. Although different degrees of interdependence are studied, the interdependence is either uniform over the entire landscape, i.e. all elements have the same range of interdependence with their neighbors, or it is randomly distributed. In the first case, all elements are indirectly interdependent. In the second case, it has been shown by Frenken et al. (1999) that even most systems with low K values are completely non-decomposable: Again, all their components are directly or indirectly interdependent, and no independent subsystems can be separated. As a consequence, *NK* models can be utilized to study the effects of variations in the uniform level of interdependence among elements, but

36. The positive effect of weak interdependencies on adaptability found by Kauffman (1993) is only reproduced in the innovation model if the number of ways in which each operation can be executed is small (Auerswald et al., 2000, p. 429).

they are not well suited to investigate decomposability in the sense of mutually independent subsystems of varying sizes.

Both lines of criticism are dealt with by the modified fitness landscape model developed by Frenken et al. (1999). These authors study the effectiveness of alternative search strategies and problem decompositions in different kinds of landscapes. To this purpose, they first develop measures of decomposability in terms of the size of independent subsystems into which the system can be broken down for parallel search (such that there are interdependencies only within, but not between subsystems). The smaller the largest independent subsystem, the higher is the decomposability of the system. It is then shown that the decomposability of a system increases the more imperfect solutions are accepted. In other words, finding 'satisficing' solutions that lie within a specified range of the global maximum is possible on the basis of more decomposed search strategies than are suitable for finding the global maximum.

The principal advantage of decomposed search strategies is that they need less time to find a solution than strategies without decomposition. To simulate the effects of rapid adaptation, Frenken et al. (1999) model the competition between populations of agents employing different search strategies for the solution of decomposable problems. Agents using decomposition strategies subdivide the system into subsystems and restrict changes to one or several elements of a single subsystem. Competition eliminates the worst performing agents and replaces them with copies of the most successful ones. It is found that in most cases those search strategies do best that use the 'true' decomposition of the problem, i.e. the decomposition that corresponds to the actual interdependence structure of the problem. In highly interdependent problems, however, decomposition strategies can have an advantage over the 'correct' non-decomposition strategy, because they allow for faster progress. Finally, the latter result is strengthened by finding that in a nearly-decomposable problem with weak interdependencies between subsystems, a simulated search strategy that ignored the interdependence outperformed the 'correct' strategy.

The results of Frenken et al. (1999) are noteworthy in two regards. First, they show that the decomposition of systems may be impossible even if they exhibit only weak interdependence between elements (low-K systems in Kauffman's terminology). Second, the finding that the decomposability of a system increases when the requirements for the 'goodness' of solutions are lowered indicates a trade-off between precision and complexity. Together with the simulations of competing search strategies, this reinforces a point made in the above discussion of modular products: the trade-off between performance and adaptability. In a competitive process that puts a premium on speed, decomposability may be advantageous because it allows for rapid changes, even if it compromises some global characteristics of the product (or adaptive system). Increasing decomposition may serve to speed up development more than it helps to find the best solution at any point in time.

6.5 MODULARITY OF TECHNIQUES

The arguments in favor of modular product designs and the findings on adaptive complex systems suggest the following question: What dynamic properties could be expected in modular production techniques defined analogously to modular designs? To answer this question, three steps are required. Modularity of techniques needs to be defined, the kinds of innovations compatible with modular techniques need to be identified, and the adaptive capacity of modular techniques has to be assessed. These tasks will be taken up in this section.

In analogy to Ulrich's (1995) definition of modular products, a technique can be defined as modular if it satisfies two conditions. First, all necessary modifications of workpiece properties have to be carried out in separate operations. This arrangement guarantees that all required changes of the workpiece are independent. Second, the interfaces between operations have to be specified and decoupled. Specification of interfaces can be given a precise meaning in the present context: It requires that the values of all production-relevant properties are determined *ex ante* for each interface between two operations.[37] It is the production-relevant properties that matter for the specification of interfaces, because the modularity of the technique is not affected if the replacement of an operation modifies its effect only with regard to user-relevant properties. Decoupling of interfaces requires that as long as the interface specifications are adhered to, each operation can be varied at will without interfering with other operations. Because of the way production-relevant properties have been defined above, decoupling of interfaces is guaranteed by their *ex ante* specification. Finally, the order of operations (i.e. the technique's 'architecture') must remain the same, unless two operations are identical in terms of the production-relevant properties of workpieces entering and leaving them. This condition may be satisfied for example by two successive operations that only modify user-relevant

---

37. In line with the discussion in section 3.3, an exception needs to be made if the value of production-relevant properties is not yet well-defined at an early stage, for example because they are related to a component yet to be added. For these properties, an arbitrary start value can be used as long as their specific value does not yet matter for the process.

properties but do not affect production-relevant ones. Changing their order would be consistent with a modular technique.

	Unchanged effect on relevant properties	**Changed effect on relevant properties**
Single operation affected	Change within operation	Replacement of operation
Sequence of operations affected	Change within sequence of operations	Replacement of sequence of operations

Source: Own compilation

Figure 6.2 Classification of process innovations in sequential production

To assess the implications of defining modular techniques in this way, consider first which of the kinds of process innovations distinguished in section 6.1 it would allow for. The different kinds of innovations are summarized in Figure 6.2. Of the four classes of process innovations, only changes within a single operation are allowable without additional restrictions in a modular technique as defined above. By contrast, for changes within sequences of operations to be consistent with the modularity of a technique, an additional condition has to be satisfied: Also within the modified sequence of operations, the interfaces between operations have to remain the same as before. If interfaces within the new sequence were allowed to change, parallel development of changes to individual operations that are part of this sequence would no longer be compatible with the new sequence. Replacements of operations and of sequences of operations that change the effects of operations on production-relevant properties are not consistent with modular techniques, because they obviously violate the condition of specified interfaces.

As can be seen from these considerations, strictly defining modularity of techniques in analogy to the modularity concept in product design seriously restricts the scope of allowable innovations. The effects of restrictions may be outweighed, however, by advantageous properties of modular techniques with regard to the allowable kinds of innovations and the speed of technological advances.

At the level of individual techniques, modular techniques can in principle be expected to have the same advantages as modular products. *Ex ante* specification of interfaces between operations allows for parallel development by introducing changes to several operations at the same time. Moreover, restricting operations to the modification of one property at a time may enhance innovation, as the resulting operations can be expected to be less complex than ones that affect multiple properties. These characteristics suggest that modular techniques may be particularly attractive for rapidly changing production processes. On the other hand, modularity excludes more far-reaching changes of techniques realized by replacements of operations and sequences that affect production-relevant properties. As in the case of modular products, modular techniques may moreover compromise economies that arise from a 'global' optimization of the technique, for example by means of shared use of factor services among several operations.

In analogy to the above argument that modular designs facilitate complementarities by allowing for standardization of components, the modularity of techniques may result in 'standardized' operations that are applicable in a variety of different techniques and production processes. The condition that each operation modifies only a single property tends to increase their range of applicability, which further enhances the likelihood of complementarities. Again, imperfect adaptation of standardized operations to the various applications is a potential drawback of standardization.

The unit operation concept of chemical engineering (see above, Chapter 3) is a prominent example of a class of modular techniques based on standardized operations that are applicable in a wide variety of production processes. As a historical illustration of how the increasing modularity of techniques may give rise to broad complementarities between production processes, consider the origins of the machine tool industry in the second half of the nineteenth century (Rosenberg, 1963). The development of a specialized machine tool industry was closely related to the introduction of interchangeable parts in mass production, which required an increased precision of the various operations, because all components had to comply exactly with the specifications. To achieve the required precision of operations, various kinds of machine tools were developed for the needs of individual industries. In turn, once these machines delivered the required precision, they could easily be adapted for use in the analogous operations of other techniques and processes. According to Rosenberg (ibid., p. 423), the emerging manufacturing industries were characterized by 'technological convergence' in that they used the same kinds of operations and faced similar problems. There were thus broad complementarities in machine-tool innovations, which resulted in machine building becoming organized as a separate industry, offering in part standardized products such as the universal milling machine.

6.6 VARIABLE AND ENDOGENOUS DECOMPOSABILITY

In the previous section, I introduced the concept of modular techniques and defined it in analogy to the modularity concept in product design. The subsequent discussion served to highlight the consequences of the analogy-based concept. It demonstrated that modular techniques are highly restrictive with regard to the kinds of process innovations that are compatible with them. In spite of the historical examples of modular techniques, increasing modularity in the above sense neither appears a good description of how production processes actually change over time, nor does it seem a generally useful prescription for how they should change over time.

The above definition of modularity does not capture all interesting dimensions of changes in sequential production processes. In the development of actual techniques, some significant patterns are discernible that are closely related to changes in the interdependencies between the individual operations, and that are not reflected by the modularity concept. Some of these developments are discussed in this section. To keep the present discussion clearly separated from the above considerations on modularity, I will in the following refer to the decomposability of techniques. Increasing decomposability of techniques just means that it becomes more feasible to change operations individually (i.e. that the degree of interdependence goes down). Decomposability does not require *ex ante* specification of interfaces or other elements of the above definition. It is a purely descriptive indicator of interdependence.

Knowledge and Decomposability

Knowledge is an important determinant of decomposability operating at different time scales. In a long-term perspective, the decomposability of techniques has been increased by fundamental changes in the state of technological knowledge. The more advanced the available scientific and engineering knowledge, the better can the functioning of individual operations and their mutual interdependencies be understood. In turn, better understanding of interdependencies creates opportunities for reducing them, and also for coping with the remaining ones.

Mokyr's (2000, p. 259) notion of a technique's 'epistemic base' is helpful to discuss the relationship between a technique and the knowledge on which it is based. The epistemic base of a technique denotes the degree of theoretical understanding that underlies the application of the technique. It can be of varying broadness, with one extreme being given by thorough understanding of all relevant scientific and engineering aspects. At the other extreme are what Mokyr calls 'singleton techniques' (ibid., p. 262), techniques about which nothing is known except the empirical fact that they work. The broadness of a technique's epistemic base directly affects the flexibility with which it can be adapted to changing circumstances and new applications, and also its potential of being further improved. Improvements of singleton techniques are possible only on the basis of trial-and-error learning and serendipitous discoveries. At the same time, in techniques with narrow epistemic bases, much of the available knowledge is likely to be tacit, so that it can only be acquired by practice. In this case, opportunities for adopting the operations of the technique in other applications are further diminished.

Mokyr uses these concepts to explain the timing of the Industrial Revolution. He argues that it was accompanied by a 'knowledge revolution' (ibid., p. 275), which was caused by the scientific revolution of the seventeenth century and the enlightenment of the eighteenth century. Mokyr suggests that changes in information processing (for example, improvements in printing and more advanced postal services) as well as in scientific practice and culture were instrumental for the subsequently achieved sustained growth, because they broadened the epistemic base of industrial production processes. Mokyr's concepts are of interest here because his argument can be generalized for the time from the Industrial Revolution to the present. In the past 200 years, the epistemic base of techniques has been further broadened through advances in the physical and engineering sciences, as well as through improved measurement and instrumentation. These changes have drastically increased the potential for decomposing and recombining techniques. They have therefore enhanced the scope of complementarities in production processes.

At a much shorter time scale, advances in knowledge have a similar effect on the decomposability of individual techniques over their life cycle. The longer a technique has been in use, the better it tends to be understood, both as a result of shop-floor learning by doing and because of the longer history of deliberate research and development efforts. Understanding that is based on practical experience with a technique is likely to increase its decomposability, as it results in an increased capacity to control the effects of the individual operations and to adapt them to slightly different uses. What this suggests is that at least some of the knowledge that determines the decomposability of a technique is generated in the very use of the technique. As a consequence, the decomposability of techniques and their potential to give rise to complementarities are partly endogenous, and there may be dynamic increasing returns in terms of decomposability.

Increasing Elasticity of Interfaces

The decomposability of techniques may increase in yet another way that is not captured by the above definition of modularity, and which also appears as an important dimension of long-term changes in real-world production processes. This kind of increase in decomposability is not based on the precise specification of interfaces between operations, but rather on their enhanced 'elasticity' in being adapted to changing circumstances, in the sense that a broader range of workpiece characteristics is compatible with the successful linking of operations. In this way, the tolerance of the technique vis-à-vis changes in operations is increased. Two recent developments may be taken as providing evidence for the empirical importance of increased elasticity of interfaces: Flexible manufacturing at the technological level, and management practices based on knowledge sharing at the organizational level.

In terms of the sequential production framework, flexible manufacturing technology increases the producer's capacity to deal with changes in production processes. Flexible manufacturing is based on equipment that can be adapted to varying workpiece properties and that can thus absorb changes in the effects of previous operations. It is typically advocated as a way to allow for more rapid change in products; and flexible manufacturing is to that extent a powerful alternative to modular product designs. However, by buffering the effects of changes in the operations of sequential production techniques, flexible manufacturing is also suited as an alternative to the modularity of techniques. It is closely related to the adaptation component of process control that was discussed as a factor service in Chapters 4 and 5. Technological innovations that allow for enhanced adaptability of operations, among which numerically controlled machines figure prominently, provide the basis of flexible manufacturing.

The elasticity of interfaces between operations is not exclusively determined by technological factors. Organizational factors that allow for a rapid and coordinated reaction may be complementary to the technological capacity to absorb changes. In this context, horizontal coordination mechanisms and the reliance on shared rather than specialized knowledge have been advocated as elasticity-enhancing organizational principles. Specific measures that favor the sharing of knowledge include long-term employment and personnel rotation between departments, characteristics that have been identified in Japanese firms (Aoki, 1990).

What emerges from this discussion, then, is that in addition to the modularity of production techniques in the way it was defined above, i.e. by an *ex ante* definition and decoupling of the interfaces between individual operations, decomposability of techniques may also result from better understanding of the process and more flexible interfaces between operations. These developments may be able to reduce problems caused by interdependencies between operations, and to increase the scope of complementarities, without imposing the restrictive specifications of strictly modular techniques. A final note on the causes of the various forms of increasing decomposability may be useful. Whereas modularity and flexibility of interfaces are two alternative strategies for deliberately reducing interdependencies in production, the discussion of the impact of knowledge on decomposability suggests that the determinants of interdependencies go beyond the level of deliberate decision making.

Integration of Operations may Decrease their Decomposability

The previous paragraphs have highlighted developments toward increasing decomposability of techniques. But even though increasing decomposability of techniques is frequently observable, it is by no means the exclusive direction in which the degree of interdependence in techniques changes over time. To the contrary, there are deliberate changes in techniques that directly reduce their decomposability. In some techniques, sequences of operations are shortened as several operations are integrated into one. In this way economies from the joint use of factors can be realized. For example, continuous casting, continuous rolling and continuous annealing have been important steel making innovations of recent decades (Burwell, 1990). They allow for the molten steel to be directly processed into finished shapes without intermittent cooling, and result in substantial savings of energy, time, transportation costs and inventories. As a manufacturing example consider powder metallurgy, in which metal parts are made through the compacting of metal powders. Powder metallurgy makes it possible to produce parts with intricate geometries in a single operation while at the same time it reduces the requirements for subsequent finishing operations (Todd et al., 1994, ch. 5).

The development of new techniques with a lower degree of decomposability than older ones suggests that the argument made above for modular techniques also holds for decomposability: Reducing the interdependence of operations may compromise the capacity to achieve the best overall technique. Rather than being a generally advantageous strategy for the setup of production processes, decomposability seems to be particularly useful under specific conditions.

6.7 CONCLUSIONS

This chapter has discussed a broad range of concepts that are related to changes in sequential production processes. I first proposed distinguishing different kinds of technological change on the basis of how they alter the effects of an operation (or a sequence of operations) on the workpiece. Process innovations changing the output of an operation may be incompatible with other operations of the technique. On the other hand, they have the potential to cause complementarities that go well beyond the specific technique or production process. As a theoretical basis for investigating the effects of interdependencies in techniques, the chapter has drawn upon the discussions of modular product designs and the decomposability of complex systems. I have shown that modular techniques can be defined in analogy to the definition of modular product designs. At the same time, the modularity concept thus arrived at did not capture all observable changes in the decomposability of techniques. In particular, the chapter has discussed two additional sources of changes in decomposability: increases in the knowledge base of the technique, which can be caused by advances in theoretical knowledge and by endogenous learning by doing, and also the increased elasticity of interfaces between operations. Finally, the observable development of new techniques that shorten the sequence of operations has been taken as an indication that decomposition comes at a cost and is neither an invariably favorable strategy nor a universal developmental regularity.

In the next chapter, three historical cases of innovations in energy technologies will be studied in more detail. The aim of these case studies is to learn more about the dynamics of introducing new kinds of factor services into sequential production processes, and to show how the characteristics of process innovations suggested in this chapter are reflected by actual historical developments.

7. A closer look at change: three historical examples of energy innovations

Chapter 5 gave a broad overview over the most important historical changes in energy technologies, and classified them according to the factor services of energy differentiated in Chapter 4. Subsequently, Chapter 6 discussed some general characteristics of technological change in sequential production processes. The present chapter takes up both lines of discussion. It looks at three historical energy innovations in some more detail: the transition from wood to coal, the adoption of the steam engine, and the electrification of industrial production. By doing so, I illustrate how the concepts developed earlier in this volume can be used to understand the complex dynamics of actual changes in energy technologies. All three cases discussed in this chapter have been the object of extensive research by economic historians. It is not the purpose of this chapter to add to the results of the historical research. The discussion is rather intended as a step towards a better integration of theoretical concepts and historical detail in the analysis of process innovations.

7.1 THE TRANSITION FROM WOOD TO COAL

With the transition from wood to coal humans began to use fossil sources of energy. The adoption of coal was the first step in the successive exploitation of the stocks of fossil fuels to satisfy human energy needs. From the sixteenth to nineteenth centuries, coal was introduced in the Western world for use in numerous production processes, and for the provision of different factor services. As will be shown in this section, the differences in factor services in which coal replaced wood also caused differences in the problems encountered.

Wood Scarcity and the Adoption of Coal

Wood, the resource that coal was to replace in many uses, was a resource of fundamental importance in pre-industrial economies. In many production

136   *The economics of energy and the production process*

processes, wood was required for the provision of thermal energy, both for the direct factor services of heating and for indirect services in thermal materials processing and manufacturing operations. In addition, wood served as the energy source for endothermic chemical materials processing, particularly in metallurgical processes. And finally, wood (timber) constituted a crucial material input in the construction of a variety of objects and buildings. By contrast, wood played no role as a source of mechanical energy in pre-industrial societies, because before the invention of the steam engine there was no feasible way of converting its chemical energy into mechanical work, and production processes depended on muscle, wind, and water power as sources of mechanical energy to do work.

The adoption of coal first started in Britain where an early period of substantial coal use can be identified after 1200. Coal use was temporarily given up later, but a sustained and large-scale return to coal began in sixteenth-century Britain (Sieferle, 1982; Fouquet and Pearson, 1998). There has been a prolonged controversy among historians about whether the second introduction of coal was triggered by the depletion of wood reserves (see Hammersley, 1973; Thomas, 1986; Fouquet and Pearson, 1998; Mokyr, 1999). The controversy has led to the conclusion that there was no dramatic wood shortage at the national level. This is indicated by the fact that a small share of Britain's forests was sufficient to satisfy contemporary timber needs (Hammersley, 1973). Nonetheless, demand for wood did increase in the sixteenth and seventeenth centuries, both because of increasing population levels – which at the same time had a negative effect on wood supply[38] – and because of increasing per capita wood consumption. Expanding applications of wood included its growing use as a domestic and commercial fuel as well as rising timber requirements for construction and ship-building (Thomas, 1986; Fouquet and Pearson, 1998). The increase in demand caused an upward movement of the prices for timber and charcoal. According to calculations made by Thomas (1986), the price of timber relative to that of industrial products increased by 41 per cent from 1600 to 1649. Similarly, sharply increasing prices for charcoal have been documented at several seventeenth century locations. A recent estimation of price changes for charcoal in Southern England concludes that real prices approximately doubled from 1630 to 1700 (Fouquet and Pearson, 1998).

In addition to the nation-wide increases in wood prices, pronounced wood scarcity occured as a regional problem. The local supply of wood was

38. A growing population increases the direct demand for wood, and also the demand for agricultural output, which in turn tends to diminish the area of land available for forestry and thus for the supply of wood (Sieferle, 1982).

restricted by the difficulties of transporting it: Since wood was costly to transport over land, forests in remote areas were useless for harvesting wood, unless the wood could be rafted down a waterway. Processing wood into charcoal did not do much to improve its transportability, because charcoal tends to disintegrate into small crumbs during transportation, and these crumbs were not suitable as a fuel, for example, in blast furnaces. As a consequence of these difficulties, the economic range of transporting wood was limited to about five miles, which turned the availability of wood into an important determinant for the geographical dispersion of energy-intensive plants. In the iron industry, charcoal supplies (together with the availability of water) restricted the size and concentration of furnaces at any particular location. Limited charcoal supply prevented both the expansion of individual iron works and the joint operation of furnaces and forges at the same location (Hammersley, 1973). Similar size restrictions caused by fuel availability also existed in other sectors.

Various strategies of dealing with wood scarcity were adopted in Britain in the sixteenth and seventeenth centuries. Increasing quantities of timber, as well as energy-intensive products such as iron, were imported from Scandinavia and Russia. At home, the planting of forests was intensified, and regulations for the use of forests were introduced. Moreover, the substitution of coal for wood began, which turned out to become the most important reaction to the pre-industrial wood scarcity. The leading role taken by Britain in the transition to coal can in part be explained by its geography. While Britain lacked big rivers on which wood could be rafted, coal was relatively easily accessible, as it was found close to the sea and could be shipped to many destinations. Even in Southern England, which lacked its own coal deposits, coal was half as expensive as charcoal by 1600, and the price differential further grew throughout the following two centuries (Fouquet and Pearson, 1998). Britain's switch to coal was additionally favored by the presence of comparatively well-established market structures, which translated cost differentials into economic incentives to use coal. These institutional prerequisites were far less developed in other European economies (Sieferle, 1982).

The Use of Coal as a Source of Thermal Energy

In spite of the incentives in favor of coal use, wood or charcoal could in many applications not simply be replaced by coal, but technologies had to be adapted to the different physical and chemical properties of the new fuel (Rosenberg, 1982b). The transition from wood to coal was made in one industry after another in a gradual process that lasted several decades and in which practical learning and incremental shop-floor innovations were of crucial importance (Harris, 1976, 1984, 1988a). Among the properties of coal causing the most severe problems were the temperatures attained in coal firing, the emissions it gave rise to, and also the peculiarities of the chemical composition of coal. The significance of the various complications differed among the applications of coal and the different factor services it provided in these applications.

Using coal for the provision of thermal energy was complicated by the fact that burning coal reaches higher temperatures than wood or charcoal. This made it necessary to construct modified furnaces that were capable of withstanding the heat. Where processes were heat-sensitive, ways of controlling and limiting temperatures had to be devised. Coal firing moreover required changes in the operation of furnaces, and a lack of operating skills could prevent its successful introduction (see Harris, 1976, p. 176, where the failed attempt by a French glass producer is discussed).

In a number of industrial uses, smoke and soot emitted by coal furnaces had adverse effects on product quality. For example, coal firing caused stains in glass and textile products, while in brewing it impaired the taste of beer. Coal could not even be easily used for residential heating, because burning coal requires a chimney – something that houses often lacked at the time. A variety of innovations made it possible to overcome these problems. Covered crucibles and reverberatory furnaces (heat-reflecting furnaces that separate the workpiece from the heat source) helped to make coal utilizable for smoke-sensitive industries. Reverberatory furnaces were introduced in glass making around 1610; they subsequently diffused to other industries. Another important step toward alleviating the emission problems of coal was made by processing coal to coke before using it, which resulted in a much purer fuel. Coke was first used around 1640 in drying malt (Smil, 1994, p. 160). It turned out to be universally applicable for a wide variety of operations.

The Use of Coke in Pig Iron Production

The substitution of coal and coke for wood and charcoal was most problematic and time-consuming in iron making. Around 1700, the iron industry was the last major industry in Britain that still depended on wood-based fuels. Iron production consisted of two major stages: First, pig iron was produced from iron ore in blast furnaces. 95 per cent of pig iron production was subsequently processed into malleable wrought iron (the remaining 5 per cent was used for casting; Harris, 1988b, p. 19). Both stages required inputs of charcoal.

In contrast to other industries, the iron industry depended on charcoal or coke not only as energy sources for thermal processes, but also to provide the chemical process energy required for the endothermic chemical reaction of reducing iron ore. In terms of the categories of Chapter 4, iron production was based on factor services of energy that differed from those used by the industries that had adopted coal and coke earlier. Since in iron smelting the ore was in direct contact with the fuel, chemical impurities of the fuel were in the chemical reaction transmitted to the iron and adversely affected its properties. New technologies had to be devised for coke-based iron smelting. However, finding ways to make coke suitable for iron production was complicated by the lack of theoretical knowledge of metallurgy. As a consequence, when problems were encountered in using coke to make iron, they could not be approached systematically, but innovations in iron making were forthcoming only from a trial-and-error process. These difficulties were further aggravated by regional variations in coal and iron ore qualities, which limited the geographic diffusion of techniques. What had proven successful at one location did not necessarily work elsewhere.

Abraham Darby first achieved successful smelting of coke-based pig iron in 1709, but his technique did not diffuse among iron works before the mid-eighteenth century. Between 1720 and 1755 British iron producers erected 22 new blast furnaces for charcoal use, but not a single one for coke-based smelting (Hyde, 1977, p. 29). After some controversies on the causes of this lack of adoption, economic historians now seem to agree that before 1750, coke pig iron was too costly to compete with charcoal pig iron, except in the niche market of castings for which Darby held a patent (Hyde, 1977, ch. 2; Harris, 1988b, ch. 3). For the much larger market of pig iron as an input to wrought iron production, coke pig iron was inferior to charcoal pig iron. Coke pig iron had a higher silicon content, which had to be removed in the further processing into wrought iron. The removal increased charcoal consumption and labor costs, and it reduced the wrought iron yield per unit of pig iron input. Therefore, although it was technically possible to use coke pig iron for wrought iron production, doing so made no economic sense before coke pig iron was substantially cheaper than charcoal pig iron. This was the case only after 1750, when the competitive situation had changed in two ways. First, the costs of producing charcoal pig iron had increased sharply, mainly as a result of increasing charcoal prices. Second, the costs of producing coke pig iron had been reduced considerably over time, both because of (temporarily) falling coal prices and because '[i]ronmasters had greatly improved their efficiency in using coal' (Hyde, 1977, p. 62). Hyde attributes one half of total cost reductions in coke pig iron production to price changes and the other to efficiency increases. The case for the impact of technical improvements on the success of coke iron is strengthened by circumstantial evidence suggesting that improvements adopted around 1750 facilitated the processing of coke pig iron into wrought iron (Harris, 1988b, p. 36f.; Rehder, 1987, p. 43).

Rehder (1987) has produced additional evidence for the impact of technical improvements on the competitiveness of coke pig iron. Using comparable data for nineteenth century US blast furnaces that used charcoal and coal intermittently, he estimates that using coke as a fuel must initially have increased the fuel consumption of Darby's furnace by almost 40 per cent, and that it must also have resulted in air requirements rising by 80 per cent. On this basis, Rehder suggests that air supply was limiting the output of Darby's blast furnace. Because air was provided by water-powered bellows, the bottleneck in air supply could be dealt with by installing water pumps (horse-powered in 1734, steam-powered in 1742). Doing so increased the production volume of Darby's furnace, which lowered capital and operating costs per unit output. Records of materials consumption in the furnace moreover show that ore inputs per ton of pig iron were halved from 1722 to 1737, while coke use went down from 6.5 tons to 2.7 tons per ton of iron produced (Rehder, 1987, p. 41). Cost reductions due to improved performance of the coke blast furnace were thus achieved along several lines. In any case, once it started after 1750, the diffusion of coke iron smelting had pronounced effects on the British iron industry. Pig iron production tripled from 1750 to 1790, with coke pig iron accounting for 90 per cent of output in 1790 (Harris, 1988b, p. 35).

The Use of Coal in Wrought Iron Production

Even after the successful adoption of coke in pig iron production, charcoal was still required for the second stage of iron making: the production of wrought iron from pig iron. Wrought iron producers suffered a profit squeeze in the 1750s, as they were hit by the increasing prices of charcoal, whereas their products were competing with imports. There were accordingly a variety of attempts to use coal instead of charcoal for wrought iron production, but technical problems delayed the switch to coke for decades (Hyde, 1974; Harris, 1988b, ch. 3).

To make wrought iron, carbon has to be removed from the pig iron. Traditionally this was done by heating the pig iron on a charcoal fire while blowing air on it to oxidize the carbon, before the iron was hammered into the desired form. Coal could not be used in this process because of its sulfur content. It would have contaminated the iron and would have caused it to become brittle when hot, thus making it impossible to hot-work the iron in further processing stages. Accordingly, new techniques had to be devised. The first successful use of coal in wrought iron production was achieved in the early 1760s, when the Wood brothers introduced the potting and stamping process (Hyde, 1974, 1977, ch. 5). In this process, coke pig iron was first heated in direct contact with coal to reduce its silicon content (which stemmed from the blast furnace process). This caused the iron to absorb sulfur from the coal. To remove the sulfur, the iron was subsequently broken into small pieces, these were mixed with lime as a flux, put into covered crucibles, and placed in a coal-fired furnace. In the furnace, the carbon contained in the iron was oxidized, while the lime absorbed the sulfur. The use of covered crucibles protected the iron against renewed contaminations. In the 1770s, the potting process was improved by using coke rather than coal for the initial heating. This change reduced the extent of sulfur contamination and eliminated the need for lime.

Potting was widely adopted because it was significantly less expensive than charcoal-based wrought iron production, but it was short-lived. In 1784, Henry Cort introduced the puddling and rolling method, which was to dominate British wrought iron making in the nineteenth century. The puddling process allowed for the conversion of pig iron into wrought iron without the use of crucibles or lime flux. It utilized a coal-fired reverberatory furnace, in which the iron was heated without having direct contact with the coal, so that it was not contaminated with sulfur. To speed up the oxidation of carbon, the pool or 'puddle' of molten pig iron had to be stirred by a skilled worker – the 'puddler' – to bring impurities to the surface. The method is referred to as the puddling and rolling process because Cort also replaced the final hammering stage of wrought iron production by use of a rolling mill.

Although the puddling method had principal advantages over potting and stamping, it was not in widespread use before 1795. The new technique was plagued with serious technical problems resulting in low quantity and quality of output, so that the cost savings of puddling over potting were initially small (Hyde, 1974, p. 202). It was only after a period of learning that the costs of puddling fell significantly. By the mid-1790s, puddling had become the most economic method of wrought iron production.

The extreme level of practical skills demanded by puddling is a recurrent theme in accounts of the eighteenth and nineteenth century iron industry. Puddling has been characterized as a 'balanced combination of physical strength and almost artistic judgement' (Harris, 1976, p. 177; see also Fremdling, 1991; Rydén, 1998). The productivity of wrought iron production was crucially dependent on the puddler's skills, which could only be acquired on a trial-and-error basis. The skill requirements of puddling are not the only aspect of iron making, however, that relied on the tacit knowledge of individual shop-floor workers. In quite similar fashion, the transition to coke depended on the ability to make heat-resistant refractory linings and crucibles. This required the use of special clays, which sometimes had to be transported over long distances and which needed appropriate preparation and mixing. Again, ways of producing workable crucibles had to be found by trial and error, and they differed between the various industries using crucibles (Harris, 1976, p. 173f.).[39]

Even when the technical problems of using coal and coke in iron making had been solved in Britain, the adoption of coal took more time elsewhere. The Continental economies were protected from international competition by tariffs and transport costs. Moreover, relative prices were less favorable to coal, so that early attempts to introduce coke-based iron making were found to be unprofitable (Fremdling, 2000). The slow diffusion of coal shows in the consumption of firewood in Silesian iron works, which increased in absolute terms until 1850. At that time wood still accounted for some 80 per cent of fuel use in that industry (Gleitsmann, 1980). Likewise, half of the iron produced in the mid-nineteenth century US was smelted with charcoal. One reason for this is that using the anthracite coal found in the Appalachians created novel problems in iron making that existing technology could not handle. They could be solved only after the hot blast technology was invented in 1828 (Chandler, 1972; Rosenberg, 1982b).

In spite of the transitional difficulties, the use of coal and coke in the production of iron and steel had far-reaching implications in the long run. It lifted the previous limitations both in the selection of locations for iron works and in their individual sizes. The output of iron could be increased by orders of magnitude, which gave rise to lower iron prices and large-scale substitution of iron for wood in construction and machine building in the Industrial Revolution. Therefore, through the increased volume of iron production made possible by coal use, coal eventually became an indirect replacement of wood even in some of its material factor services.

Characteristics of the Adoption of Coal

Four aspects of the transition from wood to coal seem most noteworthy in the context of this study. First, there was no rapid adoption of coal but a prolonged period of transition, in spite of incentives being in favor of coal use. In this transition period, it can be seen how differences in the physical and chemical properties of the different fuels frustrated attempts at substituting coal for wood. The introduction of coal moreover indicates the significance of distinguishing between the different categories of factor services provided by a particular factor of production: The problems faced in using coal as a source of thermal process energy differed from those

39. As late as in the 1930s some iron works prepared the clay for crucibles by manually treading it for several hours rather than using mechanical stirring. Treading was believed to improve clay quality (Harris, 1976).

encountered in iron production. Moreover, even within the category of thermal operations using the new fuel, the extent of difficulties varied between different kinds of production processes. As a consequence of the differences in factor services, there was no once-and-for-all solution that would have opened the way for universal adoption of coal, but specific solutions had to be found for the individual applications. At the same time, this does not imply that the adoption of coal in the various processes was entirely independent. Some of the solutions that made possible the transition in specific production processes were also helpful for the adoption of coal elsewhere. For example, coking turned out to be of quite general usefulness, and the reverberatory furnace that was originally used in glass making later became a key element of the puddling process in wrought iron production. These examples indicate the presence of complementarities between processes – the complementarities were between specific processes, however, and they did not generally eliminate the problem caused by the heterogeneity of factor services.

Second, the introduction of coke in iron making was plagued by the kind of interdependencies between individual stages of production that were emphasized in the previous chapter. Pig iron production and wrought iron production are subsequent sequences of operations used in techniques for the manufacturing of final goods made from iron. The above discussion has shown how using coke instead of charcoal resulted in qualitative changes in the output of the sequences (i.e. in the iron they produced). Consequently, in terms of the framework of Chapter 6, the introduction of coke was a replacement of the respective sequences of operations rather than a mere change within these sequences. This argument holds, first, for coke-based smelting: It made pig iron that contained more silicon than charcoal-based pig iron and that thus increased the costs of the subsequent refining into wrought iron. Second, the same is true for coal use in the refining operation. Before the techniques of potting and puddling had been invented, coke-based refining produced a qualitatively inferior wrought iron that was practically impossible to process further. The iron industry thus shows how the specific characteristics of the fuels providing the factor services of energy may affect the properties of the produced good, and how substituting one fuel for another in one operation may be incompatible with other operations of the technique.

Third, the transition to coal and coke use in the iron industry also illustrates the importance of learning and incremental innovation. The adoption of coal was made feasible by innovations that eliminated the incompatibilities between the stages of iron making. These innovations were the results of learning about how iron can be made. Therefore, the adoption of coal in iron making is also an example of a knowledge-based increase in decomposability. In addition to the major innovations, the role of gradual efficiency increases in pig iron production has been highlighted above. And also the replacement of the potting process by the puddling method took place only after puddling had been improved sufficiently. Learning by doing and shop-floor innovation played important roles in these gradual improvements of iron making, as well as in other processes based on coal use (such as glass making). In studying these developments, it has to be kept in mind that all changes in the period covered here were the result of trial-and-error learning, since the underlying laws of chemistry and physics were not known yet. Accordingly, the epistemic base of iron production was narrow. Iron production was, in Mokyr's (2000) terminology, a clear-cut case of a 'singleton technique.'

Fourth, the heterogeneity of products was an important determinant of the delayed adoption of coal and coke. The niche market for iron castings provides a good illustration for this point. For Darby's own use of pig iron in making castings, coke pig iron was qualitatively superior to charcoal pig iron. This superiority was caused by the very effects of coke use on the properties of pig iron that prevented its use in wrought iron production. The higher silicon content of coke pig iron increased its fluidity and enabled Darby to make thinner castings without incurring defects such as holes and cracks. He was thus able to produce superior products selling at higher prices, while using less inputs of iron (Hyde, 1977, p. 40). In other words, for direct casting of iron, the transition to coke caused a (static) complementarity: The change in the smelting operation directly increased the productivity of the casting operation. In turn, the niche market for castings was crucial for the further development of coke-based smelting, because it caused Darby to stick to making coke pig iron, even though others did not adopt the method for a long period of time. As has been shown above, the decades of Darby's own use of the method resulted in sufficient technological improvement in coke pig iron making to render it competitive when relative prices eventually became more favorable in the 1750s.

7.2 THE INTRODUCTION OF THE STEAM ENGINE

The steam engine was the first technology for converting the chemical energy of fuels such as wood and coal into mechanical energy that could be used to provide useful work. The revolutionary character of the steam engine as a new energy technology has already been noted above. Many popular accounts of the Industrial Revolution even see in the steam engine the decisive factor for Western industrialization, although this view has been qualified by economic historians (von Tunzelmann, 1978; see Mokyr, 1999, for a recent survey on the discussion). The beginnings of the Industrial Revolution with the mechanization of operations and the emergence of the factory system anteceded the diffusion of the steam engine, whereas the steam engine's significance lies primarily in the later decades of the Industrial Revolution in the nineteenth century.

While the steam engine was a revolutionary new technology, its adoption was much more gradual than revolutionary in character. The steam engine was not a sweeping success once the first workable exemplars became available, but its diffusion required several decades in Britain and even longer in other countries with less favorable conditions. Over time, cost reductions, qualitative improvements in power output, and also positive feedback between fuel availability, construction materials and power generation all contributed to the success of the steam engine. And when it finally did take place, the diffusion of the steam engine resulted in profound changes in the Western economies affected by it, as it allowed for an unprecedented quantitative expansion and geographic concentration of economic activity.

Major Changes in Steam Engine Design

The history of the steam engine is a history of both a series of major design changes and of numerous incremental and often anonymous technical improvements (von Tunzelmann, 1978; Hunter, 1985). The earliest practical use of steam to do mechanical work was in steam pumps that followed the basic design developed by Thomas Savery in 1695. Savery pumps were used throughout the eighteenth century to increase the capacity of water wheels by pumping water back up to re-use it. In 1712 Thomas Newcomen constructed the first steam engine equipped with a moving piston. In the Newcomen engine the piston was driven by condensing steam in the engine's cylinder, which created a partial vacuum. The piston's own weight was then sufficient to force the piston down in the cylinder, whereas the weight of the wooden transmission beam brought it back to its initial position. Mechanical work was performed only in the downward motion of the piston. The resulting work output was irregular, and the fuel efficiency of early Newcomen engines was very low (see also Table 7.1). They were nonetheless used in numerous applications, primarily in pumping water from coalmines. In this application, steam pumps could be fired with coal wastes, which because of the costs of transporting them would not have been usable for other purposes. Because of their simplicity and low capital costs, Newcomen engines also competed with the more sophisticated Watt engines for a long time after the latter engines were first introduced.

Although James Watt is sometimes credited with the invention of the steam engine, his contribution actually consisted of a number of major improvements to its earlier design.[40] Watt's most important invention was the separate condenser. Condensation of the steam outside the cylinder drastically reduced heat losses. Watt moreover enclosed the cylinder with a lid so that the engine could be operated at above-atmospheric pressure, and steam could be admitted to the cylinder from both sides of the piston. The piston thus provided work both in its upward and downward motion, a principle known as the double-acting engine. Further improvements introduced by Watt were the flyball governor that regulated engine speed through opening and closing the steam valve, a rigid mechanism for guiding the movement of the piston rod (parallel motion), and a workable design for converting reciprocating motion into rotary motion (sun and planet gearing). As a result of these improvements, the steam engine's thermal efficiency doubled (see Table 7.1), but the enhanced performance came at the price of substantially higher capital costs than those of Newcomen engines (von Tunzelmann, 1978, ch. 4).

The next major innovation in steam engine design was the high-pressure engine, which was independently developed by Richard Trevithick in Britain and Oliver Evans in the United States in 1802/03. As is indicated by its name, the high-pressure engine utilized steam at higher pressures than the Watt engine. Simple non-condensing high-pressure engines were less fuel efficient than Watt engines and wore out faster, but their price was lower, and they were smaller and lighter than the latter (Temin, 1966). In addition, high-pressure engines were more flexible in use, as the steam pressure could be varied to adapt output to current power needs. Non-condensing engines also saved on the expenses for condensing water, which amounted to 25–35 times the feedwater requirements and which restricted the range of suitable locations for Watt engines (Hunter, 1985, p. 135f.).[41] For many applications the high-pressure engine was therefore the more economic alternative. It remained the dominant steam engine type for small-scale applications in US mills and factories throughout the nineteenth century (ibid., p. 505f.). By contrast, in countries with a lower fuel price/interest rate ratio such as Britain

---

40. There are different views on how significant these improvements were in the long run (see the positions of von Tunzelmann, 1978; Hunter, 1985; Mokyr, 1990).

41. According to Halsey (1981), the high-pressure engine could be combined with a simple surface condenser, and this was frequently done after 1812, resulting in increases in both capital cost and fuel efficiency. Nonetheless, as both variables remained below the levels of the Watt engine, the basic tradeoff between the capital and operating costs of the two engine types was not eliminated.

(and possibly the Easternmost US), Watt engines were more economic than high-pressure engines in the early nineteenth century (Halsey, 1981).

With the high pressures attained by the engines of Evans and Trevithick, the expansive use of steam began to make economic sense. It was to develop into one of the most important ways of improve the steam engine's fuel economy (with some increases in capital costs). Expansive use of steam means that the admission of steam into the cylinder is 'cut off' before the piston has reached its turning point, so that its tendency to expand in the cylinder can be exploited for driving the piston. This innovation was first introduced in steam vessels in 1818; it was widely adopted in stationary uses in the 1840s. Expansive use of steam moreover provided the foundation for the automatic variable cutoff engine developed in 1849 by the American George Corliss. In the Corliss design, engine speed was regulated by varying the cutoff of steam admission. With automatic variable cutoff, the Corliss engine attained superior fuel efficiency. Moreover, it delivered rotary motion with unprecedented regularity, even under abruptly varying load. These characteristics were of particular importance to large-scale users such as steel rolling mills. Finally, yet another way of utilizing the expansive properties of high-pressure steam was found by combining two (or more) cylinders into one engine (known as compounding). In compound engines the second cylinder was fed with the steam exhausted by the first one, steam which had lost some of its pressure, but could still perform work.

Increasing engine speed was another line of development characterizing the history of the steam engine. It culminated in the Porter-Allen machine of 1862, an engine type based on a novel kind of valve gear that was suitable for high speeds. Its design was simplified in the single-valve automatic engine introduced in 1876 (Hunter, 1985, ch. 8). High-speed engines were comparatively small and could frequently be linked directly to the machinery, thereby eliminating the need for a large flywheel and extensive millwork. In addition, high-speed engines attained new levels of regularity. Both characteristics made the new kind of engine attractive for the emerging electric power industry. The advantages of the high-speed engine had to be purchased, however, at the price of greater precision requirements in construction, a shorter working life of the engine, and a fuel efficiency that did not match the performance of the most advanced Corliss and compound engines, even though it exceeded that of most low-speed engines.

Gradual Improvements of Steam Engine Design

The series of major design changes from Newcomen to the high-speed engine drastically altered the steam engine's technology. It is not to be inferred, however, that engine technology was static in between these changes. The significance of incremental technological change for engine design and engine construction can be traced over the entire history of the steam engine.

The history of incremental steam engine innovations begins at the time of the Newcomen engine, when John Smeaton introduced important improvements to the Newcomen design that modified its proportions and reduced its heat losses. In this way he managed to improve the engine's fuel efficiency markedly (von Tunzelmann, 1978, p. 17f., 69). In general, changes in steam technology resulted in gradually increasing sizes and power ratings, as well as rising efficiency. Higher efficiency was obtained by secular increases in steam pressure and speed of rotation. Incremental innovations included various modifications of boiler design, valve gear, speed regulation, and other components of the engine. In addition, advances in manufacturing technology played an important role in the incremental improvements of the steam engine. It is well known that precision boring of the engine's cylinder was a bottleneck in the construction of Watt's first engine. It was alleviated by John Wilkinson's advances in boring, but it also required experiments with various materials in order to fill the gaps between piston and cylinder (Landes, 1969, p. 103). Earlier, the production costs of Newcomen engines had been reduced through the replacement of brass cylinders by less expensive ones made of cast iron, which also required improvements in production methods. Very much the same problem, i.e. the skills needed for manufacturing suitable boilers, cylinders, and pistons, frustrated the use of high-pressure steam before 1800 (Temin, 1966). Boiler explosions caused by insufficient manufacturing quality still remained a very real danger in the nineteenth century. For the US, Hunter (1985) suggests that steam engine construction and mechanical engineering coevolved. The state of the art of mechanical engineering was sufficient for the construction of the simple mill engines that were widespread in the US, but the attainable levels of dimensional precision were limiting best practice as regards steam pressures and machine speeds.

The significance of incremental innovation for the development of US steam engine technology between 1800 and 1850 is emphasized by Hunter (1985, p. 250):

> A . . . distinctive characteristic of the early decades of engine building was the incremental and largely anonymous nature of advances in design and construction. From present evidence, patents played a minor, even negligible, role in the development of mill engines from Oliver Evans to George Corliss . . . Improvements in engine design and building were evidently far less the result of conscious intent, whether directed to specific components or the machine as a whole, than the sum of many minor changes suggested by the practical experience of builders and users and related especially to problems of maintenance and repair. The very substantial advances in engine design over the long run . . . suggest that a process of collective trial and error was at work.

In this context, it is noteworthy that the physical character of the steam engine as a heat engine was less emphasized in much of its development than were mechanical improvements (Hunter, 1985, ch. 8). The scope for systematic improvements in the thermodynamic properties of steam engines was limited by the state of theoretical knowledge of thermodynamics. It has often been noted that the founder of thermodynamics, Sadi Carnot, was an engineer concerned with the practical design of steam engines, not a theoretical scientist. This does not seem to have been the only instance in which practical knowledge of heat engines anteceded advances in theoretical thermodynamics. Another case in point is the prolonged controversy about the thermodynamic and economic superiority of the expansive working of steam engines that was going on in US engineering in the 1860s (ibid.). Given such uncertainty about the scientific principles underlying steam engine technology even in the later stages of its development, the 'process of collective trial and error' referred to by Hunter appears as the natural way for technological change to proceed.[42]

Indicators of Technological Change in Steam Engines

During the two centuries of its industrial prominence, steam engine technology advanced along a number of dimensions. A general indicator of progress in steam engine technology is the development of fuel efficiency. Some data on the thermal efficiency of steam engines between 1725 and 1903 are compiled in Table 7.1. Most of the figures given in the table are for large pumping engines used in Cornwall. These engines attained considerably higher efficiencies than industrial steam engines of the same vintage, as is indicated by the much smaller figure for the 1850 high-pressure mill engine included in the table. The numbers therefore reflect the development of best-practice technology for a particular type of engine; they are not representative of day-to-day engine performance in industrial uses. The development of maximum efficiency over time is depicted in Figure 7.1.

In addition to increasing efficiency, the development of steam engine performance was characterized by qualitative improvements. Regularity of power output was a crucial qualitative characteristic in a range of steam

---

42. Anecdotal evidence suggesting that knowledge of early steam engine technology was of a tacit character is also provided by the difficulty with which the technologies of both Newcomen and Watt engines diffused from Britain to other countries before 1800. Robinson (1974) finds that, in spite of the availability of technical literature on steam engines, industrial espionage was pervasive in the industry, which suggests that the printed material alone was insufficient to copy the British machines. Moreover, engine building abroad often relied on the skills of British engineers and on cylinders imported from Britain.

The economics of energy and the production process

Table 7.1 Thermal efficiency of steam engines, 1725–1903

Year	Type[a]	Duty[b]	Lb coal/ HP/hr	Thermal efficiency (%)
1725	unknown	3.75	45.3	0.56
1768	Newcomen	6.39	26.6	0.96
1769	unknown	4.59	37.2	0.69
1769	unknown	5.88	29.0	0.88
1769	unknown	7.44	22.8	1.12
1772	Newcomen/Smeaton	9.45	18.0	1.42
1778	Newcomen	5.77	29.5	0.86
1778	Watt	14.6	11.7	2.18
1778	Newcomen	7.04	24.1	1.06
1790	Newcomen/Smeaton	9.58	17.75	1.44
1792	Watt	26.71	6.36	4.01
1798	Watt	27.5	6.18	4.13
1805	Watt	13.5	12.6	2.02
1815	Cornish	52.3	3.25	7.85
1820	Cornish	50.4	3.37	7.56
1825	Cornish	54.0	3.15	8.1
1830	Cornish	77.9	2.18	11.69
1835	Cornish	95.8	1.77	14.37
1840	Cornish	81.7	2.08	12.26
1842	Cornish	107.5	1.58	16.13
1843	Cornish	96.1	1.77	14.42
1850	High-pressure mill engine	37.78	4.5	5.67
1893	Reynolds–Allis triple pumping	143.3	1.19	21.5
1893	Unspecified pumping	153.0	1.31	22.95
1903	Unspecified pumping	176.0	1.14	26.4

Notes
a Most figures refer to pumping engines.
b Duty is defined as the number of millions of lbs of water that can be raised one foot per bushel (84 lbs) of coal used. Duty, coal consumption per horsepower per hour and thermal (first-law) efficiency can be converted into each other. Missing values have been calculated using the conversion formulae by Hills (quoted in von Tunzelmann, 1978, p. 67)

Sources Von Tunzelmann, 1978, pp. 18, 67–69; Hunter, 1985, pp. 169, 581, 587, 605

engine applications. Improvements in regularity have already been noted for several of the major design changes. Steam power applications particularly sensitive to output variations included the cotton industry (see below), and also the electric power industry in the late nineteenth century. In the generation of electricity for lighting, irregular power supply resulted in flickering light, which was visible even to laymen and which was clearly incompatible with the luxury-good character of early electric lighting. The growing market for electricity therefore exerted pressure to improving the speed regulation of steam engines (Hunter, 1985, p. 473f.). For other uses of steam power, cost considerations and robustness of engines were more important than regularity. The growing variety of engine designs increased the number of options in the spectrum of performance characteristics. It thus broadened the range of potential uses for the steam engine.

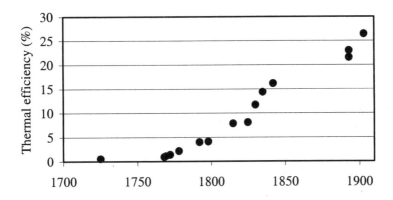

Sources: see Table 7.1

Figure 7.1   Maximum thermal efficiency of steam engines used for pumping, 1725–1903

Evidence on the development of steam engine prices as another indicator of technical change is more sketchy and suffers from problems of comparing prices across countries and points in time. In Britain there were no drastic reductions in the construction costs of steam engines in the early nineteenth century (von Tunzelmann, 1978, p. 72, 139). The (nominal) price for a 30-horsepower Watt engine was 15 per cent lower in 1835 than it was in 1795. In interpreting this change, it has to be considered that license payments accounted for almost a third of the price of the engine in 1795. The lower engine price in 1835 is entirely caused by the elimination of license payments, whereas construction costs had substantially increased since

1795.[43] More substantial price cuts have been documented for the United States. Hunter (1985, p. 64) cites a contemporary source according to which the price of an 80-horsepower engine had come down from $7600 in 1815 to $5700 in 1824 (both figures are in 1824 US dollars). There is moreover evidence for decreasing costs per horsepower coming with increasing engine size throughout the nineteenth century, i.e. after the period covered by these figures.

Obstacles to the Adoption of Steam Power

It was argued above that the steam engine was of little significance in the early decades of the Industrial Revolution in Britain. It was only in parallel to its technical development that the steam engine diffused into industries other than mining, and that total installed horsepower of British steam engines skyrocketed. The comparatively late impact of the steam engine can be shown for the cotton industry, one of the key sectors in the Industrial Revolution. Adoption of the steam engine was delayed not only by the relative cost of early steam engines, but also by qualitative problems of power supply.

The most crucial innovations in the cotton industry, i.e. the spinning jenny (1764), water frame (1769) and mule (1779) in spinning, as well as the flying shuttle in weaving, were innovations in tool operation and handling of materials. They were introduced independently of and prior to innovations in energy technology. Human labor remained the principal power source in the cotton industry, possibly as late as the 1820s (Hills, 1970; von Tunzelmann, 1978). If early cotton machinery did use a non-human energy source, it tended to be animal or water power. By contrast, early steam power was not suitable for the textile industry because its output was to irregular to drive the machinery. Regular speed of spinning machines was essential for the regularity of the yarn produced. Before automatic control of engine speed was made possible by the flyball governor (first installed in 1788), the use of steam engines in the cotton industry was limited to pumping water in order to make water-powered plants more independent of fluctuating water availability (Hills, 1970). In 1800, at most one quarter of the power needs of spinning in Britain was provided by steam (von Tunzelmann, 1978, p. 179).

---

43. The extent of the price reduction in real terms is hard to evaluate. From 1795 to 1835, the price level fell by some 6 per cent (Phelps Brown and Hopkins, 1956), implying that the price reduction in steam engines is real. However, prices sharply increased between 1795 and 1800 before they fell again, so that the real price of the steam engine in 1835 was higher than in 1800, a fact stressed by von Tunzelmann (1978, p. 139f.).

The eventual dominance of steam power in the cotton industry came in combination with the self-acting mule. Adoption of the self-acting mule began after 1830, but it was substituted for hand spinning of finer yarns only after 1850 because it had a higher hazard of breaking threads, which resulted in higher labor costs. With further technical improvements both in cotton machinery and in the regularity of power supply by steam engines, however, the yarn quality produced by self-acting mules eventually surpassed that of hand-spun yarn. The qualitative improvement of the self-acting mule also was instrumental for the mechanization of weaving, because the even quality of the yarn produced by self-actors facilitated the adoption of the power loom (von Tunzelmann, 1978, p. 194). Full substitution of power looms for hand looms did not occur before 1850, when power looms and steam engines had been improved sufficiently to make steam-powered weaving attractive to investors (von Tunzelmann, 1978, ch. 7; Lyons, 1987).

The Competitiveness of Steam and Water Power

In addition to the overcoming of technical problems, the adoption of steam engines also depended on the costs of competing energy sources, most importantly water power. Economic historians have conducted extensive research into the relative costs of steam and water power. They found that in Britain, water remained competitive with steam as an energy source to drive cotton machines at least through the 1850s (von Tunzelmann, 1978, ch. 6). From 1839 to 1858, the capacity of water power installed in the British textile industry increased by almost 50 per cent. After 1850, however, the growth of steam power was much more rapid than that of water power. By 1870, water power had begun to decline not only in relative, but also in absolute terms, and it represented a mere 5 per cent of total power use in the British textile industry (Fouquet and Pearson, 1998).

In the US the relative competitive positions of steam and water power differed widely between regions and even specific locations. Temin (1966) quotes a contemporary comparison of steam and water costs in New England cotton mills around 1840, which is based on assuming favorable locations for each type of power. According to this estimate, water power had a slight cost advantage over steam. Its variable costs were much lower, but it had higher capital costs than steam power. Of the capital costs of water power in the estimate, 40 per cent are payments for water rights. These payments indicate that water power had a substantial (technical) cost advantage, which allowed the owners of water rights to extract rents from them (von Tunzelmann, 1978, ch. 6, makes a similar point for Britain in 1800). By contrast, good sites for water power were scarce in the Midwest, where coal was cheaper and capital more expensive than in New England. The steam engine consequently was more widely adopted in the West than in the East.

The difference in variable costs of water and steam power was primarily caused by the fuel costs of steam engines. Therefore, the competitiveness of steam power was directly affected by changing coal prices. Again, it is difficult to make general statements on the development of coal prices, because coal quality differed widely and the deficient transport infrastructure before the large-scale construction of railways gave rise to large geographical differences in coal prices.[44] The available figures suggest, however, that changes in coal prices were not decisive for the steam engine's increasing competitiveness. In 1800, British coal prices varied between counties from 76 to 560 pence per ton. The location of steam-powered cotton mills later closely followed the pattern of coal price differences (von Tunzelmann, 1978, p.66, 148). According to Fouquet and Pearson (1998), both British coal prices and consumer prices declined somewhat between 1800 and 1870, with the real price of coal slightly increasing, and variations in coal prices being less pronounced than changes in general price levels. In the US, the development of coal prices varied between regions. Coal prices generally increased from the 1830s to the 1870s and then fell again. In New England, the nominal mean price of coal in the 1890s was equal to that in 1830. In all other regions it was higher than in 1830 (Atack et al., 1980, p. 298).[45]

Atack et al. (1980) construct estimates of the competitiveness of steam and water power in the nineteenth century US from data on individual cost components. Because of a lack of unique data on individual cost items, they rely on Monte Carlo simulations to calculate probability distributions of total costs for both energy sources. The estimated ranges of per-horsepower costs of water and steam power thus estimated overlap for all regions and points in time (for a 95 per cent confidence interval), an indication that cost differences were of limited magnitude. Both alternatives had decreasing costs over the entire period covered (1830s through 1890s), with an exception for steam in the 1870s caused by temporarily rising coal prices. The decreasing trend in steam costs is obviously to be expected given the increases in fuel efficiency detailed above. In water power, the substitution of turbines for waterwheels resulted in similar cost reductions, and falling prices of water rights reflected

44. Wood was used for some applications of steam in the US, particularly for steamships and railways. By contrast, the use of wood in industrial steam engines was limited by concurrent increases in wood prices (Hunter, 1985, ch. 7).

45. These numbers can be compared because US price levels did not change much between 1830 and 1890 (according to consumer price index data cited in Nordhaus, 1997, p. 46).

the growing competitive pressure by steam. Atack et al. (1980) moreover find large regional differences of power costs, and a decreasing gap between the costs of the two alternatives in the individual regions. Overall, the relative competitive position of steam power improved after 1850. In the Midwest, it clearly was cheaper than water power. By contrast, water power remained (on average) the least-cost alternative in the East.

Although these figures indicate that water power could still be competitive in 1890, the share of steam power increased continually. By 1870 US steam power led water power both in installed capacity and in new investment. Another 30 years later, direct use of water power (outside electricity generation) had been reduced to a marginal role limited to small businesses and traditional industries (Hunter, 1985). Steam was even adopted in New England, where energy costs favored water power. The inelastic supply of water power at existing locations is one explanation given for this development (Atack et al., 1980). It could force expanding plants at water power sites to install steam engines for their additional energy needs. The larger pattern of energy use moreover reflected the Westward shift of economic activity in the US.

Perhaps the most important factor in the adoption of steam was that it suitable for the beginning urbanization of manufacturing in the nineteenth century. US steam power was an urban phenomenon. In 1838 one-third of total installed steam power capacity was concentrated in six cities located on the Atlantic coast and the Ohio River (Hunter, 1985, p. 88). These urban centers had previously developed as commercial centers because of their location near navigable waterways. Before steam was available, the lack of available energy sources had prevented industrialization at these locations. But once energy needs could be satisfied through the introduction of steam power, the commercial cities were attractive locations for industry. Rosenberg and Trajtenberg (2001) produce econometric evidence for the impact of the Corliss steam engine on the urbanization of US industrial production after 1850. They show that the use of this engine type, which dominated the market for large steam engines, was heavily concentrated in urban centers, and that its presence at a specific location was moreover correlated with the location's subsequent population growth. These authors conclude that the steam engine's importance primarily consisted in relaxing the constraints imposed by water power on the choice of location and the size of individual plants.

The finding of prolonged competitiveness of water power also seems to hold outside Britain and the US. Landes (1969, p. 182) argues that before 1850, Continental manufacturers relied on water power wherever they could. As an example, he notes that cotton manufacturers in Southern Germany persistently stuck to water power even after 1850. In a case study of the

Swedish sawmill industry, Johansson (1998) shows that steam engines did not have dramatic cost advantages over water power throughout the nineteenth century. Best-practice water turbines were technically and economically competitive with steam engines until the 1880s. As in the US, their use was limited, however, by the growing scarcity of suitable locations.

Finally, the eventually dominant role of steam power as an industrial prime mover does not imply that steam was suitable for all industrial uses (Hunter and Bryant, 1991, ch. 1). In particular, steam was not competitive in small-scale applications of the 1–5 horsepower range, both because of capital costs and operating expenses. Steam engines had to be attended, and their operation required skills that were often not available in small workshops. Moreover, the intermittent use of steam engines was bothersome and expensive. As a consequence, by 1900, two-thirds of all manufacturing establishments in the US were employing no sources of mechanical energy other than human labor and work animals (ibid.).

Characteristics of the Adoption of Steam Power

In summary, several characteristics of the introduction of steam power seem noteworthy. First, the steam engine constituted a radically new way of providing a factor service, based on a new energy conversion: It generated mechanical energy from the chemical energy of wood and coal, which could be used to provide mechanical work that had previously been done by water power, human labor and work animals. However, the economic importance of this innovation was also due to the contemporary innovations in the mechanization of tool operation and the handling of materials, beginning in the textile industry. Without these, there would initially have been little use for steam engines other than in mining.

Second, the history of the steam engine shows the importance of improvement over time for the competitiveness of a technology. It is evident that the steam engine was not a sweeping success as soon as it had been invented. Early steam engines were competitive only in particular applications such as mine drainage, and the steam engine had to compete with water and even with muscle power over most of the nineteenth century. The history of the steam engine highlights the role of technological factors in its development; its improved competitiveness was caused more by cost reductions through improved fuel efficiency than by falling prices for coal and engines. It was moreover shown that, in addition to a series of profound design changes, development of steam engine technology was driven by numerous incremental innovations based on practical experimentation and learning by doing. These findings are in line with the suggestion made in Chapter 6 that in industries with pervasive learning effects, the relative position of competing technologies may develop endogenously and be characterized by dynamic increasing returns to adoption.

The increasing variety of designs was an important aspect of the improvements over time in steam technology. It allowed for the factor services provided by steam power to be adapted to the requirements of the particular production technique, both in terms of alternative options in the tradeoff between fixed and variable costs and in terms of qualitative dimensions. In particular, the increasingly regular supply of energy by high-quality steam engines broadened the range of potential applications, as it reduced the problems caused by interdependencies. This development can again be expressed in terms of the abstract framework of the previous chapter. Mechanical energy provided by a steam engine and a suitable fuel provided a factor service in the production of goods such as cotton yarn. Its introduction in a particular technique was a replacement of the respective operation(s) as long as the yarn produced with steam power differed qualitatively from that produced manually or with water power. Because of the irregular power supply of early steam engines, the use of steam lowered the quality of the yarn output or even made its further processing into cloth impossible. The introduction of steam thus caused an incompatibility problem. By contrast, later in the steam engine's history, the yarn quality produced by steam-powered self-acting mules surpassed that of hand spinning. At this stage of development, use of the self-acting mule facilitated the adoption of the power loom in the subsequent operation of weaving. The incompatibility had turned into a (static) complementarity. As a consequence, the further adoption of the steam engine was not only due to cost advantages, but also to its qualitative superiority.

Furthermore, as is emphasized by Rosenberg and Trajtenberg (2001), the steam engine gave rise to dynamic complementarities that were of crucial importance for the subsequent pattern of industrial development. The most important complementarities may have been the opportunities for geographic concentration of production which would not have been possible without steam power, at least not before electricity became available for the inexpensive long-range transmission of energy (see below). Steam power therefore was an important factor underlying urbanization. In addition, large-scale plants such as the rolling mills of the steel industry would have been difficult to operate without steam. Finally, steam played an important role in the complex set of mutually reinforcing interrelations between mining (which used steam pumps for drainage), iron production (where steam was instrumental in supplying air in the blast furnace; see Rosenberg, 1982b) and railway transportation. The interplay of the various elements in this network of technologies was crucial for the sustained growth of production after the Industrial Revolution.

7.3   THE ELECTRIFICATION OF INDUSTRIAL PRODUCTION

The Challenge of Energy Transmission

After 1850 the industrial utilization of mechanical energy was more severely restricted by transmission problems than by shortcomings of the available generation technologies (Hunter and Bryant, 1991, ch. 3). The energy transmission bottleneck would only be eliminated by the introduction of electricity.

At this time, factories had one central supply of energy, typically based on water power or a steam engine, and the energy was transmitted to the machinery through a mechanical system of shafts, pulleys and belts (the so-called 'millwork'). This configuration is known as direct drive or line shaft drive. It had a large number of shortcomings. The most severe problem of direct drive was that a large share of mechanical work output was lost because of friction in the transmission system. The size of the transmission losses varied between industries. In the textile industry they were less pronounced than for example in machine shops, where losses in the range of 40 to 50 per cent of total work output were incurred even in the best designed and maintained establishments (ibid., p. 124). In the Baldwin Locomotive Works in Philadelphia, apparently one of the leading US engineering establishments, steam-based direct drive in 1889 had transmission losses in the order of some three-quarters of total output (ibid., p. 139).

Besides transmission losses, numerous other factors added to the costs of direct drive (Hunter and Bryant, 1991, ch. 3). The weight of the millwork required massive structural support, thus increasing the construction costs of plants. Energy transmission problems restricted the size of individual plants and complicated later extensions. There were only limited possibilities of varying the speed of direct drive transmission. The system required substantial labor input for maintenance and lubrication, and the whole line shaft had to rotate continuously no matter how many machines were actually in operation. Breakdowns in single parts of the system could result in the temporary shutdown of the entire plant. Shafts and belts moreover obstructed the headroom of the plant, which impaired illumination, ventilation and cleanliness, and made the operation of cranes impractical. The multitude of moving shafts and belts created severe risks of work accidents. And finally, since power transmission required connections between rooms and floors, fire hazards in factories were increased, or else costly belt towers had to be built. These shortcomings of direct drive were recognized most strongly in large and dispersed plants, where the millwork was most complex.

Given the problems of direct drive, it is not surprising that various attempts at developing alternative systems of energy transmission were made before electricity became available for this purpose (ibid.). One widespread approach to the transmission problem utilized ropes made from hemp, cotton and wire as replacements for shafts and belts. Wire ropes allowed for transmitting energy up to several kilometers, and several thousand wire rope transmission systems were in operation in Continental Europe by 1869. They were also used for the first transmissions of water power from remote locations. Other producers experimented with decentralized energy supply based on several small steam engines all fed by a central boiler and connected by a network of steam pipes. This kind of arrangement intended to capture the scale economies of larger boilers while benefiting from the flexibility of having several steam engines. It was plagued, however, by maintenance requirements and steam losses that rendered it uneconomical. A variety of liquids and gases were used for the transmission of mechanical energy. High-pressure hydraulic systems based on water were introduced from 1846 on for the operation of cranes in British docks and railway yards, as well as in heavy industry. They were limited by the velocities attainable without incurring prohibitive losses from friction, and also by difficulties encountered in converting pressure into rotary motion. In addition to high-pressure systems, both the existing low-pressure public water supply systems and the distribution systems for gas lighting were tapped for driving small motors in the mid-nineteenth century. Compressed air was even introduced as a medium for the transmission of energy. It was easy and safe to use, but heat losses incurred in compressing the air were substantial (45 to 60 per cent of energy input in the early 1890s; Hunter and Bryant, 1991, p. 175). Distribution systems for compressed air were established in several European cities after 1881. In Paris compressed air was more widespread than electricity as a medium of energy transmission even at the turn of the twentieth century.

The Introduction of Electric Energy

The use of electricity as a transmission technology for mechanical energy requires the availability of both dynamos to generate electricity from mechanical energy and electric motors to convert it back into mechanical energy. The first workable dynamo was constructed in 1870, and the electric motor was first used for manufacturing purposes in 1883. By 1890 all the equipment necessary for DC power transmission was available and operational. Subsequently the efficiency of electric equipment increased rapidly, and further innovations made possible a broader application of electric transmission. Introduction of the AC induction motor (in 1895) and

160   *The economics of energy and the production process*

of the rotary converter (invented in 1888, produced in the early 1890s) were instrumental for the transmission of electricity over very long distances. Based on AC transmission, large-scale exploitation of water power in remote locations such as the Alps and the American West became economical. From this time on, electricity represented a viable substitute for the direct use of water and steam, and an alternative to competing ways of energy transmission.

A contemporary comparison of the costs of alternative transmission technologies for the range from 5 to 100 horsepower made in 1883 (see Tables 7.2 and 7.3) shows the relative competitive status of electricity in its earliest days. These calculations suggest that both in terms of capital outlays and total costs, electricity was less expensive than water, air and wire ropes

Table 7.2 Capital costs per horsepower for alternative transmission technologies (in pounds sterling; estimates for 1883)

Maximum horsepower transmitted	System of transmission	Over a distance of					
		100 m	500 m	1000 m	5000 m	10 000 m	20 000 m
5	Electric	75.1	78	81	108	142	210
	Hydraulic	41	66	97	358	610	1280
	Pneumatic	73	96	210	600	1090	2060
	Wire rope	6.5	31	61	305	760	1220
10	Electric	52	54	56	77	103	154
	Hydraulic	30	45	65	220	416	806
	Pneumatic	60	72	88	213	369	680
	Wire rope	5.1	23	47	231	460	925
50	Electric	40	41	42	55	69	100
	Hydraulic	16	21	30	91	170	325
	Pneumatic	31	36	42	88	147	265
	Wire rope	1.8	7.2	14	69	136	272
100	Electric	32	33	35	45	59	87
	Hydraulic	14	20	28	88	164	310
	Pneumatic	26	30	34	67	109	192
	Wire rope	1.1	4.3	8.4	41	81	162

Source: Gisbert Kapp, *Electric Transmission of Energy*, London, 1891. Reproduced in Hunter and Bryant, 1991, p. 189

Table 7.3 Price paid at the receiving station per horsepower hour transmitted using various technologies (in pence; estimated for 1883)

Max. horse-power trans-mitted	System of trans-mission	Steam Power Transmitted over a distance of						Water Power Transmitted over a distance of						Cost of steam power at receiving staton
		100m	500m	1000m	5000m	10000m	20000m	100 m	500 m	1000 m	5000 m	10000m	20000m	
5	Electric	2.25	2.33	2.41	2.87	3.29	5.20	0.35	0.36	0.37	0.44	0.52	0.84	3.80
	Hydraulic	2.50	2.84	3.15	6.52	10.50	19.00	0.29	0.38	0.48	1.38	2.50	4.79	
	Pneumatic	2.70	2.96	3.30	5.25	9.53	16.72	0.40	0.47	0.58	1.27	2.40	4.45	
	Wire rope	1.13	1.45	1.88	5.45	10.40	22.70	0.11	0.19	0.30	1.25	2.50	4.86	
10	Electric	1.98	2.07	2.14	2.53	3.10	4.85	0.27	0.28	0.29	0.36	0.47	0.71	2.63
	Hydraulic	2.38	2.55	2.79	5.08	7.70	14.30	0.25	0.30	0.37	0.95	1.54	3.17	
	Pneumatic	2.54	2.69	2.87	4.48	6.25	10.40	0.35	0.38	0.44	0.88	1.42	3.97	
	Wire rope	1.12	1.38	1.70	4.50	8.50	19.10	0.09	0.17	0.25	0.96	1.91	4.00	
50	Electric	1.87	1.94	1.99	2.28	2.74	4.25	0.23	0.24	0.26	0.29	0.31	0.55	1.02
	Hydraulic	1.63	1.70	1.80	2.90	4.21	7.80	0.15	0.18	0.22	0.46	0.76	1.43	
	Pneumatic	2.02	2.11	2.18	2.87	3.54	5.30	0.22	0.24	0.28	0.44	0.65	1.08	
	Wire rope	1.08	1.18	1.30	2.54	4.51	11.10	0.09	0.11	0.13	0.38	0.72	1.61	
100	Electric	1.79	1.85	1.91	2.18	2.63	4.08	0.20	0.22	0.23	0.26	0.32	0.50	1.02
	Hydraulic	1.62	1.70	1.78	2.87	4.15	6.84	0.16	0.17	0.19	0.43	0.72	1.14	
	Pneumatic	2.00	2.04	2.09	2.63	3.10	4.50	0.22	0.23	0.24	0.36	0.48	0.93	
	Wire rope	1.07	1.14	1.22	2.21	3.83	9.73	0.08	0.10	0.11	0.28	0.48	1.19	

Source: see table 7.2 No further information on the methods of calculation underlying these estimates is available

161

for transmission distances above 5000 meters. The data also show that long-distance electric transmission of water power could compete with on-site steam engines. On the other hand, electricity was initially not competitive for short-distance power transmission and for use within plants. The data in Tables 7.2 and 7.3 indicate that for 100-meter transmissions the capital costs of electricity (per horse power transmitted) were at least ten times that of wire rope systems, whereas total costs were at least twice as high as for wire ropes. According to these estimates, there was thus no cost advantage of electricity for use as a distribution technology within individual plants, at least not in plants where power needs reached the minimum size of practicable steam engines of some five horsepower. Electricity was no challenge to the usual practice of self-generation of mechanical energy (by means of water or steam) and direct drive transmission. On the other hand, it was able to attain a foothold in niche uses where attempts had been made before to circumvent the transmission problems of direct drive. These included applications in which its cleanliness, ease of control, and the feasibility of maintaining a steady speed were particularly important.

The diffusion of electric lighting was another crucial ingredient into the electrification of industrial production. Electric lighting itself was not primarily introduced for cost considerations. It was rather its qualitative superiority to the then dominating gas lighting systems that made electric light attractive (Nye, 1990; Gugerli, 1996). For the widespread adoption of electric lighting, however, its costs had to be brought down. One way to achieve this was to extend the market for electricity beyond the early morning and evening hours when the demand for lighting was peaking. In this way, the load factor of electricity supply systems could be improved, and capital costs could be spread over a broader base of sales. A straightforward (albeit often only reluctantly exercised) option for broadening demand consisted in selling electricity to industrial users of mechanical energy. Electricity generated and sold by central power stations was particularly attractive for small urban businesses that had practically been excluded from the use of steam engines and that had no access to water power either. Thus, small businesses purchasing electricity from utilities provided another early niche market for electricity.

Although comparatively rapid, the diffusion of electricity as a source of mechanical energy in manufacturing required several more decades. Electric motors accounted for 5 per cent of total mechanical horsepower in US manufacturing in 1899. They had reached a share of 25 per cent by 1909, 55 per cent by 1919, and 82 per cent of total horsepower by 1929 (Rosenberg, 1982b). Costs of electric energy fell dramatically during the diffusion period, both because of increasingly efficient equipment in the electricity-using industries and because of technological improvements in electricity generation – which were not least caused by the advances in steam engine design detailed in the previous section and by the subsequent development of steam turbines. Electric power generation is moreover characterized by scale and network economies. Increasing the size of power plants and distribution networks helped to reduce the costs of electricity supply. In the process of diffusion, the character of electric energy use in production was itself altered substantially. This change caused a fundamental reorganization of industrial energy supply.

From Direct Drive to Unit Drive

Electrification can be subdivided into three stages (Devine, 1983; Hunter and Bryant, 1991; see also Du Boff, 1967; David, 1990a, 1990b). In the first stage of electrification, a single electric motor replaced a steam engine or water power as the central energy supply in the plant, whereas the existing system of energy distribution remained in place. At this stage, electricity was primarily used as a comparatively inexpensive means of long-range energy transmission.

In the second stage of electrification, electric group drive of machinery helped to overcome the above-mentioned problems of the line shaft drive. Group drive, which was already being advocated by some engineers in the 1890s, means that the manufacturing process was organized around several groups of machines each driven by a separate electric motor. It became viable because reasonably efficient small-size electric motors were being marketed at competitive prices. The lower efficiency of smaller motors was moreover compensated by the reduction in transmission losses resulting from the smaller millwork. Compared to steam-based direct drive, group drive increased overall energy efficiency by some 20 to 25 per cent. However, these efficiency differences were of rather minor significance for total production costs because energy costs represented only a small fraction of them. More significant changes resulted from the reorganization of production made possible by group drive. Machines could now be grouped according to production requirements rather than considerations of energy supply, and individual groups of machines and workshops could be operated independently of each other.

Electric unit drive as the third phase of electrification basically extended the principle of group drive by equipping each individual machine with an electric motor. Unit drive was the subject of extended discussion among engineers in the 1890s and early 1900s, and group drive persisted for a prolonged time in many applications (Hunter and Bryant, 1991, p. 235). Unit drive implied that the aggregate power capacity of the whole plant had to increase substantially because averaging effects of shared motors were lost and each motor had to be of sufficient power to fulfill the maximum energy need of the machine.[46] Although relatively inexpensive AC induction motors were available, capital costs of unit drive were accordingly higher than those of group drive. In addition, the efficiency and steadiness of unit drive could suffer from the loss of averaging effects. On the other hand, savings resulted from a variety of factors. Transmission losses were minimized. The construction of plants became cheaper as it no longer needed to reflect transmission loss considerations, and less expensive, one-story buildings could be erected. The capacity of a given plant size increased because all space in the plant became usable for production. In addition, power supply considerations no longer prevented the extension of plants. Reduced maintenance costs and increased organizational flexibility could be achieved in pretty much the same way as in the earlier transition from line shaft drive toward group drive. In the long-term perspective, unit drive was a prerequisite of the twentieth century revolutions in production methods such as the assembly line. Again, therefore, indirect effects of the changing energy technology seem to have been more significant than direct savings in energy costs, even more so because electricity prices were sharply decreasing at the same time due to the spread of central power stations, so that the impact of energy costs was further circumscribed.

It was only after World War I that electric unit drive became the dominant form of energy supply in industrial production. Several factors seem to have slowed down the transition to electric unit drive. First, a simple problem of irreversible investment was present, as unit drive could not be retrofitted to earlier plants, and the cost savings did not generally justify the replacement of functioning plants. Second, to fully reap the efficiency potentials of unit drive, adaptations in the machinery were necessary, but machine tools specifically designed for use with electric motors were not immediately available (Devine, 1983, p. 369). Third, the enthusiasm that engineers had for unit drive was not universally shared by entrepreneurs and managers who moreover, given the state of the art in measurement technology, tended to possess only vague knowledge of the size of the losses incurred by the installed transmission system (Hunter and Bryant, 1991, p. 232). Finally, the engineering principles of unit drive were not readily available, and its implementation required adaptations to the specific conditions of each individual project. The expertise of architects and engineers thus had to be

---

46. This development implies that using installed horsepower bases of electric motors as a measure of their diffusion, as was done above, somewhat overstates their actual spread because total capacity requirements of electric unit drive are, all other things being equal, higher than those of direct drive based on steam or water power.

developed gradually in learning by doing (David, 1990b). Some electric power companies facilitated the transition to unit drive by selling consulting services to their customers (Devine, 1983, p. 370). In addition the process of learning was accompanied by the emergence of engineering schools and industrial research facilities, so that the development of manufacturing practice and the science of electrical engineering was closely intertwined (Hughes, 1983, pp. 148ff.).

Characteristics of Electrification

What lessons can be learnt from the history of electrification? First, it has to be noted that the introduction of electricity did not change the factor service provided by energy in the affected operations. The electric motor provided mechanical energy, in the form of rotary motion, in the same way as the steam engine did. Accordingly there were no incompatibility problems in adopting electricity, just the disadvantage of early electricity in terms of its costs. There is thus a notable difference between electricity on the one hand, and coal and the steam engine on the other. Whereas in the cases of coal and steam, specific properties such as chemical impurities and irregular power supply at first limited the applicability of the new technologies, electricity matched the qualitative features of the competing factor services from the outset.

Electricity rather is a prime example of complementarities caused by the specific characteristics of an energy technology (Rosenberg, 1982b). The complementarities it gave rise to were mostly of the dynamic kind. One crucial advantage of electric motors was that they could provide factor services in small-scale applications where steam was not practical and mechanization of energy supply had therefore not been viable before. Its suitability for small-scale uses turned electric energy into a highly flexible technology, which was the key factor for many subsequent innovations. Additional special characteristics of electric motors, such as their capacity to start and stop almost instantly, and their safety, cleanliness and silence in use, were valuable in particular production processes. In some cases, for example in the textile industry, these properties had an advantageous effect on the quality of the product. In others they were necessary to allow mechanization to happen at all. The electrification of mechanical operations moreover facilitated the subsequent use of electric energy for factor services other than those of electric motors. As was shown in Chapters 4 and 5 above, electric energy is used to provide factor services in thermal and chemical operations of manufacturing and materials processing, and also in information processing and process control. The adoption of the electric motor was complementary to the other uses of electric energy. The same physical infrastructure for electricity generation, transmission and distribution was utilized, and the development of these additional uses benefited from the research efforts that accompanied the adoption of electric energy in mechanical manufacturing.

Second, the use of electricity in industrial production constitutes another case in which the superiority of a technology was not given in advance, but developed during its use. As with the steam engine, the development of electric energy systems was characterized by dramatic technological improvements, which resulted in cost reductions in electricity generation as well as in electric motors and their applications. The cost reductions achieved over time were instrumental in turning electricity from its modest beginnings as a niche technology to its being the most widely used source of mechanical energy in manufacturing. Realizing the potential benefits to be reaped from decentralized energy supply was an additional aspect of technological advance. It was based on a process of learning among engineers and industrial users, supported by the emergence of engineering sciences and industrial research facilities.

Third, the decentralized energy supply made possible by electricity also increased the decomposability of industrial processes. Independent energy supply by unit drive of individual operations facilitated changes in the power supply of individual operations and allowed for the selective replacement of machinery. Furthermore, a particular episode in the development of electricity distribution and utilization provides another example of the endogenous decomposability of a technique: the rotary converter that allowed for the interconnection of AC and DC systems of electricity distribution (see David and Bunn, 1988, who characterize it as a 'gateway technology' because of the interconnecting it enabled). The two systems had been incompatible and competing before the rotary converter allowed the transformation of AC into DC. The interface for AC and DC systems which it created made it possible to combine AC transmission with DC motors that had some specific advantages over AC motors (ibid.).

7.4 CONCLUSIONS

The characteristics identified in the three historical cases of energy innovations are not unknown to economists, but they have not been systematically integrated into production theory. For concluding this chapter, it seems appropriate to recapitulate the usefulness of the concepts developed earlier in the volume for the discussion of the historical cases. This also indicates how the concepts can be used as building blocks for a more general analysis of process innovations in a production-theoretic context.

The notion of factor services has played a major role in the present study. It was developed to specify the way in which a particular factor of production is useful for the production of a good. The cases discussed in this chapter suggest that by using this concept, important information on production processes can be captured that is lost in the standard aggregation of inputs into broad factor categories. This emerged most clearly in the study of coal. It was shown above that coal was used in factor services of thermal energy and for the provision of chemical process energy in iron making, and that the difficulties of adopting coal differed between these uses. These differences are not reflected by the aggregate factor category 'energy' alone.

The usefulness of the sequential framework for studying production processes also showed most clearly in the case of coal, particularly in the transition from charcoal to coke in iron production. It was indicated above how the repercussions of coke use in individual operations of iron making gave rise to adverse effects in later operations. In an aggregate representation of the technique in terms of inputs and outputs only, these incompatibility problems would not be visible. To include the effects of interdependence in production models, some disaggregation is necessary, both in terms of the categories of inputs and outputs and in terms of the production process. The same argument holds for complementarities. To see how different techniques and processes may benefit from each other, it is helpful to describe them in more detail than is present in aggregate production models.

Third, in all three cases there were significant effects of gradual improvements of techniques, and also of learning from practical experience. The more experience had been accumulated with a new energy technology, the better was its absolute and relative performance. In economic terms, learning by doing gave rise to dynamic increasing returns: The productivity of the techniques was not a priori given but developed endogenously. In addition to improvements in general dimensions, such as costs and fuel efficiency, learning also broadened the range of applications for the new energy technologies. In general, it may well be that a technique using a new factor service or operation, although it is in general inferior to an existing technique, has a cost advantage in a specific niche application. It may accordingly be introduced in that niche, which gives rise to learning processes that also increases its competitiveness in other applications. This description fits the above cases; it holds for coke-based iron smelting which developed in the niche market for castings, for the early steam engine that was profitable to use only in mining, and also for the initial use of electric energy as a solution to specific energy transmission problems.

It was furthermore argued in Chapter 6 that the decomposability of a technique is variable in the long run. The cases studied in the present chapter lend support to this conjecture. Again, it was the use of coal in iron making that most vividly showed the impact of the general state of technological knowledge (the epistemic base of a technology) on decomposability. The lack of metallurgical knowledge was an important factor that delayed coal use in iron production, because it prevented the systematic solution of the encountered interdependence problems. In addition, it was argued in Chapter 6 that increases in decomposability may be achieved over the life cycle of a technology. Evidence for this development was found in the increasingly broad applicability of steam engines made possible by more regular power supply. The interconnection of AC and DC power systems based on the rotary converter is an example of an interdependence problem that was deliberately tackled by means of an incremental innovation. In both the steam engine and the electrification cases practical use of the new energy technologies began before they were fully understood theoretically. The practical application of these technologies moreover provided an important motivation for the research efforts into their theoretical foundations. Again, the advances made in this research can therefore be seen as at least partially endogenous.

Another implication of the discussed cases is that process innovations may widely differ in the range of their impact, i.e. the spectrum of techniques and production processes affected by them. With the general purpose technologies concept, economics has made a step toward incorporating these differences into production and growth theories. The complementarity concept suggested in this study is closely related to that concept, but it is more general. The scope of complementarities caused by changes in an operation depends on the range of applications of the modified operations and factor services. Identifying and classifying operations and factor services can help to generate systematic findings on the scope of complementarities. All energy innovations discussed here were related to broadly used factor services, and the potential range of complementarities was accordingly wide. In addition, there were even pervasive complementarities that linked the three energy innovations discussed in this chapter. Coal was used to fire steam engines, and in turn steam engines were first used in coal mining. Steam-powered air pumps increased the capacity of blast furnaces in iron making. Iron was required for steam engine production and for railway construction. The railway was driven by steam power, and it facilitated the transport of coal. Moreover, electricity generation demanded that steam engines (which were powered by coal) supplied power that did not fluctuate, which affected the development of steam technology. Improvements in one of these technologies thus tended to have indirect advantageous effects on the other ones.

As a general result, the discussion of the historical cases illustrated their multifaceted character. Their significance is not done justice by simply referring to how much they increased the quantity of energy available for human purposes, but the various kinds of qualitative changes brought about or enabled by them also have to be taken into consideration. The relative importance of quantitative factors for the overall impact of the energy innovation differed between the three cases. It was greatest in the case of coal. Scarcity of alternative fuels was crucial for its first adoption, and the quantitative expansion of industries such as iron and steel production realized after the Industrial Revolution would not have been possible on the basis of wood alone. Coal moreover became necessary as a fuel for the widespread use of the steam engine. In the case of the steam engine, the quantitative effect was only part of the importance of the new energy technology. Further significant aspects of steam power consisted in the concentration of production, the independence from water power sites and the urbanization of industry that it allowed. Finally, the electrification of industrial production processes derived most of its impact from non-quantitative factors. Electricity did not make a new primary source of energy available to humans. The energy sources used for electricity generation had all been used before. They were only used more indirectly after electric power became available. It was the different characteristics of this indirect use (in particular, the flexibility it enabled in terms of locations and sizes of production processes) that brought about the importance of electricity for economic development.

These considerations suggest that major innovations in energy technology involve more than just making more energy available for production. In this respect, the case studies support the general point made in this book: The role of energy in production cannot be captured by exclusive reliance on physical concepts and measures. The perspective of the present study and the analytical tools developed above can help to better understand it.

8. Conclusions

8.1 ENERGY IN THE PRODUCTION PROCESS

The present book studied the role of energy in the production of useful goods. This statement involves more than it may seem to at first glance. The production of useful goods, as it was understood in this volume, has received little attention in economics. As I have argued in the introduction, most of economic production theory analyzes production processes at the level of prices and subjective valuations. One consequence of this choice for the level of analysis is that energy is not normally considered as an important input into production, because its share in total factor costs tends to be small. Alternative approaches that do treat energy as a significant input typically analyze production processes at the physical level. Some of these approaches were discussed in Chapter 2. They have helped to establish general properties of production processes. For example, the physical necessity of low-entropic energy inputs into all production processes can be deduced from the laws of thermodynamics. The problem with the physical level of analysis lies in the difficulty of linking it to the economic level. Where the analysis remains at the physical level, it risks being dismissed as irrelevant by economists. Where the link to the economic level of analysis has been attempted, it all too often resulted in reducing economics to a branch of physics. By contrast, it was a central tenet of the present approach that production, and economics in general, cannot be studied independently of the nature of human needs and desires. Physical concepts alone cannot distinguish whether or not processes result in an output that humans consider useful. They can specify necessary conditions of production processes, but not all processes that satisfy these conditions are production processes.

In the endeavor to link but not reduce economics to the underlying physical processes this book returned to the old economic concept of use value. It emphasized that production is the production of useful goods. In order for a physical process to qualify as a production process, it must result in a good that is useful, i.e. capable of satisfying human wants. And to show that a physical factor like energy is relevant in the production process, one must identify how its use contributes to processes that turn out useful goods. This can hardly be done without taking the human factor into account.

To study the role of energy in the production of useful goods, a series of steps had to be made in the above argument. First, a stylized conceptual framework for the representation of production processes was developed in Chapter 3. This framework allows for an abstract description of both the nature of goods and the way in which they are produced. Adopting an approach analogous to Lancasterian consumer theory, goods were first characterized by a set of user-relevant properties. For a good to be useful, these properties have to attain particular states. This is where production steps in: Production is the process in which the properties of goods are manipulated in such a way that the goods become useful, i.e. that they acquire the capacity to satisfy human wants. The manipulation of properties takes place in a series of operations that successively turn the object of production – which has been referred to as a 'workpiece' above – into a useful good. In addition, in a specific sequence of operations – called a 'technique' – changes to further, 'production-relevant,' properties of the workpiece may be required for technical reasons.

Operations are the basic building blocks of a production process. An operation can be specified in terms of its 'function,' i.e. the way in which its modification of the workpiece contributes to the purpose of the production process. It is crucial for the present approach that material statements can be made about the functions of operations in production processes. To substantiate the claim that this is possible I referred to classifications of operations developed in engineering. In these classifications, the functions of operations are indeed specified in considerable detail. Starting from an operation's function in the production process, the required inputs into the operation can then be derived. Again drawing on engineering literature, I have argued that for each function there are only a limited number of suitable kinds of operations, which are each based on the provision of a particular set of 'factor services.' Factor services are understood as the specific contributions by which inputs contribute to the increasing use value of the good that is being produced. For example, the factor services needed for a turning operation in manufacturing include a sharp edge made from a suitable material to remove chips from the workpiece, and mechanical energy (rotary motion) to do the necessary physical work on the workpiece. Finally, the factors of production in the operation are determined as those agents, objects and substances that are capable of providing the respective factor services. Their status as factors of production is thus deduced from their actual usefulness in executing an operation. It differs between different kinds of operations – with some factor services being more broadly applicable than other ones – and is dependent on the state of technology. When innovations make new production processes and operations available, the variety of factors of production may increase.

Factor services clearly are a less aggregated concept than the traditional categories of factors of production. In principle, the factor services required for an operation may be specified with an arbitrary degree of precision. However, as is indicated by the engineering classifications, meaningful abstractions of the particular factor services for operations can be developed. Based on their capacity to provide broad classes of factor services, a proposal was made in Chapter 3 to distinguish four broad categories of factors of production: tools, human labor, energy and materials. In their broadness, these categories correspond to the traditional factors. They are nonetheless fundamentally different, because at the level of use value, factors cannot simply be aggregated in the way this is possible at the price-theoretic level. This is also the reason why the notion of capital has not been adopted in Chapter 3. Tools are quite different in their suitability for various kinds of operations. The broad category 'tools' cannot provide factor services, but only the elements it contains can – each in its specific way.

Chapter 4 used the sequential framework to identify the factor services provided by energy. As a first step, energy inputs into production were classified according to the physical distinctions between energy forms: nuclear energy, chemical energy, thermal energy, mechanical energy, light and electricity. The crucial task then consisted in demonstrating the factor services provided by the various energy forms. Chapter 4 discussed two ways to approach this task.

The first way of identifying factor services of energy input departed from the nature of the produced good. It was based on the evolutionary approach to consumer theory developed by Ulrich Witt (2001) which traces consumer behavior back to a series of learning processes starting from a set of universally shared human wants. This approach to consumer behavior allows for material statements on the nature of goods. Some properties of some goods can only be brought about on the basis of energy inputs of a specific form. The inputs required to produce these energy-dependent properties have been referred to as the 'direct' factor services of energy. They include the energy inputs into food production, heating and lighting, and also the mechanical energy necessary for personal mobility. To provide any of these direct factor services, a specific form of energy is needed. Using other energy forms is possible only if they can be (and actually are) converted into the required energy form.

There are two reasons why not all factor services of energy use can be identified in this 'direct' way, starting from the nature of goods. First, not all goods can easily be related to universally shared human wants to make them amenable to material statements regarding their nature. And second, the nature of a good often does not determine the way in which it is produced. A second approach to the identification of factor services of energy was therefore developed in Chapter 4. It was based on the notion of 'indirect' factor services. Indirect factor services are used in operations that require energy inputs even though the workpiece properties they modify are not related to energy. In the case of indirect factor services, it is the operation rather than the good that is energy-dependent. Broad classes of operations for which indirect factor services of energy are required include the processing of materials, the manufacturing of solid objects, the transportation of materials and objects, and also the processing of information. The identification of factor services in these classes of operations, and of the energy forms by which they can be provided, was again based on concepts and classifications from engineering. These concepts characterize operations in an abstract way and independently of the good that is being produced. They are based on actual technological practice. Accordingly, the indirect factor services of energy have been identified at the, as it were, phenomenological level. The need for specific energy forms in particular operations is not derived from universal physical laws, but from the technological feasibility and economic viability of real world techniques. It can be (and actually is) modified by innovations.

Chapter 5 tracked long-term developments in the provision of the factor services. It also stressed the heterogeneity of energy forms. In all the distinguished factor services (with the exception of energy for food production), innovations have over time expanded the range of suitable energy forms and energy sources. It was moreover shown in Chapter 5 that only a minority of energy innovations resulted in the complete substitution of the earlier technology. New energy technologies often replaced earlier ones only in a subset of their applications, so that the variety of technologies in use grew over time, and the application of individual energy technologies became increasingly specialized. Together with secular increases in absolute levels of energy use and in the energy efficiency of individual processes, this increase in variety is instrumental in explaining the empirical developments in primary fuel use over the past 200 years. In contrast to stage theories of energy use, which suggest that the typical historical pattern of energy use is the successive displacement of one source of energy after another, absolute levels in the use of traditional fuels such as wood and coal have not decreased in the long run. Their partial substitution in some uses, and their increasingly efficient utilization in others, was offset by the overall growth of production volume.

In Chapter 6 the focus of the argument shifted from the individual operations to the entire sequence of the technique. Particular emphasis was put on interdependencies between operations and on their implications for process innovations that modify the technique. These issues were approached within the sequential framework of Chapter 3, which allows for an abstract distinction between different kinds of process innovations and forms of interdependence. I set out by developing some concepts to analyze innovational dynamics in sequential production processes with interdependent operations. Changes to operations were distinguished according to whether or not they modify the operation's effect on the workpiece. If the effect of the operation is altered, making the change may have repercussions on other operations. Such interdependencies may occur within the modified technique, but they may also extend to other techniques and production processes. They may take one of several forms.

Changes in individual operations may be incompatible with other operations of the same technique. This form of interdependence was approached by exploring its parallels to the notions of modularity in product design and decomposability in complex systems theory. To do so I first developed a definition of modular techniques that was closely analogous to the definition of modular product designs. Modularity thus defined turned out to be very restrictive in its implications for technological change. And although some real-world techniques are well described as modular in this sense, the concept did not capture some important developments in sequential production processes. Accordingly, the weaker notion of decomposability of techniques, which may be variable and in part endogenous, was distinguished from modularity, which is static and has to be specified *ex ante*. In particular, I argued that the decomposability of techniques may be varied by changes in the state of knowledge, and also by the increasing elasticity of interfaces between operations.

In addition to incompatibility problems within a technique, the effects of interdependencies may go beyond the boundaries of the modified technique, if changes in operations may have beneficial effects on other techniques or production processes. This form of interdependence was discussed under the heading of complementarities. I made a further distinction between static complementarities, where the beneficial effect on other techniques and processes can be reaped without making additional adaptations, and dynamic ones that cause a potentially beneficial effect but require supplementary changes to the adopting techniques or production processes.

Based on the sequential representation of production processes, the discussion of Chapter 6 thus integrated a variety of concepts from quite different backgrounds and brought them into an explicit production-theoretic context. For discussing these issues of technological interdependence, the present level of analysis seems more appropriate than the price-theoretic level at which these issues are normally approached in economics (if at all). From the interest in the nature of production processes and their inputs, it follows naturally to ask how the various operations of the process are interrelated, and what concrete elements of the elements cause the interdependence.

Finally, the previously developed concepts were applied in Chapter 7 to three cases of major historical energy innovations: the transition from wood to coal, the introduction of the steam engine, and the electrification of industrial production. In discussing these innovations, the distinction between different factor services of energy was helpful for understanding the patterns of timing in the adoption of the new energy technologies. In the transition from wood to coal, problems faced in processes where coal was used to provide thermal energy differed from those encountered where coal was used as an energy source for chemical reactions. Moreover, significant obstacles delaying the introduction of coal-based techniques resulted from incompatibility problems.

The steam engine is a prominent case of an energy innovation based on a new conversion technology. It allowed the generating of mechanical energy from the chemical energy of fossil fuels. A new way of providing factor services of mechanical energy (i.e. mechanical work), which are of pervasive use in production processes, was thus made available. The steam engine moreover constituted a good example of the successive improvement of a technology during its use. This development can be discerned in quantitative terms, but it also involved a qualitative improvement. The qualitative improvement broadened the spectrum of steam engine uses by eliminating incompatibility problems of early engines. It was therefore instrumental in the steam engine's success.

Finally, the economic significance of the electric motor was primarily caused by its special characteristics. It was suitable for the provision of small-scale inputs of mechanical energy and thus created opportunities for the mechanization of numerous different operations requiring physical work. Because of the pervasive changes in production processes that were made possible by the use of electric motors, the electrification of industrial processes was suggested as a prime example of how a new factor input opens a broad range of complementarities across techniques and production processes.

The three case studies of Chapter 7 illustrated the multi-faceted character of energy innovations. The significance of energy innovations for economic development cannot be reduced to their quantitative effect. To fully appreciate the impact of energy innovations, the complementarities they give rise to also have to be taken into consideration. Much of the importance of steam power was due to its effect on the geographical concentration of production. Likewise, the long-term economic impact of electricity in industrial production was largely caused by the fact that small-scale electric motors created the basis for pervasive technological and organizational changes. The sequential approach to production, the distinction between different factor services, and the interdependence concepts utilized in this book help to identify and organize these qualitative effects of energy innovations.

8.2   USE VALUE AND LONG-TERM ECONOMIC DEVELOPMENT

Early in the history of economics a distinction was made between the use value and the exchange value of goods. It was argued that use value is a necessary but not a sufficient condition for a good to have exchange value. As I noted in the introduction to this book, Carl Menger's example indicates that the discussion of goods and their usefulness was present even after the subjectivist revolution of neoclassical economics. It was soon given up afterwards. The later development of economics increasingly concentrated on the level of exchange value. Powerful price-theoretic concepts were developed that are based on the subjective evaluations of agents. Moreover, price theory was extended to production theory with the development of production functions constructed in analogy to the utility functions of consumer theory. The present book has returned to the old issue of use value. It has studied the conditions of producing goods that have use value. By using material hypotheses on the nature of goods and on regularities in the production processes, it was possible to characterize the role of energy inputs into production processes.

To identify the nature of the contribution made by inputs into production processes – captured in the factor services concept – is particularly important for a long-term perspective in economics. Knowledge of the nature of goods and of factors of production helps both in understanding past economic development and in evaluating the conditions and potential problems of future economic development. In this sense the present study is only a small piece in a larger ongoing effort. Just to give an example that has been touched upon in this book: The nature of the produced goods determines whether factor services of energy are of the direct or indirect kind. In turn, the kind of factor service makes a difference with regard to the substitutability of individual energy forms and also of energy inputs as a whole. In a dynamic perspective, the extent to which future economic development is energy-dependent is influenced by the kind of goods on which future demand will concentrate. If future demand concentrates on goods whose properties are directly energy-dependent (such as the distance of journeys, or the size of residences to be heated), the scope for innovations that reduce the need for energy inputs into production will be more circumscribed than if demand concentrates on goods whose production only requires indirect factor services of energy. In indirect factor services, the modification of the respective property does not hinge on a specific energy input, but only the (presently) known operations to perform the modification do. New operations with entirely different energy requirements may be devised. This example also indicates how linking use-value considerations with physical concepts may help in analyzing the kind of issues that physical approaches to economics have traditionally been most interested in, i.e. the need for physical resources in economic activities and the environmental implications of economic development.

8.3 THE PRODUCTION OF USEFUL GOODS: TOWARDS A THEORY

The present book suggested an evolutionary approach toward a production theory that can accommodate long-run concerns because it allows for material statements on the nature of goods and their production, and because it also has room for process innovations that qualitatively change a production process. In the course of its investigation, the study has touched upon a number of issues that have not been dealt with in sufficient detail. The approach taken here, however, can be extended in several dimensions, some of which appear to be particularly promising.

First, other categories of factors of production can be studied in the same way as energy. Their principal factor services can be identified, and the changes in how they have been provided over time can be traced. In this way, a comprehensive dynamic theory of the factors of production can be developed. This extension of the present study would seem particularly valuable for human labor. As I have briefly argued in Chapter 3, the disaggregation of human labor in the distinctive services it provides in production processes appears an adequate way to deal with the role of knowledge in production. This approach promises to be more insightful than the dichotomy between skilled and unskilled labor or the introduction of an aggregate factor knowledge. Likewise, identifying and categorizing the kinds of factor services that are provided by tools and materials seems a challenging but worthwhile endeavor. Eventually a comprehensive taxonomy of factor services may be developed in this way, which would help to clarify the extent to which factors from different categories are mutually substitutable.

A second dimension of potential extensions relates to the kind of production processes on which the analysis concentrates. Although the present book was based on an inclusive concept of production that encompassed the production of immaterial goods, the discussion of concrete production processes focused on materials processing and manufacturing. For a book dealing with the economics of energy and the production process, this bias was perhaps unavoidable, as the importance of energy use is greater in these kinds of processes than it is in other sectors. Nonetheless, the basic approach taken here, based on the identification of factor services for broad classes of operations, can also be applied to a more thorough analysis of the production of services. With the brief discussion of information processing in Chapters 4 and 5, a modest start into this direction has been made. But clearly there is much more to be said about services and their production.

Third, more complex structures than the strictly sequential framework assumed in this study can be investigated, and the temporal dimension of stages of production can be combined with the multiplicity of product components in order to develop an encompassing picture of interdependencies in the production of goods. This would also result in a more realistic treatment of assembly processes than the one suggested here.

Fourth, the above suggestion that the decomposability of techniques is variable and partly endogenous to adoption and further development of the technique seems another issue whose further extension seems particularly worthwhile. There are two aspects to this issue. On the one hand, detailed comparative work on process innovations and changes in the extent of interdependence would seem useful in light of the conjecture that decomposability may have secularly increased. A comparative study of innovations from different historical epochs would be suitable to test this conjecture. On the other hand, the endogenous nature of decomposability that has been proposed above is one aspect of the dynamics of production processes that could be integrated into formal production models. More generally, approaches to the modeling of production and the modeling of innovation seem more detached from each other than is warranted by the close relation between these two issues. Dynamic production models that incorporate characteristics of innovation processes and allow for the endogenous change of techniques due to learning would be helpful to bridge this gap.

References

Adams, R.N. (1981), 'Natural selection, energetics, and "cultural materialism",' *Current Anthropology*, **22**: 603–608.

Adams, R.N. (1988), *The Eighth Day: Social Evolution as the Self-Organization of Enèrgy*, Austin: University of Texas Press.

Akin, W.E. (1977), *Technocracy and the American Dream. The Technocrat Movement, 1900–1941*, Berkeley: University of California Press.

Allee, W.C., A.E. Emerson, O. Park, T. Park and K.P. Schmidt (1949), *Principles of Animal Ecology*, Philadelphia and London: W.B. Saunders.

Alting, L. (1994), *Manufacturing Engineering Processes*, 2nd edn, New York: Marcel Dekker.

Antonelli, C. (1995), *The Economics of Localized Technological Change and Industrial Dynamics*, Dordrecht: Kluwer.

Aoki, M. (1990), 'Toward an economic model of the Japanese firm,' *Journal of Economic Literature*, **28**: 1–27.

Argote, L. and D. Epple (1990), 'Learning curves in manufacturing,' *Science*, **247**: 920–924.

Arrow, K.J. (1962a), 'Economic welfare and the allocation of resources for invention,' in R.R. Nelson (ed.), *The Rate and Direction of Inventive Activity*, Princeton, NJ: Princeton University Press, pp. 609–625.

Arrow, K.J. (1962b), 'The economic implications of learning by doing,' *Review of Economic Studies*, **29**: 155–173.

Arrow, K.J. and F.H. Hahn (1971), *General Competitive Analysis*, Amsterdam: North-Holland.

Arthur, W.B. (1984), 'Competing technologies and economic prediction,' *Options*, 1984/2: 10–13.

Arthur, W.B. (1989), 'Competing technologies, increasing returns, and lock-in by historical events,' *Economic Journal*, **99**: 116–131.

Atack, J., F. Bateman and T. Weiss (1980), 'The regional diffusion and adoption of the steam engine in American manufacturing,' *Journal of Economic History*, **40**: 281–308.

Atkinson, A.B. and J.E. Stiglitz (1969), 'A new view of technological change,' *Economic Journal*, **79**: 573–578.

Auerswald, P., S. Kauffman, J. Lobo and K. Shell (2000), 'The production recipe approach to modeling technological innovation: An application to learning by doing,' *Journal of Economic Dynamics and Control,* **24**: 389–450.

Ayres, R.U. (1978), *Resources, Environment, and Economics. Applications of the Materials/Energy Balance Principle,* New York: Wiley.

Ayres, R.U. (1990), 'Technological transformations and long waves,' *Technological Forecasting and Social Change,* **37**: 1–37 and 111–137.

Ayres, R.U. (1994a), 'Toward a non-linear dynamics of technological progress,' *Journal of Economic Behavior and Organization,* **24**: 35–69.

Ayres, R.U. (1994b), *Information, Entropy and Progress,* New York: American Institute of Physics Press.

Ayres, R.U. (1998), 'Eco-thermodynamics: economics and the second law,' *Ecological Economics,* **26**: 189–209.

Ayres, R.U. (1999), 'The second law, the fourth law, recycling, and limits to growth,' *Ecological Economics,* **29**: 473–483.

Ayres, R.U. and A. V. Kneese (1969), 'Production, consumption, and externalities,' *American Economic Review,* **59**: 282–297.

Ayres, R.U. and B. Warr (2001), 'Accounting for growth: the role of physical work,' Paper presented at the workshop 'Reappraising Production Theory: Concepts, Cases and Models,' Max Planck Institute for Research into Economic Systems, Jena, 29 November –1 December 2001.

Bahk, B.-H. and M. Gort (1993), 'Decomposing learning by doing in new plants,' *Journal of Political Economy,* **101**: 561–583.

Baldwin, C.Y. and K.B. Clark (1997), 'Managing in an age of modularity,' *Harvard Business Review,* September–October: 84–93.

Baldwin, C.Y. and K.B. Clark (2000), *Design Rules. Volume I: The Power of Modularity,* Cambridge, MA and London: MIT Press.

Baumgärtner, S. (2000), *Ambivalent Joint Production and the Natural Environment,* Heidelberg and New York: Physica.

Baumgärtner, S., H. Dyckhoff, M. Faber, J. Proops and J. Schiller (2001), 'The concept of joint production and ecological economics,' *Ecological Economics,* **36**: 365–372.

Beaudreau, B. (1998), *Energy and Organization. Growth and Distribution Reexamined,* Westport, CT: Greenwood Press.

Binswanger, M. (1992), *Information und Entropie. Ökologische Perspektiven des Übergangs zu einer Informationswirtschaft,* Frankfurt/Main and New York: Campus.

Böhm-Bawerk, E. ([1884] 1959), *Capital and Interest. Volume I: History and Critique of Interest Theories,* South Holland, IL: Libertarian Press.

Boulding, K.E. (1981), *Evolutionary Economics,* Beverly Hills, CA and London: Sage.

Breidbach, O. (2000), 'Alle für Eines. Der Monismus als wissenschaftsgeschichtliches Problem,' in P. Ziche (ed.), *Monismus um*

1900. Wissenschaftskultur und Weltanschauung, Berlin: Verlag für Wissenschaft und Bildung, pp. 9–22.

Bresnahan, T. and M. Trajtenberg (1995), 'General purpose technologies "Engines of growth"?' *Journal of Econometrics*, **65**: 83–108.

Brusoni, S. and A. Prencipe (2001), 'Unpacking the black box of modularity: technologies, products and organizations,' *Industrial and Corporate Change*, **10**: 179–205.

Buenstorf, G. (2000), 'Self-organization and sustainability: energetics of evolution and implications for ecological economics,' *Ecological Economics*, **33**: 119–134.

Buenstorf, G. (2003), 'Processes of knowledge sharing: from cognitive psychology to economics,' in E. Helmstädter (ed.), *The Economics of Knowledge Sharing. A New Institutional Aproach*, Cheltenham, UK and Northampton, MA: Edward Elgar, pp. 74–99.

Burwell, C.C. (1990), 'High-temperature electroprocessing: steel and glass,' in S.H. Schurr, C.C. Burwell, W.D. Devine and S. Sonenblum (eds), *Electricity in the American Economy. Agent of Technological Progress*, Westport, CT: Greenwood Press, pp. 109–129.

Cameron, R. (1993), *A Concise Economic History of the World. From Paleolithic Times to the Present*, 2nd edn, New York and Oxford: Oxford University Press.

Cantner, U., H. Hanusch and G. Westermann (1996), 'Detecting technological performance and variety: an empirical approach,' in E. Helmstädter and M. Perlman (eds), *Behavioral Norms, Technological Progress, and Economic Dynamics*, Ann Arbor, MI: University of Michigan Press, pp. 223–246.

Carlaw, K.I. and R.G. Lipsey (2002), 'Externalities, technological complementarities and sustained economic growth,' *Research Policy*, **31**: 1305–1315.

Chandler, A.D. (1972), 'Anthracite coal and the beginnings of the industrial revolution in the United States,' *Business History Review*, **46**: 142–181.

Chapman, P.F. and F. Roberts (1983), *Metal Resources and Energy*, London: Butterworth.

Chenery, H.B. (1949), 'Engineering production functions,' *Quarterly Journal of Economics*, **63**: 507–531.

Chenery, H.B. (1953), 'Process and production functions from engineering data,' in W. Leontief (ed.), *Studies in the Structure of the American Economy*, New York: Oxford University Press, pp. 297–325.

Cheng, B.S. (1996), 'An investigation of cointegration and causality between energy consumption and economic growth,' *Journal of Energy and Development*, **21**: 73–84.

Cleveland, C.J. (1999), 'Biophysical economics: from physiocracy to ecological economics and industrial ecology,' in K. Mayumi and J.M. Gowdy (eds), *Bioeconomics and Sustainability. Essays in Honor of Nicholas Georgescu-Roegen*, Cheltenham, UK and Northampton, MA: Edward Elgar, pp. 125–154.

Cohen, W.M. and D.A. Levinthal (1990), 'Absorptive capacity: a new perspective of learning and innovation,' *Administrative Science Quarterly*, **35**: 128–152.

Cordes, C. (2003), 'An evolutionary analysis of long-term qualitative change in human labor,' PhD dissertation, Friedrich Schiller University, Jena.

Costanza, R. (1980), 'Embodied energy and economic evaluation,' *Science*, **210**: 1219–1224.

Costanza, R. (1982), Reply to: D.A. Huettner: 'Economic values and embodied energy,' *Science*, **216**: 1143.

Costanza, R. and R.A. Herendeen (1984), 'Embodied energy and economic value in the United States economy: 1963, 1967 and 1972,' *Resources and Energy*, **6**: 129–163.

Cottrell, F. (1955), *Energy and Society. The Relation between Energy, Social Change, and Economic Development*, New York: McGraw-Hill.

Cowan, R. (1987), 'Backing the wrong horse: sequential technology choice under increasing returns,' PhD dissertation, Stanford University.

Cowan, R. and D. Foray (1997), 'The economics of codification and the diffusion of knowledge,' *Industrial and Corporate Change*, **6**: 595–622.

Cowan, R. and S. Hultén (1996), 'Escaping lock-in: the case of the electric vehicle,' *Technological Forecasting and Social Change*, **53**: 61–79.

Dasgupta, P. and G. Heal (1974), 'The optimal depletion of exhaustible resources,' *Review of Economic Studies*, **41**: 3–28.

David, P.A. (1975), *Technical Choice Innovation and Economic Growth*, London and New York: Cambridge University Press.

David, P.A. (1990a), 'The dynamo and the computer: a historical perspective on the modern productivity paradox,' *American Economic Review*, **80**: 355–361.

David, P.A. (1990b), 'General-purpose engines, investment and productivity growth: from the dynamo revolution to the computer revolution,' in E. Deiaco, E. Hornell and G. Vickery (eds), *Technology and Investment: Crucial Issues for the 1990s*, New York: Columbia University Press, pp. 141–154.

David, P.A. and J.A. Bunn (1988), 'The economics of gateway technologies and network evolution: lessons from electricity supply history,' *Information Economics and Policy*, **3**: 165–202.

De Bruyn, S.M. and J.B. Opschoor (1997), 'Developments in the throughput–income relationship: theoretical and empirical observations,' *Ecological Economics*, **20**: 255–268.

De Vries, L. and H. Kolb (1978), *Dictionary of Chemistry and Chemical Engineering*, 2nd edn, vol.1, Weinheim and New York: Verlag Chemie.

Depew, D.J. and B.H. Weber (1995), *Darwinism Evolving. Systems Dynamics and the Genealogy of Natural Selection*, Cambridge, MA and London: MIT Press.

Deutsches Institut für Normung (1985), *DIN 8580: Fertigungsverfahren: Begriffe; Einteilung*, Entwurf vom Juli 1985.

Devine, W.D. (1983), 'From shafts to wires: historical perspective on electrification,' *Journal of Economic History*, **43**: 347–372.

Devine, W.D. (1990a), 'Electricity in information management: the evolution of electronic control,' in S.H. Schurr, C.C. Burwell, W.D. Devine and S. Sonenblum (eds), *Electricity in the American Economy. Agent of Technological Progress*, Westport, CT: Greenwood Press, pp. 43–70.

Devine, W.D. (1990b), 'Early developments in electroprocessing: new products, new industries,' in S.H. Schurr, C.C. Burwell, W.D. Devine and S. Sonenblum (eds), *Electricity in the American Economy. Agent of Technological Progress*, Westport, CT: Greenwood Press, pp. 77–98.

Du Boff, R.B. (1967), 'The introduction of electric power in American manufacturing.' *Economic History Review*, **20**: 509–518.

Dudley, L. (1999), 'Communications and economic growth,' *European Economic Review*, **43**: 595–619.

DuVall, J.B. (1996), *Contemporary Manufacturing Processes*, South Holland, IL: Goodheart Willcox.

Ebeling, W. and R. Feistel (1992), 'Theory of selforganization and evolution: the role of entropy, value and information,' *Journal of Non-Equilibrium Thermodynamics*, **17**/4: 303–332.

Ellinger, T. and R. Haupt (1996), *Produktions- und Kostentheorie*, 3rd edn, Stuttgart: Schäffer-Poeschel.

Energy Information Administration (2002), *Annual Energy Review 2001*, Washington, DC: U.S. Department of Energy.

Erdmann, G. (1995), *Energieökonomik. Theorie und Anwendungen*, 2nd edn. Zürich and Stuttgart: Vdf Hochschulverlag and Teubner.

Etemad, B. and J. Luciani (1991), *World Energy Production 1880–1985*, Geneva: Libraire Droz.

Faber, M., R. Manstetten and J. Proops (1996), *Ecological Economics*, Cheltenham, UK and Brookfield, VT: Edward Elgar.

Faber, M., H. Niemes and G. Stephan (1995), *Entropy, Environment and Resources*, Berlin: Springer.

Faber, M., J. Proops and S. Baumgärtner (1998), 'All production is joint production – a thermodynamic analysis,' in S. Faucheux, J. Gowdy and I. Nicolai (eds), *Sustainability and Firms*, Cheltenham, UK and Lyme, USA: Edward Elgar, pp. 131–158.

Foreman-Peck, J. (1996), '"Technological lock-in" and the power source for the motor car,' *Oxford University Discussion Papers in Economic and Social History*, No. 7.

Forsund, F. (1999), 'On the contribution of Ragnar Frisch to production theory,' *Rivista Internazionale di Scienze Economiche e Commerciali*, **46**: 1–34.

Foster, J. (1994) 'The self-organization approach in economics,' in P. Burley and J. Foster (eds), *Economics and Thermodynamics: New Perspectives on Economic Analysis*, Dordrecht: Kluwer, pp. 183–201.

Foster, J. (1997), 'The analytical foundations of evolutionary economics: From biological analogy to economic self-organization,' *Structural Change and Economic Dynamics*, **8**: 427–451.

Fouquet, R. and P.J.G. Pearson (1998), 'A thousand years of energy use in the United Kingdom,' *Energy Journal*, **19**: 1–41.

Frankel, M. (1955), 'Obsolescence and technological change in a maturing economy,' *American Economic Review*, **45**: 296–319.

Fremdling, R. (1991), 'The puddler – a craftman's skill and the spread of a new technology in Belgium, France and Germany,' *Journal of European Economic History*, **20**: 529–567.

Fremdling, R. (2000), 'Transfer patterns of British technology to the Continent: The case of the iron industry,' *European Review of Economic History*, **4**: 195–222.

Frenken, K. (2001a), 'Understanding product innovation using complex systems theory,' academic thesis, University of Amsterdam.

Frenken, K. (2001b), 'Technological complexity, modularity, and vertical disintegration,' Paper presented at the workshop 'Reappraising Production Theory: Concepts, Cases and Models,' Max Planck Institute for Research into Economic Systems, Jena, 29 November – 1 December, 2001.

Frenken, K., L. Marengo and M. Valente (1999), 'Interdependencies, nearly-decomposability, and adaptation,' in T. Brenner (ed.), *Computational Techniques for Modelling Learning in Economics*, Boston, MA: Kluwer, pp. 145–165.

Fritsch, B. (1992), 'Evolutionsökonomische Aspekte des Energie- und Umweltproblems,' in U. Witt (ed.), *Studien zur evolutorischen Ökonomik II*, Berlin: Duncker and Humblot, pp. 117–144.

Frondel, M. and C.M. Schmidt (2002), 'The capital-energy controversy: An artifact of cost shares?' *Energy Journal*, **23**: 53–79.

Georgescu-Roegen, N. (1970), 'The economics of production,' *American Economic Review*, **60**: 1–9.

Georgescu-Roegen, N. (1971), *The Entropy Law and the Economic Process*, Cambridge, MA and London: Harvard University Press.

Georgescu-Roegen, N. (1979), 'Energy analysis and economic valuation,' *Southern Economic Journal*, **44**: 1023–1058.

Georgescu-Roegen, N. (1986), 'The entropy law and the economic process in retrospect,' *Eastern Economic Journal*, **12**: 3–25.

Gleitsmann, R.-J. (1980), 'Rohstoffmangel und Lösungsstrategien: Das Problem vorindustrieller Holzknappheit,' *Technologie und Politik*, **16**: 104–154.

Gugerli, D. (1996), *Redeströme. Zur Elektrifizierung der Schweiz 1880–1914*, Zürich: Chronos.

Gutenberg, E. ([1951] 1983), *Grundlagen der Betriebswirtschaftslehre. Vol. I: Die Produktion*, 24th edn, Berlin and Heidelberg: Springer.

Haeckel, E. (1870), 'Über Entwicklungsgang und Aufgabe der Zoologie,' *Jenaische Zeitschrift*, **5**: 353–370.

Hall, C., D. Lindenberger, R. Kümmel, T. Kroeger and W. Eichhorn (2001), 'The need to reintegrate the natural sciences with economics,' *BioScience*, **51**: 663–673.

Halsey, H.I. (1981), 'The choice between high-pressure and low-pressure steam power in America in the early nineteenth century,' *Journal of Economic History*, **41**: 723–744.

Hammersley, G. (1973), 'The charcoal iron industry and its fuel, 1540–1750,' *Economic History Review*, **26**: 593–613.

Harris, J.R. (1976), 'Skills, coal and British industry in the eighteenth century,' *History*, **61**: 167–182.

Harris, J.R. (1984), 'The rise of coal technology,' *Scientific American*, **231**: 92–97.

Harris, J.R. (1988a), 'The diffusion of English metallurgical methods to eighteenth-century France,' *French History*, **2**: 22–44.

Harris, J.R. (1988b), *The British Iron Industry 1700–1850*, Basingstoke and London: Macmillan Education.

Helpman, E. (ed.) (1988), *General Purpose Technologies and Economic Growth*, Cambridge, MA; London: MIT Press.

Hemming, W. (1998), *Verfahrenstechnik*, 8th edn, Würzburg: Vogel.

Henderson, R.M. and K.B. Clark (1990), 'Architectural innovation: the reconfiguration of existing product technologies and the failure of established firms,' *Administrative Science Quarterly*, **35**: 9–30.

Hills, R.L. (1970), *Power in the Industrial Revolution*, Manchester: Manchester University Press.

Hotelling, H. (1931), 'The economics of exhaustible resources,' *Journal of Political Economy*, **39**: 137–175.

Huettner, D.A. (1982), 'Economic values and embodied energy,' *Science*, **216**: 1141–1143.

Hughes, T.P. (1983), *Networks of Power. Electrification in Western Society, 1880–1930*, Baltimore, MD and London: Johns Hopkins University Press.

Hunter, L.C. (1985), *A History of Industrial Power in the United States, 1780–1930. Volume Two: Steam Power*, Charlottesville, VA: University Press of Virginia.

Hunter, L.C. and L. Bryant (1991), *A History of Industrial Power in the United States, 1780–1930. Volume Three: The Transmission of Power*, Cambridge, MA and London: MIT Press.

Hyde, C.K. (1974), 'Technological change in the British wrought iron industry, 1750–1815: a reinterpretation,' *Economic History Review*, **27**: 190–206.

Hyde, C.K. (1977), *Technological Change and the British Iron Industry 1700–1870*, Princeton, NJ: Princeton University Press.

IEA (International Energy Agency) (1999), *Energy Balances of OECD Countries 1996–1997*, OECD, Paris.

IEA (International Energy Agency) (2002), *Energy Balances of OECD Countries 1999–2000*, OECD, Paris.

Islas, J. (1997), 'Getting round the lock-in in electricity generating systems: the example of the gas turbine,' *Research Policy*, **26**: 49–66.

Johansson, A.O. (1998), 'Why change to steam power? Institutional constraints, risk-aversion and path-dependence in the Swedish sawmill industry, 1850–1900,' in M. Berg and K. Bruland (eds), *Technological Revolutions in Europe*, Cheltenham, UK and Lyme, USA: Edward Elgar, pp. 207–229.

Joskow, P.L. (2001), 'California's electricity crisis,' *NBER Working Paper 8442*, Washington, DC: National Bureau of Economic Research.

Kaberger, T. and B. Mansson (2001), 'Entropy and economic processes – physics perspectives,' *Ecological Economics*, **36**: 165–179.

Kauffman, S. (1993), *The Origins of Order. Self-organization and selection in evolution*, New York and Oxford: Oxford University Press.

Kazanas, H.C., G.E. Baker and T. Gregor (1981), *Basic Manufacturing Processes*, New York: McGraw-Hill.

Klepper, S. (1996), 'Entry, exit, growth and innovation over the product life cycle,' *American Economic Review*, **86**: 562–583.

Klepper, S. and K.L. Simons (1997), 'Technological extinctions of industrial firms: an inquiry into their nature and causes,' *Industrial and Corporate Change*, **6**: 379–460.

Kloock, J. (1975), Entry 'Input–Output-Analyse,' in E. Grochla and W. Wittmann (eds), *Handwörterbuch der Betriebswirtschaft*, 4th edn, Stuttgart: Schaeffer-Poeschel, columns 1953–1966.

Knight, F.H. (1921), *Risk, Uncertainty, and Profit*, Boston: Houghton Mifflin.

Knoedler, J. and A. Mayhew (1999), 'Thorstein Veblen and the engineers: a reinterpretation,' *History of Political Economy*, **31**: 255–272.

Koopmans, T.C. (1951), 'Analysis of production as an efficient combination of activities,' in T.C. Koopmans (ed.), *Activity Analysis of Production and Allocation*, New Haven and London: Yale University Press.

Krautkraemer, J.A. (1998), 'Nonrenewable resource scarcity,' *Journal of Economic Literature*, **36**: 2065–2107.

Krugman, P. (2003), 'Delusions of power,' *New York Times*, March 28.

Kümmel, R. (1998), *Energie und Kreativität*, Stuttgart and Leipzig: Teubner.

Kümmel, R., W. Strassl, A. Gossner and W. Eichhorn (1985), 'Technical progress and energy dependent production functions,' *Zeitschrift für Nationalökonomie*, **45**: 285–311.

Kümmel, R., D. Lindenberger and W. Eichhorn (1997), 'Energie, Wirtschaftswachstum und technischer Fortschritt,' *Physikalische Blätter*, **53**: 869–875.

Lancaster, K.J. (1966), 'Change and innovation in the technology of consumption,' *American Economic Review*, **56**: 14–23.

Landes, D.S. (1969), *The Unbound Prometheus. Technological Change and Industrial Development in Western Europe from 1750 to the Present*, Cambridge: Cambridge University Press.

Landesmann, M. and R. Scazzieri (1996), 'The production process: description and analysis,' in M. Landesmann and R. Scazzieri (eds), *Production and Economic Dynamics*, Cambridge, UK and New York: Cambridge University Press, pp. 191–228.

Langlois, R.N. (1992), 'Transaction-cost economics in real time,' *Industrial and Corporate Change*, **1**: 99–127.

Langlois, R.N. (2003), 'The vanishing hand: the changing dynamics of industrial capitalism,' *Industrial and Corporate Change*, **12**: 351–385.

Langlois, R.N. and P.L. Robertson (1992), 'Networks and innovation in a modular system: Lessons from the microcomputer and stereo component industries,' *Research Policy*, **21**: 297–313.

Lipsey, R.G., C. Bekar and K. Carlaw (1998), 'What requires explanation?' in E. Helpman (ed.), *General Purpose Technologies and Economic Growth*, Cambridge, MA and London: MIT Press, pp. 15–54.

Lotka, A. (1922), 'Contribution to the energetics of evolution,' *Proceedings of the National Academy of Science (U.S.A.)*, **8**: 147–151.

Lozada, G. (1999), 'The role of entropy and energy in natural resource economics,' in K. Mayumi and J.M. Gowdy (eds), *Bioeconomics and Sustainability. Essays in Honor of Nicholas Georgescu-Roegen*, Cheltenham, UK and Northampton, MA: Edward Elgar, pp. 326–351.

Lyons, J.S. (1987), 'Powerloom profitability and steam power costs: Britain in the 1830s,' *Explorations in Economic History*, **24**: 392–408.

Marchetti, C. (1987), 'Infrastructures for movement,' *Technological Forecasting and Social Change*, **32**: 373–393.

Marshall, A. ([1890] 1997), *Principles of Economics*, 8th edition, Great Minds Series, Amherst, NY: Prometheus Books.

Martinez-Alier, J.M. (1987), *Ecological Economics*, Oxford and Cambridge, MA: Blackwell.

May, E. (1992), *Dynamische Produktionstheorie auf der Basis der Aktivitätsanalyse*, Heidelberg: Physica.

McCabe, W.L., J.C. Smith and P. Harriott (2001), *Unit Operations of Chemical Engineering*, 6th edn, New York: McGraw.Hill.

Meadows, D.H., D.L. Meadows, J. Randers and W.W. Behrens III (1972), *The Limits to Growth. A Report for the Club of Rome's Project on the Predicament of Mankind*, New York: Universe Books.

Melosi, M.V. (1982), 'Energy transitions in the nineteenth-century economy,' in G.H. Daniels and M.H. Rose (eds), *Energy and Transport. Historical Perspectives on Policy Issues*, Beverly Hills, CA: Sage, pp. 55–69.

Menger, C. ([1871] 1950), *Principles of Economics*, Glencoe, IL: Free Press.

Metcalfe, J.S. (2001), 'Consumption, preferences and the evolutionary agenda,' *Journal of Evolutionary Economics*, **11**: 37–58.

Milgrom, P. and J. Roberts (1990), 'The economics of modern manufacturing: technology, strategy, and organization,' *American Economic Review*, **80**: 511–528.

Mirowski, P. (1988), 'Energy and energetics in economic theory: a review essay,' *Journal of Economic Issues*, **22**: 811–830.

Mirowski, P. (1989), *More Heat than Light*, Cambridge, UK: Cambridge University Press.

Mokyr, J. (1990), *The Lever of Riches. Technological Creativity and Economic Progress*, New York and Oxford: Oxford University Press.

Mokyr, J. (1999), 'Editor's introduction: the new economic history and the Industrial Revolution,' in J. Mokyr (ed.), *The British Industrial Revolution. An Economic Perspective*, 2nd edn, Boulder, CO: Westview Press, pp. 1–127.

Mokyr, J. (2000), 'Knowledge, technology, and economic growth during the Industrial Revolution,' in B. Van Ark, S.K. Kuipers and G.H. Kuper (eds), *Productivity, Technology and Economic Growth*, Boston: Kluwer, pp. 253–292.

Morroni, M. (1992), *Production Process and Technical Change*, Cambridge, UK: Cambridge University Press.

Morroni, M. (1999), 'Production and time: a fund-flow analysis,' in K. Mayumi and J.M. Gowdy (eds), *Bioeconomics and Sustainability. Essays in Honor of Nicholas Georgescu-Roegen*, Cheltenham, UK and Northampton, MA: Edward Elgar, pp. 194–228.

Nelson, R.R. (1959), 'The simple economics of basic scientific research,' *Journal of Political Economy*, **67**: 297–306.

Nordhaus, W.D. (1973), 'The allocation of energy resources,' *Brookings Papers on Economic Activity*, 529–570.

Nordhaus, W.D. (1997), 'Do real-output and real-wage measures capture reality? The history of lighting suggests not,' in T.F. Bresnahan and R.J. Gordon (eds), *The Economics of New Goods*, Chicago: University of Chicago Press, pp. 29–66.

Nye, D.E. (1990), *Electrifying America. Social Meanings of a New Technology, 1880–1940*, Cambridge, MA and London: MIT Press.

Odum, H.T. (1971), *Environment, Power, and Society*, New York: Wiley.

Odum, H.T. and R.C. Pinkerton (1955), 'Time's speed regulator: the optimum efficiency for maximum power output in physical and biological systems,' *American Scientist*, **43**: 331–343.

Pavitt, K. (2002), 'Knowledge about knowledge since Nelson & Winter: a mixed record,' *SPRU Electronic Working Paper Series* No. 83, University of Sussex.

Phelps Brown, E.H. and S.V. Hopkins (1956), 'Seven centuries of the prices of consumables, compared with builders' wage-rates,' *Economica*, **23**: 296–314.

Pimentel, D. and M. Pimentel (eds) (1996), *Food, Energy, and Society*, Niwot, CO: University Press of Colorado.

Polanyi, M. (1966), *The Tacit Dimension*, New York: Doubleday.

Porter, M.E. (1985), *Competitive Advantage. Creating and Sustaining Superior Performance*, New York: Free Press.

Pratt, J.A. (1981), 'The ascent of oil: The transition from coal to oil in early twentieth-century America,' in L.J. Perelman, A.W. Giebelhaus and M.D. Yokell (eds), *Energy Transitions. Long-Term Perspectives*, Boulder, CO: Westview Press, pp. 9–34.

Prigogine, I. (1976), 'Order through fluctuation: self-organization and social system,' in E. Jantsch and C.H. Waddington (eds), *Evolution and Consciousness: Human Systems in Transition*, London: Addison-Wesley, pp. 93–133.

Prigogine, I. and I. Stengers (1984), *Order out of Chaos*, Boulder, CO: New Science Library.

Prigogine, I., G. Nicolis and A. Babloyantz (1972), 'Thermodynamics of evolution,' *Physics Today*, **25**/11: 23–28 and **25**/12: 38–44.

Proops, J.L.R. (1983), 'Organisation and dissipation in economic systems,' *Journal of Social and Biological Structures*, **6**: 353–366.

Proops, J.L.R. (1986), 'The physical input to economics,' *Mondes en Développement*, **14**/54–55: 245–252.

Rant, Z. (1956), 'Exergie, ein neues Wort für "technische Arbeitsfähigkeit",' *Forschung auf dem Gebiete des Ingenieurwesens*, **22**: 36–37.'"tralala"

Rant, Z. (1957), 'Bewertung und praktische Verrechnung von Energien,' *Allgemeine Wärmetechnik*, **8**: 25–32.

Rehder, J.E. (1987), 'The change from charcoal to coke in iron smelting,' *Journal of the Historical Metallurgy Society*, **21**: 37–43.

Reynolds, T.S. (1983), *75 Years of Progress: A History of the American Institute of Chemical Engineers*, New York: American Institute of Chemical Engineers.

Reynolds, T.S. (1986), 'Defining professional boundaries. Chemical engineering in the early 20th century,' *Technology and Culture*, **27**: 694–716.

Rifkin, J. (1980), *Entropy: A New World View*, New York: Viking Press.

Robinson, E.H. (1974), 'The early diffusion of steam power,' *Journal of Economic History*, **34**: 91–107.

Rosenberg, N. (1963), 'Technological change in the machine tool industry, 1840–1910,' *Journal of Economic History*, **23**: 414–443.

Rosenberg, N. (1969), 'The direction of technological change: inducement mechanisms and focusing devices,' *Economic Development and Cultural Change*, **18**: 1–24.

Rosenberg, N. (1979), 'Technological interdependence in the American economy,' *Technology and Culture*, **20**: 25–50.

Rosenberg, N. (1982a), 'Learning by using,' in *Inside the Black Box: Technology and Economics*, Cambridge and New York: Cambridge University Press, pp. 120–140.

Rosenberg, N. (1982b), 'The effects of energy supply characteristics on technology and economic growth,' in *Inside the Black Box: Technology and Economics*, Cambridge and New York: Cambridge University Press, pp. 81–103.

Rosenberg, N. (1998), 'Chemical engineering as a general purpose technology,' in E. Helpman (ed.), *General Purpose Technologies and Economic Growth*, Cambridge, MA and London: MIT Press, pp. 167–192.

Rosenberg, N. and M. Trajtenberg (2001), 'A general purpose technology at work: the Corliss engine in the late 19th century US, *NBER Working Paper 8485*, Washington, DC: National Bureau of Economic Research.

Ruprecht, W. (2001), 'Towards an evolutionary theory of consumption: conceptual considerations and empirical evidence,' PhD dissertation, Friedrich Schiller University, Jena.

Rydén, G. (1998), 'Skill and technical change in the Swedish iron industry, 1750–1860,' *Technology and Culture*, **39**: 383–407.

Sartorius, C. (1999), 'Energie- und Stoffflüsse im ökologischen und ökonomischen Zusammenhang.' *Jahrbuch Ökologische Ökonomik*, **1**: 425–452.

Saviotti, P.P. (1996), *Technological Evolution, Variety and the Economy*, Cheltenham, UK and Brookfield, VT: Edward Elgar.

Saviotti, P.P. and J.S. Metcalfe (1984), 'A theoretical approach to the construction of technological output indicators,' *Research Policy*, **13**: 141–151.

Scazzieri, R. (1993), *A Theory of Production. Tasks, Processes, and Technical Practices*, Oxford: Clarendon Press.

Schrödinger, E. (1945), *What Is Life?* Cambridge and New York: Cambridge University Press and Macmillan.

Schurr, S.H., C.C. Burwell, W.D. Devine and S. Sonenblum (eds) (1990), *Electricity in the American Economy. Agent of Technological Progress*, Westport, CT: Greenwood Press.

Setzer, M. (1998), *Wirtschaftliche Entwicklung und Energieintensität*, Marburg: Metropolis.

Sieferle, R.P. (1982), *Der unterirdische Wald. Energiekrise und Industrielle Revolution*, Munich: C.H. Beck.

Simon, H.A. ([1962] 1996), 'The architecture of complexity,' *Proceedings of the American Philosophical Society*, **106**: 467–482. Reprinted in revised form in H.A. Simon, *The Sciences of the Artificial*, 3rd edn, Cambridge, MA and London: MIT Press, pp. 183–216.

Smil, V. (1994), *Energy in World History*, Boulder, CO: Westview Press.

Soddy, F. (1933), *Wealth, Virtual Wealth and Debt. The Solution of the Economic Paradox*, New York: E.P. Dutton & Co.

Söllner, F. (1996), *Thermodynamik und Umweltökonomie*, Heidelberg: Physica.

Solow, R.M. (1974a), 'The economics of resources or the resources of economics,' *American Economic Review*, **64**: 1–14.

Solow, R.M. (1974b), 'Intergenerational equity and exhaustible resources,' *Review of Economic Studies*, **41**: 29–45.

Spiegler, K.S. (1983), *Principles of Energetics*, Berlin: Springer.

Stabile, D.R. (1986), 'Veblen and the political economy of the engineer: the radical thinker and engineering leaders came to technocratic ideas at the same time,' *American Journal of Economics and Sociology*, **45**: 41–52.

Stern, D.I. (2000), 'A multivariate cointegration analysis of the role of energy in the US macroeconomy,' *Energy Economics*, **22**: 267–283.

Stigler, G.J. (1940), Contribution to: 'Round table on cost functions and their relation to imperfect competition,' *American Economic Review*, **30** (Supplement): 400–402.

Stiglitz, J. (1974), 'Growth with exhaustible natural resources: efficient and optimal growth paths,' *Review of Economic Studies*, **41**: 123–137.

Szargut, J., D.R. Morris and F.R. Steward (1988), *Exergy Analysis of Thermal, Chemical, and Metallurgical Processes*, New York: Hemisphere.

Taylor, P.J. (1988), 'Technocratic optimism, H.T. Odum, and the partial transformation of ecological metaphor after World War II,' *Journal of the History of Biology*, **21**: 213–244.

Temin, P. (1966), 'Steam and waterpower in the early nineteenth century,' *Journal of Economic History*, **26**: 187–205.

Thomas, B. (1986), 'Was there an energy crisis in Great Britain in the 17th century?' *Explorations in Economic History*, **23**: 124–152.

Todd, R.H., D.K. Allen and L. Alting (1994), *Fundamental Principles of Manufacturing Processes*, New York: Industrial Press.

Tribus, M. and E.C. McIrvine (1971), 'Energy and information,' *Scientific American*, **225**: 179–187.

Ulrich, K. (1995), 'The role of product architecture in the manufacturing firm,' *Research Policy*, **24**: 419–440.

US Bureau of the Census (1997), *Historical Statistics of the United States. Colonial Times to 1970*, Electronic edition by S. Carter, S. Gartner, M. Haines, A. Olmstead, R. Sutch and G. Wright (eds), Cambridge and New York: Cambridge University Press.

Varian, H. (1992), *Microeconomic Analysis*, 3rd edn, New York and London: W.W. Norton.

Vauck, W.R.A. and H.A. Müller (2000), *Grundoperationen chemischer Verfahrenstechnik*, 11th edn, Stuttgart: Deutscher Verlag für Grundstoffchemie.

Von Tunzelmann, G.N. (1978), *Steam Power and British Industrialization to 1860*, Oxford: Clarendon Press.

Weber, M. ([1909] 1985), 'Energetische Kulturtheorien,' in *Gesammelte Aufsätze zur Wissenschaftslehre*, 6th edn, Tübingen: Mohr (Siebeck), pp. 400–426.

Weinel, I. and P.D. Crossland (1989), 'The scientific foundations of technological progress,' *Journal of Economic Issues*, **23**: 795–808.

Weissmahr, J.A. (1992), 'The factors of production of evolutionary economics,' in U. Witt (ed.), *Explaining Process and Change*, Ann Arbor, MI: University of Michigan Press, pp. 67–79.

White, L.A. (1943), 'Energy and the evolution of culture,' *American Anthropologist*, **45**: 335–356.

Wibe, S. (1984), 'Engineering production functions: a survey,' *Economica*, **51**: 401–411.

Wicken, J.S. (1980), 'A thermodynamic theory of evolution,' *Journal of Theoretical Biology*, **87**: 9–23.

Wicken, J.S. (1986), 'Evolutionary self-organization and entropic dissipation in biological and socioeconomic systems,' *Journal of Social and Biological Structures*, **9**: 261–273.

Witt, U. (1985), 'Coordination of individual economic activities as an evolving process of self-organization,' *Economie Appliquée*, **36**: 569–595.

Witt, U. (1991), 'Economics, sociobiology, and behavioral psychology on preferences,' *Journal of Economic Psychology*, **12**: 557–573.

Witt , U. (1997), 'Self-organization in economics – what is new?' *Structural Change and Economic Dynamics*, **8**: 489–507.

Witt, U. (1999), 'Bioeconomics as economics from a Darwinian perspective,' *Journal of Bioeconomics*, **1**: 19–34.

Witt, U. (2000), 'Genes, culture, and utility,' *Papers on Economics and Evolution*, No. 0009, Max Planck Institute for Research into Economic Systems.

Witt, U. (2001), 'Learning to consume – a theory of wants and the growth of demand,' *Journal of Evolutionary Economics*, **11**: 23–36.

Witt, U. (2003a), ' "Production" in nature and production in the economy – second thoughts about some basic economic concepts,' *Papers on Economics and Evolution*, No. 0301, Max Planck Institute for Research into Economic Systems.

Witt, U. (2003b), *The Evolving Economy*, Cheltenham: Edward Elgar.

Wright, G. (1997), 'Towards a more historical approach to technological change,' *Economic Journal*, **107**: 1560–1566.

Index

localized technological change 118
long-term economic development 176
Lotka, A. 17–18
Lozada, G. 33
Luciani, J. 117
Lyons, J.S. 153

Mansson, B. 26, 39
manufacturing 47–8, 51–3, 59, 61,
    64, 83, 85–9, 97–100, 103,
    111, 136, 165, 173, 177
Marchetti, C. 103
Marshall, A. 5
Martinez-Alier, J.M. 15
material transformation function
    (Chenery) 54–5
materials processing 47–51, 53, 59,
    83–7, 97–100, 103, 136, 165,
    177
maximum power principle (Odum) 18
May, E. 58
Mayhew, A. 16
McCabe, W.L. 49
McIrvine, E.C. 24, 28, 86
Meadows, D.H. 1, 11
Melosi, M.V. 98
Menger, C. 5–7, 176
Metcalfe, J.S. 61–2
Milgrom, P. 116n
Mirowski, P. 4–6, 11n, 15, 55
modular innovation 122
modularity 109, 120, 122–3, 127–30,
    132, 134, 174
    of products 9, 122–3, 127, 132,
        134, 174
    of techniques 127–30, 132–4, 174
Mokyr, J. 93, 102, 130–31, 136, 144,
    146n
monism 15
morphological process model (Alting)
    51
Morroni, M. 56
Müller, H.A. 48–50

nearly decomposable systems 123
Nelson, R.R. 70
neoclassical economics 4, 7, 11n, 176
Newcomen, T. 145–9
niches 106, 167
NK models 124–5

non-renewable resources *see*
    exhaustible resources
non-shaping manufacturing
    operations 51, 85
Nordhaus, W.D. 12, 93, 95, 154n
novelty 8, 27, 37
nuclear energy 1
Nye, D.E. 93, 162

Odum, H.T. 18
OECD 77, 105
oil price shocks 1–2, 17, 19, 105
open systems 10, 18, 20, 25, 33–4,
    37, 43
operations *defined* 62
    change within 112–5, 120, 125,
        128, 143
    elasticity of interfaces between
        132, 134, 174
    replacement of 112–5, 120, 125,
        127, 129, 143, 157
    sequences of 53, 109, 113, 128,
        143
Opschoor, J.B. 14
Ostwald, W. 15–17

Pavitt, K. 71
Pearson, P.J.G. 136–7, 153–4
Phelps Brown, E.H. 152n
physiocrats 11
pig iron 138–44
Pimentel, D. 91
Pimentel, M. 91
Pinkerton, R.C. 18
Planck, M. 15
Podolinsky, S. 15
Polanyi, M. 71
Porter, M.E. 58
potting and stamping 140–41
Pratt, J.A. 94
Prencipe, A. 122–3
Prigogine, I. 24n, 34–7
process control 83, 87, 101, 103, 132,
    165
process energy 51–2, 83–8, 90, 97,
    138, 142, 167
process innovation 9, 109–10, 113–4,
    125, 128, 130, 134–5, 166,
    168, 173, 177–8
product architecture 120